Death in the Literature of Unamuno

Death in the Literature of UNAMUNO

By Mario J. Valdés

UNIVERSITY OF ILLINOIS PRESS, URBANA AND LONDON, 1966

Originally published as Volume 54 in the Illinois Studies
in Language and Literature.
© 1964 by the Board of Trustees of the University of Illinois.
Manufactured in the United States of America. Library
of Congress Catalog Card No. 64-63023.

ACKNOWLEDGMENTS

I wish to express my sincere appreciation to Professor William H. Shoemaker for his criticism and most valuable advice throughout the course of the research and writing of the original study on which this book is based.

Also, I wish to thank Professor Oskar Kubitz for his many valuable suggestions in my philosophical orientation.

I am further very grateful to the members of the Board of Editors of the University of Illinois Studies in Language and Literature, and especially to Professor Philip Kolb, for their recommendation to publish this work.

NOTE ON ABBREVIATIONS

The following abbreviations will be used throughout this study to refer to the texts of Unamuno. The multiplicity of texts is necessary since there is no complete collection. The two editions of the *Obras completas* are not interchangeable in any volume, but rather complement each other since many essays such as *La fe, Mi religión, Del sentimiento trágico,* and *La agonía del Cristianismo* that appear in the 1950 edition are not yet in the 1958 edition and on the other hand many speeches and prologues appear for the first time in the 1958 edition. The latter edition is under the direction of Manuel García Blanco and is planned for sixteen volumes. However, at this time only the first twelve have been published.

Of Unamuno's original publications of poetry only the very rare *Rimas de dentro* has not been accessible, but thanks to Luis Felipe Vivanco's anthology of 1947 we have all of its contents. Most of the poetry that Unamuno left unpublished is now available in Federico de Onís' edition of the *Cancionero* and García Blanco's *Don Miguel de Unamuno y sus poesías. Estudio y antología de poemas inéditos o no incluídos en sus libros.*

AP   *Antología poética.* Madrid: Escorial, 1947.

C   *Cancionero.* Buenos Aires: Losada, 1953.

CV   *El Cristo de Velázquez.* Buenos Aires: Espasa-Calpe, 1947.

FP   *De Fuerteventura a París.* París: Excelsior, 1925.

OC 1a.   *Obras completas.* Vols. I–V. Madrid: Afrodisio Aguado, 1950.

OC 2a. *Obras completas.* Vols. I–XII. Barcelona: Vergara, 1958.

P *Poesías.* Bilbao: Rojas, 1907.

PI "Poemas inéditos," *Don Miguel de Unamuno y sus poesías. Estudio y antología de poemas inéditos o no incluidos en sus libros,* ed., Manuel García Blanco. Salamanca: Universidad de Salamanca, 1954, pp. 365–424.

RD *Romancero del destierro.* Buenos Aires: Alba, 1928.

RSL *Rosario de sonetos líricos.* Madrid: Imprenta española, 1911.

T *Teresa.* Madrid: Renacimiento, 1926.

CONTENTS

INTRODUCTION

This study deals with the theme of death in the literature of Miguel de Unamuno: that is, with death as a motivating force in the thinking of the man and also with death as an element of the literary creation. The aim is both philosophical and literary: to elucidate the philosophy of Unamuno in its relation to the death theme and to show how that thinking process is based on the esthetic experiences of death as created in the literature. The division of the study into the two disciplines of philosophy and literary criticism is made as a matter of logical necessity to prevent a falsification of Unamuno's creation. The literary study begins with the philosophical framework and proceeds to the literary works.

The materials used are the entire corpus of the writings of Unamuno which were accessible. There are no selective omissions since the intention is to prove that the theme of death pervades all of Unamuno's creative expression and that, in effect, this is a literature of death. However, due to Unamuno's fecundity, not all of these writings are treated directly in the text, but they are all indirectly accounted for in the course of Chapters One, Two, Three, and Four. All the principal works are included, that is, the longer essays, the novels, the plays, and the longer poems. All the minor and brief works are also studied, but directly only through the analysis of representative selections.

Of the some 1,500 books and articles about Unamuno and studies and reviews which are available, all the longer ones have relevance to this study, and their relevance is indicated wherever appropriate in the text; most of the shorter reviews and notes are also found to be pertinent to the scope of this study. And quite obviously the few outstanding studies—those of Blanco Aguinaga, Ferrater Mora, García Blanco, Marías, Zubizarreta—play a very important rôle in the orientation and analysis used here. But whenever there is a serious difference of interpretation between a published opinion and this text, the scholar is answered in the notes.

These considerations have resulted in a plan of five chapters. Chapter One presents Unamuno's philosophy of death as stated in the essays. Because of the writer's intention of convincing his reader, the essay can be approached with the methods of philosophical study. It is not that creative writing cannot contain philosophical truth, for it certainly does, and most especially Unamuno's literature does; but its truth must be studied through different methods of analysis—those of literary criticism.

In order to answer the question of philosophical consistency in Unamuno's treatment of death, the following methods of study are used: first, the chronological ordering of fifty years of essay-writing according to the date of completion; and, second, the classification for analysis of these materials in the following considerations: problems treated, kinds of proof offered, methods of presentation, and support used from the history of philosophy. This preliminary examination of the essays suggests that (1) there are three changes in the direction of Unamuno's inquiry; (2) these changes complement each other since each moves into a new area of consideration; (3) the changes are gradual, for parts of one anticipate the other; (4) a culmination of each direction will be seen in *En torno al casticismo* (1895), *Del sentimiento trágico de la vida* (1912), and *La agonía del Cristianismo* (1925).

Careful examination of the data, thus, establishes a framework for a philosophy which is based on the directions of Unamuno's thought. These directions are philosophical perspectives, and each of the three, besides being a functioning part of the philosophy, also carries with it a corresponding spirit and tone. Therefore, the philosophical framework has also the possibility of being the outline for Unamuno's creative process. This spirit is a literary attitude which appears as predominant in the literary creations of a given period. Thus, at this point, it appears that Unamuno's thinking is the intellectual expression of esthetic intuitionistic experiences which is realized in three successive periods, each period enriching the whole by one more direction of expression. Consequently, this framework is a calculated hypothesis to be proved or disproved by a literary analysis of the entire corpus of Unamuno's imaginative literature. The problem is one of establishing a historical and spiritual correspondence between the three intellectual culminations and the esthetic experiences of the literary creation.

The primary interests in this study are literary, but in trying to understand such a profound problem as the meaning of death, the study has been initiated from the nonliterary disciplines as outlined above and for the reasons already stated. In Chapters Two, Three, and Four, the study is finally in the position to undertake the direct analysis of the world of the literary creation as the validity of the hypothesis is tested.

The literature treated in each of these three chapters is arranged in the chronological order of the actual writing. In cases where there is a difference in time between composition and publication, the work appears in its chronological place based on the writing, and the bibliographical datum is given in the notes. Some works were in process over a number of years. For such cases the works are entered at the date of completion and the periods of the writing are indicated in the text. There are a few instances where a work was written and published and then rewritten and republished; those works appear in both chronological places with the more detailed study postponed for the final entry.

Aside from the differences in scope which the attitudes dictate in each of these three literary chapters, the internal distribution of the chapters is the same. The literature is studied under the divisions of narrative prose, dramatic prose, and lyric verse. Each of these is a functionally determined grouping and has no relation to the normalistic precepts derived from Aristotle. Each work of literature is treated as a unit in the literary analysis. Stylistic analysis is used in a few cases, but for the most part the study is thematic.

Although each of the literary chapters has a summary, this is an enumeration of the findings and not a conclusion. Chapter Five is the conclusion to this study where the initial question as to the meaning of death is answered after giving a résumé of the literary forms used in the expression of death.

I refer the interested scholar to an excellent bibliography which has all the major books, articles, and reviews pertinent to the study of Unamuno, his life, and his works. The compilation has been effected by Federico de Onís and it appears in "Homenaje a Miguel de Unamuno," *La Torre*, IX, 35–36 (Universidad de Puerto Rico, 1961), 601–636.

CHAPTER ONE

UNAMUNO'S PHILOSOPHY OF DEATH

UNAMUNO AS A PHILOSOPHER

Most commentators [1] divide Unamuno's life and works into three stages of philosophical development: (1) an inner calm resting on faith; (2) a period of shifting and realignment from 1884 to 1910; and (3) the final maturity after 1910. However, this simple division leaves far too many unexplained problems which have led Blanco Aguinaga to consider two parallel developments in Unamuno—"el Unamuno contemplativo" and "el Unamuno agónico." [2] This opinion deals with Unamuno's literary attitudes and will be studied in the next chapter.

The Early Years

Although it is quite true that Unamuno's early faith was demolished by the impact of empirical Positivism, especially Herbert

---

[1] The first stage has been well documented in all the biographical chapters of the studies devoted to Unamuno. See J. Ferrater Mora, *Unamuno: Bosquejo de una filosofía* (Buenos Aires: Sudamericana, 1957), pp. 19–22; Jacinto Grau, *Unamuno, su tiempo y su España* (Buenos Aires: Ediciones Alda, 1946), pp. 23–24; René Marill, *Miguel de Unamuno*, trans., P. Matthews (Buenos Aires: Editorial La Mandrágora, 1952), pp. 22–48; S. Serrano Poncela, *El pensamiento de Unamuno* (México: Fondo de Cultura Económica, 1953), pp. 7–12; C. Blanco Aguinaga, *El Unamuno contemplativo* (México: El Colegio de México, 1959), pp. 18–19. The second stage demands more than logical supposition. This documentation has been given by Armando F. Zubizarreta, *Tras las huellas de Unamuno* (Madrid: Taurus, 1960), pp. 15–32, which is the study of an unpublished manuscript of this period entitled "La filosofía lógica." Ferrater Mora, *Unamuno: Bosquejo de una filosofía*, pp. 23–27, suggests that the years of the second stage be treated in three parts: 1884–97 as a period of positivism, 1897–1905 as one of personal crisis and an attempted return to Catholicism, and 1905–12 as the formation of the mature Unamuno that would lead him through life. Also of value as to the dating of Unamuno's emotional crisis of 1897: Hernán Benítez, *El drama religioso de Unamuno* (Buenos Aires: Universidad de Buenos Aires, 1949), p. 15; and Antonio Sánchez Barbudo, *Estudios sobre Unamuno y Machado* (Madrid: Guadarrama, 1959), pp. 15–79.

[2] See Blanco Aguinaga, *El Unamuno contemplativo*, pp. 9–12.

Spencer's philosophy, and this nineteenth-century philosophy did destroy his belief in Catholicism, it did not supplant the faith. It was even before Spencer that the philosophical language and frame of mind of the dialectic of Hegel had left a lasting imprint in the young mind of Unamuno. Referring to these early years, Unamuno later wrote:

La doctrina de Hegel acerca de la identidad entre el ser puro y la pura nada, cosas eran que producían vértigo a mi alma tierna y sin balancín todavía para sostenerse a aquellas alturas en la maroma metafísica [*Recuerdos de niñez y de mocedad*, 1908; *OC*, 2a, I, 310].

In 1901 he wrote to his friend Federico Urales:

Aprendí alemán en Hegel, en el estupendo Hegel, que ha sido uno de los pensadores que más honda huella han dejado en mí. Hoy mismo creo que el fondo de mi pensamiento es hegeliano.[3]

And, years later, in 1925, he was to write in *La agonía del Cristianismo:*

El modo de vivir, de luchar, de luchar por la vida y vivir de la lucha, de la fe, es dudar. . . .

¿Y qué es dudar? *Dubitare* contiene la misma raíz, la del numeral *duo*, dos, que *duellum*, lucha. La duda, más la pascàliana, la duda agónica o polémica, que no la cartesiana o duda metódica, la duda de vida—vida es lucha—y no de camino—método es camino—, supone la dualidad del combate.

Desnacer es morir y desmorir es nacer. Y esto es una dialéctica de agonía [*OC*, 1a, IV, 833–835].

This dialectical pattern of thought was to color much of Unamuno's writings throughout his life. However, it is of the utmost importance to realize that when he refers to a dialectic, Unamuno is not considering the logic of Hegel that assumes a hierarchy of thesis-antithesis leading to synthesis which is the thesis of another level, and so forth. Unamuno sees no synthesis but only a continued struggle between the opposing parts of whatever he is treating. This manner of thinking and writing will explain some of the otherwise unanswerable complexities of the Unamunian philosophy.[4]

[3] See Zubizarreta, *Tras las huellas de Unamuno*, p. 21.

[4] F. Meyer in his study of Unamuno's philosophy, *L'ontologie de Miguel de Unamuno* (Paris: Presses Universitaires de France, 1955), p. 1, presents the following interpretation of the dialectic as the basis of the philosophy: "L'être concret, le seul être concret existant, est partout et toujours, pour Unamuno, contradictoire, polémique et agonique. Il n'y a nulle part de refuge ontologique pour l'être plein. Tel est le sens du sentiment tragique de la vie ou du sentiment agonique de l'être, et ce malheur essentiel de la conscience d'être n'est pas seulement un 'malheur de la conscience,' une dépression ontologique creée au sein de l'être et de l'absolu par l'avènement à la conscience de soi, il n'est pas davantage l'effet d'une chute par laquelle la conscience éprouverait sa séparation de l'être

The year 1884, which marks the end of Unamuno's university studies, is also the beginning of a gradual development of three philosophical perspectives which succeeded each other in their moments of greatest influence in three outstanding essays: *En torno al casticismo* (1895), *Del sentimiento trágico de la vida* (1912), and *La agonía del Cristianismo* (1925). But it is significant to note that each came out of a literary attitude that Unamuno was to maintain in parallel, and often interacting, currents, as will be demonstrated in subsequent chapters.

Unamuno and His Critics

The polemics and disagreements that surround Unamuno's thought stem from the fact that many minds have attempted to simplify the most complex literary figure of contemporary Spain. Unamuno was not Lutheran,[5] atheistic,[6] nihilistic,[7] nor a disciple of Nietzsche [8] or of Kierkegaard,[9] nor a pragmatist,[10] a mystic,[11] nor

---

et son péché d'origine; c'est bien d'un malheur, ou si l'on veut d'une monstruousité de l'être qu'il s'agit, et c'est la structure ontologique elle-même qui est contradiction et agonie sans espoir. L'intuition originelle qui commande toute la pensée d'Unamuno est toute entière dans le sentiment d'un être en conflit avec lui-même, ennemi de lui-même et qui ne peut être que dans et par ce conflit, en l'exaspérant, en l'assumant et en le pourtant à son comble par une passion désespérée et contradictoire."

[5] For the opinion on the Lutheranism of Unamuno see José L. Aranguren, "Sobre el talento religioso de don Miguel de Unamuno," *Arbor*, XI, 36 (1948), 485–503.

[6] For Unamuno as an atheist, see P. Nemesio González Caminero, S.J., *Unamuno, Trayectoria de su ideología y de su crisis religiosa* (Comillas: Universidad Pontífica, 1948). There is a long list of articles and books by the Catholic clergy in general condemnation of Unamuno, but they have nothing more to offer as criticism. For the most recent, see Joan Manyà, *La teología de Unamuno* (Barcelona: Vergara, 1960). For an excellent review of ecclesiastic criticism, see Antonio González O.P., "¿Unamuno en la hoguera?," *Asomante*, XII (1961).

[7] The label of nihilism has often been applied to Unamuno for his numerous statements that he seeks war and not peace. Superficial readers who do not grasp the meaning of the Unamunian *agonía* may well be led to think that Unamuno is calling for destruction when it is precisely the opposite that he seeks, that is, eternal action, and a living, constantly changing flux. For such readers and commentators, see Frank Sedwick, "Unamuno the Essayist and His Detractors," *Modern Language Forum*, XLII, 2 (1957), 101–112.

[8] For documentation and the extent of the relations between Unamuno and Nietzsche, see "Presencia y ausencia de Nietzsche en Unamuno" in the excellent article by Manuel García Blanco, "La cultura alemana en la obra de Miguel de Unamuno," *Romanistisches Jahrbuch*, VIII (Hamburg, 1957), 326–330.

[9] See the fully documented study of Jesús-Antonio Collado that establishes the similarities and differences between the two philosophers: *Kierkegaard y Unamuno* (Madrid: Gredos, 1962).

[10] The many comments linking Unamuno and William James have been

a primitive Christian,[12] although by taking any one passage from his writings and subscribing only to the literal meaning of the words a good case may be made for the above categorical types. Unamuno was a man—in his own words "nada menos que todo un hombre, un hombre de carne y hueso"—who opened his mind to the widest spectrum of Western philosophy and literature. The misleading factors have been his language, which must be examined as a pattern of oppositions and the multiplicity of perspectives which were reformations and regroupings to attack the same problem: the immortality of existence.[13] With a few notable exceptions, most critics of Unamuno can be put in two categories: (1) those who have concentrated on his relations with the individuals whom he found to have an affinity to his way of thinking, and (2) others who have focused on his preoccupation with the problem of immortality. The former group are those who try to force Unamuno into a set type. But, there is no evidence of anything more than a recognized affinity in thought with these writers. The latter group of critics, because of the lack of system, because of the multiplicity of sources, have been led to conclude that Unamuno was an eclectic semiphilosopher who concerned himself with the problems of philosophy, but who did not write philosophy. In this manner Julián Marías has studied the only central concern—the immortality of existence—and he has not been sidetracked by the mere company Unamuno kept.[14] Marías finds that the problem of immortality is the intellectual unity of Unamuno. And as a consequence of the lifelong confrontation with this problem, a personal way of thought slowly developed with a central core which was the personal awareness of death of the individual man.[15] This is seen

brought together for a conscientious examination of the thought of both men by Pelayo Hipólito Fernández, *Miguel de Unamuno y William James* (Salamanca: Cervantes, 1961).

[11] See Agustín Esclasans, *Miguel de Unamuno* (Buenos Aires: Juventud, 1947), p. 214.

[12] See Alain Guy, "Miguel de Unamuno, Pélerin de l'Absolu," *Cuadernos de la cátedra Miguel de Unamuno,* I (1948), 100.

[13] Reference is made to the one problem of immortality as the opening to a philosophy, not as a conclusion, for this problem is not resolved—it cannot be resolved. Thus, from this doorway into the existence of man, Unamuno implicitly writes an ontology and explicitly an anthropology.

[14] See Julián Marías, *Miguel de Unamuno* (Madrid: Espasa-Calpe, 1943), pp. 14–16.

[15] In his *Miguel de Unamuno,* Marías states (pp. 14, 19, 20): "Y la repetición es, en efecto, la forma unificadora del pensamiento de Unamuno. . . . [de] ese tema único del hombre que muere. . . . se hace ese tema *El* de la filosofía. Se trata, pues, del problema del hombre, de la persona humana, y de su perduración.

not as a concept of death, but rather as a driving force that thrust Unamuno into the most diverse corners in search of an answer to the unanswerable question: After I die, what?

Since Marías' study in 1943 [16] this opinion has prevailed among the serious students of Unamuno. However, Unamuno's writings also have been examined by Ferrater Mora, who because he has penetrated into the multifaceted core of Unamunian thought, has insisted on Unamuno's place as a philosopher.[17] Here, the task will be to bring out this philosophy which has been outlined but not presented by Ferrater Mora, for it is an implicit rather than an explicit philosophy which is dispersed over fifty-two years of writings.

Ferrater Mora sums up his opinion in these words:

This [the concrete eternal] can be understood in two ways. First, as something whose permanence is being continuously produced or created; true permanence is, Unamuno believes, the result of an effort, of an act of will, of a conatus to such an extent that there is no fundamental difference between being and wishing to be. Second, as something whose duration is constantly threatened by annihilation; just as war is the guarantee of peace, death—the imminence of death—is the guarantee of life. To last forever is not to go on existing, to continue to be, it is to conquer unceasingly its own being. This explains why for Unamuno to live is primarily "to agonize," namely, to fight against death.[18]

Thus, although two Unamunian views of reality are given, the commentator does not develop the correspondence or relation they may have to each other, nor does he connect them to the different perspectives that Unamuno realized. It is our contention that these two views are parts of a philosophy which Unamuno developed over the years and which manifested itself from three perspectives, but with each of these in turn, it used the same open dialectic of oppositions on the same problem before him: immortality and death or non-being.

The dialectic language dramatized the basic thought of Unamunian philosophy: that being is essentially an "in-struggle" fact

Y quien plantea esta cuestión es la muerte: se trata de saber qué es morir, si es aniquilarse o no."

[16] Marías, *Miguel de Unamuno*, pp. 9–22. Marías repeats the same interpretation in *El existencialismo en España* (Bogotá: Ediciones Universidad Nacional de Colombia, 1953), pp. 88–89.

[17] Ferrater Mora, *Unamuno: Bosquejo de una filosofía*, pp. 46–48, 55–56; also in "On Miguel de Unamuno's Idea of Reality," *Philosophy and Phenomenological Research*, XXI, 4 (June, 1961), 514–520.

[18] Ferrater Mora, "On Unamuno's Idea of Reality," p. 520.

of existence. Thus, this philosophy is not a system [19] nor an eschatology [20] of a world mind, but a dynamic surge which is "a being-in-struggle" without end. The perspectives are not counter-resolutions to the same problem, but rather complementary manifestations of the problem as (1) world, (2) the individual man, and (3) the accumulating tradition of man's thought.

The Three Philosophical Perspectives

The perspectives follow clearly if one keeps in mind that "in-struggle" is the formulation of being and that there is no end such as a solution or a victory, but instead being is continuous struggle: (1) in order that the totality of reality may persist in existence there must be a continuous effort keeping the "in-struggle" going and thus there is a constant negating of non-being; (2) for the personal *yo* of Unamuno, which is his living consciousness, to exist he must continue "in-struggle," but it is only when he becomes aware that he as an individual struggles against death that he is authentic and absorbs his living environment; (3) for the continued re-creation of Unamuno's thoughts in others there must be continued activity by others to keep this mind from oblivion. Thus, this is a philosophy that considers existence from three different perspectives. However, since we are attempting to penetrate the perspectives that were operative in Unamuno's mind, it is necessary to study each as an individual problem of philosophical inquiry as it developed in his reflective life. The literary attitudes which were the creative expressions for this philosophy can better be discussed in the light of the philosophical perspectives. Thus, before the literature can

[19] Unamuno's philosophy is not a system in the sense that this term usually carries of a metaphysical statement of the limitations and observations of the substance of this existence that man encounters empirically. In Unamuno's philosophy there is no such abstraction of reality, but rather the intuition into the continuity of existence itself viewed from the three perspectives of inter-history, man, man's thought. See Meyer, *L'ontologie de Miguel de Unamuno*, pp. 1–24, where the basis of the dialectic is established; pp. 25–58, where the dialectic is studied in direct application to the existential *yo;* pp. 59–80, where Meyer gives an outline of the Unamunian anthropology; and pp. 81–108, which examine the Unamunian epistemology. The only difficulty is that Meyer examines all of Unamuno's philosophy from one perspective—the second point of view of the personal *yo.* He does this by giving the dialectical basis in general terms and then shifting to the existential *yo.* This transition in actuality took place from 1895 to 1912. Meyer writes on p. 2: "L'être concret se confond avec la conscience." This statement is followed with quotations from *Del sentimiento trágico.* This opinion is well taken for this essay, but not for *En torno al casticismo.*

[20] This philosophy cannot be an eschatology since death is not treated as a finality but rather as a dialectic force.

be studied in the following chapters, these trains of thought must be firmly established, and before each perspective is textually reconstructed in this chapter the complementary relation of each to the philosophy must be clarified.

The first perspective is that of the metaphysical problem of existence in the totality of reality. When Unamuno concerns himself with this thought, he embarks on a quest into reality using intuition as a means of knowing. The position reached in *En torno al casticismo* (1895) is that of a reality that is ever changing flux in a stream of projection that has only an eternal now as time. When Ferrater Mora's analysis is applied to this perspective, it can be stated in these terms: (1) the stream of flux which is reality is being continuously produced and (2) the continuous affirmation of this totality is a constant negation of non-being. Since there is no personal consciousness in this perspective, there is only one view, one time, and one interrelationship—the totality of existence. This is seen as an eternal stream of struggle. It is "in-struggle" because as existence it is always reconquering its being. Here, the Unamunian dialectic pattern is at its broadest scope, for all there is, was, or can be is one constant affirmation of being and negation of non-being. This philosophical inquiry is not rational but necessarily intuitive since reason distorts reality into an abstraction. To a certain extent Unamuno anticipated Henri Bergson in this perspective; this philosophical relationship will be discussed in the next section of this chapter.

In the second perspective Unamuno takes the starting point of the individual man who is there in the world with his environment. No longer is metaphysics the traditional quest for the essence of existence, but rather existence is put first in the position of the individual's being cast there in the world. Ferrater Mora's two points in this perspective become the following: (1) existence is the fact that precedes all other facts, but continued existence is the result of an act of the individual's will; the force of the will to exist is what projects the individual existent so that there is no difference between being and wishing to be since man is absolutely free and is always making himself. But the *yo* that Unamuno thinks he is is the same as the *yo* that he wants to be because he has the authentic awareness of death which would open his *yo* to the world. And this leads to the second point of Ferrater Mora: (2) the existence of the *yo* is the unceasing reconquest of its being from non-being. In this perspective this is the individual *yo*'s struggle unto death.

All *yos,* whether they realize it or not, are plunging forth toward death, propelled by their own making. Many individual *yos* are in a state of self-delusion and rationalization and are not aware that their death is their impending end that could be utter annihilation and that they are making their existence. It is only as the *yo* becomes aware of the struggle that he becomes authentic. Then the realization of the *yo*-will's utter freedom [21] gives the *yo* the awareness that he is forging his own future. And directly allied to the awareness of death and the realization of the will's freedom is the commitment of the *yo* to the world. This commitment takes the form of a personalization [22] and absorption of the world by the *yo.* Thus, the second perspective does not utilize the intuition of the first; here there is a phenomenological awareness [23] of everything around the *yo* which results from its commitment.

[21] This existential freedom which was first developed by Kierkegaard (1813–55) as the passion of freedom—see *Afsluttende uvidenskabelig Efterskrift til de Philosophiske Smuler,* which is available in an English translation by D. F. Swenson as *Concluding Unscientific Postscript to the Philosophical Fragments* (Princeton: Princeton University Press, 1944), pp. 176–182, 312–318—is in Unamuno's philosophy nothing more than a self-awareness by the individual *yo* of the movement of life by which he uproots the things around him and deals with other individuals. There is no given freedom—this would be an abstraction. Each individual man must win this "inner victory" continuously over his opposing passions, over the obstacles and barriers which things or tools present, and in his relations with his fellowmen.

[22] Unamuno uses the verb *personalizar* in the sense of observing the object like a person. What this means is that the personal *yo,* once aware of his inner freedom, realizes that he is his own *de-venir* and also comprehends that his entire existence is his own doing. With this thought, the sense of responsibility and commitment follow. Thus, this is no longer the world, but my world, my fellow man, my enemy, and so forth. This is the process of making reality over in a personalization. Every human and material relationship consequently takes on new values. The *yo* in this process cares about his work, his friends, that is, his living in his world, because all of this is dependent on him—the irreplaceable *yo*—for its existence. On the first page of *Del sentimiento trágico,* Unamuno writes: "...el hombre. El hombre de carne y hueso, el que nace, sufre y muere— sobre todo muere. . . . Porque hay otra cosa, que llaman también hombre, y es el sujeto de no pocas divagaciones más o menos científicas. . . . Un hombre que no es de aquí o de allí, ni de esta época o de la otra, que no tiene ni sexo ni patria, una idea, en fin. Es decir, un no hombre. El nuestro es el otro, el de carne y hueso; yo, tú, lector mío; aquel otro de más allá, cuantos pesamos sobre la tierra. Y este hombre concreto, de carne y hueso, es el sujeto y el supremo objeto a la vez de toda filosofía, quiéranlo o no ciertos sedicentes filósofos." The *yo* is also the starting point for Heidegger in 1927: "El ente cuyo análisis es nuestro problema somos en cada caso nosotros mismos. El ser de este ente es, en cada caso, mío," *El ser y el tiempo,* trans., J. Gaos (México: Fondo de Cultura Económica, 1951), p. 49.

[23] By this term we mean the awareness of the phenomena of life and not abstractions such as "the average American," and so forth.

It is in this perspective that Unamuno's philosophy may be considered to be a forerunner of the Existentialists.[24] For here man finds himself in the world—his existence precedes all else—and when he begins to function he is absolutely free as he makes his continued existence. When he has become aware of the impending

[24] Unamuno, of course, owes much of his existentialist orientation to Kierkegaard. However, he is a forerunner of the philosophies of Martin Heidegger, Karl Jaspers, Jean-Paul Sartre, Gabriel Marcel, and Paul Tillich. The general similarities between Unamuno's second perspective and the views of these contemporary philosophers are obvious to any reader of Heidegger's *Sein und Zeit*, Sartre's *L'Être et le néant*, Jaspers' *Der philosophische Glaube*, Marcel's *Le mystère de l'être*, or Tillich's *The Courage to Be*. However, there is a much deeper affinity linking Unamuno and this subsequent current of thought: a philosophical sensitivity to the modern individual's reality which Unamuno developed into an existentialist anthropology.

The importance of Unamuno's anticipation has not yet been fully appreciated by our age largely because of the fact that he wrote in Spanish. Very briefly stated, this connection of Unamuno to Existentialism can be seen by concentrating on his second perspective and on the works of the two leading exponents of this philosophy today—Heidegger and Sartre. Heidegger himself has recognized this affinity in an interview with Cruz Hernández: "Y en Friburgo, Heidegger, mientras me señalaba los volúmenes de Unamuno alineados en su biblioteca, me decía que era el pensador español que más le había preocupado. Al mismo tiempo que Dilthey y Brentano—y bien que los tres se ignorasen entre sí— Unamuno se rebela contra aquel aséptico sujeto cognoscente, inventado por Descartes, perfeccionado por Locke y Hume, alquitarado por Kant y deformado por los positivistas," Miguel Cruz Hernández, "La misión socrática de Don Miguel de Unamuno," *Cuadernos de la cátedra* . . . , III (1952), 46.

Although the idea of the authentic man is a basic part of Unamuno's second perspective, it was given a more widely known exposition a few years later, in 1927, when Heidegger expressed these same observations in somewhat more professional language. See *El ser y el tiempo*, p. 147.

The *yo*-awareness is to Unamuno and to Heidegger primarily the result of an awareness of death as the impending possible annihilation. Unamuno, thus, had the same ontological basis as Heidegger has later. But in contrast to Heidegger, Unamuno is also concerned with the practical aspects inherent in his view of existence as the individual is in a continued struggle to be. The question is: how can men live by the traditional moral and ethical norms in a world that has destroyed the basis for these? By an immortal God that promises heaven or hell? Nietzsche would destroy the accepted norms of morality since he had destroyed God. However, Unamuno creates his own personal God and subsequently bases his anthropology on the creative force that sustains this God—the personal *yo*'s will, the *querer ser*. The personal *yo* that wills God into existence because of his thirst for immortality realizes that he is living his own life in his own world for which he alone is responsible. By accepting this inner freedom the *yo* also accepts the commitment to his living environment, thus the result is an existentialist ethic: the *yo* struggles with himself to gain an inner freedom which tells him that he is his own maker and is responsible for his making; therefore, the authentic *yo* will always choose the good. And what is the good? Simply stated, nothing is good for the *yo* without being good for all, since all is his. It is in this practical development of Unamuno's philosophy that he is akin to the French philosopher Jean-Paul Sartre. The similarities are sometimes striking;

possibility that can end all possibilities—death—he becomes authentic and realizes his freedom and his commitments to the world; this is what opens the man to the world as he personalizes it. As the personal *yo* engulfs all of his world, this world is put into a dialectic of oppositions, except that now this pattern is the *yo*'s reconquest of its being as long as the "in-struggle" remains. This authentic light of the *yo* is the tragic sense of life.

The third perspective does not concern the totality of existence nor the personal *yo* in its world, but rather the spiritual reality of the current of man's thoughts. This is the universe of ideas, traditions, and memories which all co-exist in the minds of men. But, primarily, it deals with an individual's thought. Upon death, what happens to all of the ideas and thoughts which a personal *yo* has generated during a lifetime? Some will be remembered for a time and then will be disseminated, losing the unity of being the thought of that particular individual. This individual *yo*-will which created the thought may thus be lost into oblivion. But, if the thought of the *yo*-will has been expressed in written words, then there is the possibility of a continued re-creation by others. There is also implicit in this perspective the doctrine that this spiritual brotherhood is an ever enriching continuum leading to an ever greater spiritual Universe. Of course much that is written is also destined for oblivion, but that which expresses truth to others will be read and re-created by others. Thus in this perspective Ferrater Mora's views apply in this way: (1) through the efforts of others, words that express a human truth will continuously re-create the *yo;* and (2) the words of the *yo* are always threatened by oblivion since they are "in-struggle" to be re-created. The words which express the intimate feelings of man are the truth to Unamuno and these will conquer unceasingly a continued existence. Perhaps the best way to bring this philosophy of three perspectives into view is to borrow a metaphorical expression from Unamuno's *Niebla* (1914) (*OC,* 2a, II) and to explain it.[25]

The eternal flux (which is reality) is a dialectic of oppositions between being, which is the constant affirmation of existence, and

---

Sartre writes in the conclusion of *Being and Nothingness,* trans., H. E. Barnes (New York: Philosophical Library, 1956), p. 627: "But ontology and existential psychoanalysis . . . must reveal to the moral agent that he is the being by whom values exist. It is then that his freedom will become conscious of itself and will reveal itself in anguish as the unique source of value and the nothingness by which the world exists."

25 For the study of this metaphor as part of the literary creation in *Niebla,* see Chapter Three, p. 89.

non-being, which is the continuous negation of existence. This does not make nothingness a positive factor, for it does not exist. "Non-being is a linguistic necessity to denote the undoing, negating, activity inherent within existence. Therefore, if a focal point can be put on an individual part within this flux, it would become an abstraction when removed from the context of the whole, for totality is set in an eternal "now" and individuality is necessarily temporal and finite. It is precisely this problem which makes it necessary to use a metaphor such as a stream. Consequently, man can reach an intuition of this first philosophical perspective by the intuitive contemplation of the whole of reality where he becomes a mere insignificant speck. Thus, death here merely means that this speck is arrested from the continuity and is caught in the countercurrent of constant negation, which is, however, never achieved because the affirmation of being continues.

Cuando el hombre se queda a solas y cierra los ojos al porvenir, al ensueño, se le revela el abismo pavoroso de la eternidad. La eternidad no es porvenir. Cuando morimos nos da la muerte media vuelta en nuestra órbita y emprendemos la marcha hacia atrás, hacia el pasado, hacia lo que fué. Y así, sin término, devanando la madeja de nuestro destino, deshaciendo todo el infinito que en una eternidad nos ha hecho, caminando a la nada, sin llegar nunca a ella, pues que ella nunca fué [OC, 2a, II, 836].

Now, if one takes the same metaphor of the countercurrents in flux and applies it to the existential reality of the second perspective —the individual personal yo— there is the following result:

Por debajo de esta corriente de nuestra existencia, por dentro de ella, hay otra corriente en sentido contrario; aquí vamos del ayer al mañana, allí se va del mañana al ayer. Se teje y se desteje a un tiempo [OC, 2a, II, 837].

The personal yo of man is temporal and only man of all that is being "exists," that is, only man has a future (por-venir) which is a personal projection, since only man has an individual awareness of self. The personal yo is always moving from his yesterday (memory) to his tomorrow (projection) until death cuts him off, and then the remains, physical and spiritual, become part of the counter-current; note the change from vamos to se va. But before the yo meets death he has a life which, as long as it lasts, is also in dialectic struggle (se teje y se desteje a un tiempo). Man's life is the constant affirmation of his being-there-in-the-world, while man's death is the counterforce of the threatening negation. But during life these two countercurrents of the dialectic pull man in various directions of the serlo todo, the ser nada, and the no ser nada. The first two are authentic insofar as man is aware of the dialectic and of his yo.

But the third one is unauthentic since it is the result of not confronting the dialectic. Again using the countercurrents to the spiritual legacy of man, it is formulated as follows:

Y de vez en cuando nos llegan hálitos, vahos y hasta rumores misteriosos de ese otro mundo, de ese interior de nuestro mundo. Las entrañas de la historia son una contrahistoria, es un proceso inverso al que ella sigue. El río subterráneo va del mar a la fuente [OC, 2a, II, 837].

From the countercurrent of personal existence which is death, there comes a re-creation of the word of a past *yo,* a distant echo of what he was. But man's history has at every moment the dialectic of opposition from the countercurrent of oblivion.

Thus, in conclusion, existence is a current which is countered with an opposing current. In the first perspective the currents are being and non-being, while in the second perspective they are life and death, and in the third they become re-creation and oblivion.[26] These three perspectives of the philosophy of Unamuno in their foundation are all nonintellectual and can best be considered intuitive, empathic, and emotive. The framework in which they are expressed is an open dialectic of oppositions, and whatever the perspective may be, in effect, there is a dynamic "in-struggle" continuum where the being of this existence must reconquer itself from non-being. It is the very state of "in-struggle" that is the affirmation of existence and the negation of non-being. But the threat is there in the form of non-being to the totality, of death and possible nothingness to the personal *yo,* and of oblivion to the thought of the *yo* expressed in words.

The Three Literary Attitudes

The literary attitudes, which are the sources of the philosophical perspectives, are the creative states of mind of Unamuno expressing what he considered to be the truth—that philosophy can only describe but literature can create for the reader to re-create.

[26] The new dialectic which rips open the neat Hegelian abstraction of a logical synthesis can be seen in Heidegger's philosophy after *Sein und Zeit* in "What Is Metaphysics?," in the volume of selected writings, *Existence and Being,* ed., Werner Brock (Chicago: H. Regnery, 1949), pp. 329–349; the work originally appeared as "Was ist Metaphisik?" in 1929. Also see *The Question of Being,* trans., introd., W. Klubach and J. T. Wilde (New York: Twayne Pub., 1958), pp. 33–109 (German-English texts together). Sartre recognizes this development also: "We might on the contrary emphasize the reciprocal forces of repulsion which being and non-being exercise on each other, the real in some way being the tension resulting from these antagonistic forces," *Being and Nothingness,* p. 16.

Unamuno was well aware of the different attitudes that he was capable of adopting, as will be demonstrated in Chapters Two, Three, and Four. The first one was a quiet attitude of contemplation where the powerful *yo*-will was abandoned as he became engrossed in the intuition of the totality of existence.[27] Very often it was the landscape that stirred an evocation of this feeling for the overwhelming continuity of existence. Of necessity this literary creation is highly metaphorical.

In the second attitude the *yo* that is the universe unto itself is the Unamunian expression of directness and force; there are basically two types of fictional characters in this attitude: (1) those who have the tragic sense of life and thus are aware that they want to be eternal, and (2) those who "unauthentically" are not aware of their death. For the authentic characters, that is, those with the tragic sense, life is a battleground which is always in "in-struggle." However, the characters are completely free and they may choose death over life. This active assertion of will in choosing death is what Unamuno calls *noluntad*.

Finally, in the third attitude, there is a sense of a participation in a brotherhood of creators of the word and of the flesh. This cannot be taken as an answer to the enormous thirst for immortality that the authentic character of the second attitude has, for it is quite clear that this *yo* that will be re-created in others is not the personal *yo* that must die. This attitude is expressed in the themes of motherhood, thirst for fame, and the writer's creation of a spiritual *yo* that is to be re-created by others every time it is read.[28]

The following table is an outline of the entirety of our undertaking. It is presented here so that the reader can follow the analy-

---

[27] Blanco Aguinaga has given the most valid and objective analysis of Unamuno's writings on this *yo* that exists in reality in his study, *El Unamuno contemplativo*. He demolishes the previous writings of negative critics with precision, logic, and documentation. If there be a point of dissent with Blanco Aguinaga it is that he limits Unamuno to a man who struggles and then rests from the fatigue giving in to an escape into nothingness. Unamuno saw struggle in everything but only in one attitude was he, the man, consciously in struggle.

[28] One of the best-known studies of Unamuno's themes is Serrano Poncela's *El pensamiento de Unamuno* (México: Fondo de Cultura Económica, 1953); see especially pp. 145–262. Also see Carlos Clavería, "Sobre el tema de Caín en la obra de Unamuno," *Temas de Unamuno* (Madrid: Gredos, 1953), pp. 93–122; J. L. Cano, "Unamuno y sus temas," *Insula*, VIII, 96, December 15, 1953; Julio de la Calzada, "Temas unamunianos," *Boletín de edificación* . . . , 17, 18, 19, 21, 22 (Paris, 1953–54); M. Fernández Almagro, "Crítica y glosa: temas de Unamuno," *ABC* (Madrid, November 6, 1953); F. Sedwick, "Unamuno and Womanhood," *Hispania*, XLIII, 309–313; Blanco Aguinaga, *El Unamuno contemplativo*, pp. 97–220; J. Chicharro de León, "Temas unamunianos: El sentimiento de la naturaleza," *Presencia*, I, 2 (Paris, May, 1962).

	(A) PHILOSOPHICAL PERSPECTIVES	(B) LITERARY ATTITUDES	(C) IMAGE OF MAN
I The threat of death to the world	Existence is continuous because it is eternal flux that is a continuous negation of non-being and an affirmation of being.	Reality is expressed as an intuition seen in nature with the metaphor—rain falls upon the lake.	This is the *yo* as seen from the totality of existence, i.e., a mere speck, a raindrop on the lake.
II The threat of death to the individual	The individual *yo* is the starting point of all philosophy. The *yo* exists cast there in the world, but it is his world. And it is the *yo* and his creation of the world, i.e., his life which is threatened with total annihilation. This is a continuous struggle unto death.	Life is a battleground for the *yo* but only some are aware that they are "in-struggle." These men have the tragic sense of life.	There is the *yo* that one thinks he is—this is the realization of the brute fact of existence. There is also the *yo* that wants to be—this is the *yo*-will's thirst for immortality.
III The threat of death to the thought of the individual	Man exists in others as a memory or his ideas as part of their thinking process, but only as long as others remember him or re-create his thought. The latter leads to the participation in a brotherhood of thought.	The re-creation of the *yo* can be sought through one's children or one's fame, but the only meaningful re-creation is fulfilled through the word.	There is the *yo* others think one is. This *yo* is entirely created and re-created by others.

sis of the multiple facets of Unamuno's writings, for in a detailed
study such as this there is always the danger that the reader may
lose sight of the whole because of the concentration on the parts.

The horizontal divisions are the focal points from which the
whole is examined: (a) is the philosophical perspective, the direct
statement on the problems of existence and being; (b) is the literary
attitude which is the creative expression of the Unamunian mind;
(c) is the image of man which is already contained within the two
other considerations, and is presented separately only in this table
in order to mark the broad implications of Unamuno's writings.[29]

The vertical divisions are the chronological confrontations of this
thinking process with the threat of death. In the first, being is
threatened by non-being; in the second, the *yo* must face possible
annihilation; and in the third, the *yo*'s re-created thought must
overcome oblivion.

THE FIRST PERSPECTIVE—THE AFFIRMATION OF "BEING" IN A CONTINUOUS EFFORT

Unamuno rejects reason as a way of achieving an insight into
reality and in its place uses the metaphor of poetic intuition. After
his break with empirical Positivism, Unamuno formulates his first
philosophical perspective, which is a metaphysical focus on the
totality of existence in *En torno al casticismo* of 1895.

In this collection of essays, Unamuno develops his theory of
eternal history: the *intrahistoria*. Upon close study it can be seen
that the metaphysical basis is a totality which is an eternal push
that is everchanging and continuous. Unamuno writes: "Pero lo
que pasa queda, porque hay algo que sirve de sustento al perpetuo
flujo de las cosas" (*OC*, 2a, III, 184).

[29] We acknowledge Frank Sedwick's penetrating study of the levels of personality in Unamuno's literary creation—"Unamuno, the Third Self, and Lucha,"
Studies in Philology, LIV, 3 (July, 1957), 464–479. Sedwick has very accurately
presented what we consider to be Unamuno's second philosophical perspective:
"the individual who exists and who is an end in himself. He is an end in his own
individuality, but he is also responsible for the rest of mankind. The great
responsibility was a part of Unamuno's anguish" (p. 474). However, Sedwick
does not consider the other perspectives adopted by Unamuno. He thus leaves
his thesis open to the challenge of Blanco Aguinaga: how do you account for
the Unamuno of the inner calmness, of the intuition into the process of reality?
Also omitted from consideration is the disturbing opinion of Sánchez Barbudo:
if this position of struggle be the Unamunian point of view, then we must consider much of this talk about immortality as a mere pretense, as a self-created
myth. Again we repeat that these conflicts of scholarly opinion arise due to the
limitations of thought and creativity which have been imposed on Unamuno.

The continuity of the everchanging is the totality of existence, and it is this core that must be reached. Not yet having the vocabulary to deal with this metaphysical breakthrough, Unamuno adds this tentative remark: "Un momento es el producto de una serie, serie que lleva en sí, pero no es el mundo un calidoscopio" (OC, 2a, III, 184). A moment has the infinite stream within it, for the reality Unamuno has grasped is not a kaleidoscope of fragments in a series; thus, it is not a moment in itself but only becomes a moment when man intellectually abstracts it and isolates it out of the continuum. Unamuno realized that the only way possible to express this metaphysical perspective was through metaphor; therefore rational discourse was forsaken and he proceeded through intuition to build the metaphor of the sea:

Las olas de la historia, con su rumor y su espuma que reverbera al sol, ruedan sobre un mar continuo, hondo, inmensamente más hondo que la capa que ondula sobre un mar silencioso y a cuyo último fondo nunca llega el sol. Todo lo que cuentan a diario los periódicos, la historia toda del "presente momento histórico," no es sino la superficie del mar, una superficie que se hiela y cristaliza en los libros y registros, y una vez cristalizada así, una capa dura, no mayor con respecto a la vida intra-histórica que esta pobre corteza en que vivimos con relación al inmenso foco ardiente que lleva dentro [OC, 2a, III, 185].

Throughout the literary attitude that inspires this metaphysics, the sea will be the most used metaphor. Here, in its first philosophical use, it gives the intuition of the ever changing reality that gives man only a limited surface view: the contemporary situation. And when man removes this surface view—the waves—from the continuum—the surging sea—it is no longer reality, but rather a human rational isolation. Unamuno senses the strength of his metaphor and continues it: "Una ola no es otra agua que otra, es la misma ondulación que corre por el mismo mar" (OC, 2a, III, 186). He realizes that he is dealing with an eternal time that is one never broken, continuous now:

En este fondo del mar, debajo de la historia, es donde vive la verdadera tradición, la eterna, en el presente, no en el pasado, muerto para siempre y enterrado en cosas muertas [i.e., man's rational isolations]. En el fondo del presente hay que buscar la tradición eterna, en las entrañas del mar, no en los témpanos del pasado, que al querer darles vida se derriten, revertiendo sus aguas al mar. Así como la tradición es la sustancia de la historia, la eternidad lo es del tiempo, la historia es la forma de la tradición como el tiempo la de la eternidad. Y buscar la tradición en el pasado muerto es buscar la eternidad en el pasado, en la muerte, buscar la eternidad de la muerte [OC, 2a, III, 186–187].

To attempt to find reality in the rational individual isolations is absurd to Unamuno; these die and pass, for they are the superficial change that man forms from his intellectual limitations—reality is an eternal flux; in Unamuno's metaphor it is the sea. A concrete eternal is not anything new in philosophy, but Unamuno's attempt at a continuous time of an eternal flux which he expresses in a metaphorical language significantly anticipates Bergson's *élan vital*.[30]

Thus, Unamuno formulates an eternal flux of reality through tradition and history as Bergson is to do through the biological process of evolution. In "La gloria de don Ramiro" of 1909, only two years after Bergson's *L'évolution créatrice,* Unamuno writes these lines about it:

En esta obra admirable se traza una distinción luminosísima entre el instinto y la inteligencia. . . . "es al interior mismo de la vida adonde nos conduciría la *intuición,* es decir, el instinto hecho desinteresado" [*OC,* 2a, I, 488].

With intuition, and not with logic, Unamuno will approach the phenomena of existence. This direct relationship to the reality

[30] The view of reality as a constant stream, as an eternal flux of continuous change, is not new with either Unamuno or Bergson; it dates back to 500 B.C. to Heraclitus of Ephesus. See W. T. Jones, *A History of Western Philosophy* (New York: Harcourt, Brace and Co., 1952), pp. 38–40. Also see Unamuno's article, "Heráclito, Demócrito y Jeremías" (1915), *OC,* 2a, IX, 64–69. The eternal now which Unamuno is developing in *En torno al casticismo* is also brought out by Henri Bergson in *Creative Evolution,* trans., A. Mitchell (New York: H. Holt, 1911), p. 11. There is no evidence of an influence of one philosopher's thought on the other. What we have is a parallel development in two contemporary philosophers who reacted to the same thoughts. Unamuno (1864–1936) and Bergson (1859–1941) both initiated their philosophical development with the study of Herbert Spencer; see Zubizarreta, *Tras las huellas de Unamuno,* p. 21, and Bergson, *La pensée et le mouvant* (Paris: Alcan, 1934), p. 8. Unamuno sees Spencer historically, but Bergson is struck by the biological evolution. Both men, in reaction to the Positivism of their times, reject the intellect as the means of knowing reality and seek it through intuition. See my article "El residuo Spenceriano en Unamuno," *Insula,* 200–201, July–August, 1963. The use of *intuition* by Bergson is comparable to Unamuno's *sentimiento;* both are knowing processes that start with the subject and go out to the subject's surrounding world. In a recent study of Bergson's philosophy, Ramón Xirau writes this interpretation: "Y es que Bergson piensa, y así lo afirma en *Las dos fuentes,* que toda verdadera doctrina, toda verdadera inteligencia, tiene que originarse en una gran emoción," "Metafísica de Bergson," *Revista de la Universidad de México* (November, 1959), 17. The parallel between these two philosophers has been studied by Meyer, *L'ontologie de Miguel de Unamuno,* pp. 116–117, and by Miguel Cruz Hernández, "Bergson et Unamuno," *Bulletin de la Société Française de Philosophie* (1959), 81–83; and has been mentioned by Blanco Aguinaga, *El Unamuno contemplativo,* p. 172.

of the eternal struggle is carried through by Unamuno in this first perspective.

But, how can Unamuno refer to this perspective of continuous flux known only through an intellectual sympathy or empathy in terms of the negation of non-being and the affirmation of being? The answer is clear: this dialectic pattern is not a means of knowing, but rather an *a priori* framework of thought into which all the Unamunian philosophy will be formulated in the three perspectives.

Unamuno does not use reason as a method, but since he is using language he must use the logic of thought to express himself. It is true that intuition gives the insight, but this insight is placed into the pattern of oppositions. Consequently, the metaphors of Unamuno can be misconstrued if they are not regarded as the linguistic attempt to capture the essence of an intuition. When we comment on the eternal flux of the opposition of being and non-being, it is never intended to indicate two positive entities in struggle as one would consider one man pushing another. What this expression indicates is a driving force which is at work—the work of being—and has as a basic partner the force of change and destruction. Therefore, together the forces are an eternal flux.

The pattern of thought of the dialectic accounts for some of the differences between Bergson and Unamuno's perspective; however, Unamuno himself thought that Bergson was close to his thought. He writes of Bergson in *Del sentimiento trágico:*

¿Qué son los esfuerzos de un Bergson, verbigracia, sobre todo en su obra sobre la evolución creadora, sino forcejeos por restaurar al Dios personal y la conciencia eterna? Y es que la vida no se rinde [*OC*, la, IV, 577].

Unamuno obviously felt that Bergson also tried to achieve the concept of the personal creator but failed, and then created a self-propelling totality. The first perspective of Unamuno which was stated in *En torno al casticismo* was given a solid philosophical frame by Bergson in *L'évolution créatrice* of 1907 [31] so that by 1912 when Unamuno wrote *Del sentimiento trágico* he could reaffirm his first perspective, but in Bergsonian language:

Es una cosa terrible la inteligencia. Tiende a la muerte como a la estabilidad la memoria. Lo vivo, lo que es absolutamente inestable, lo absolutamente individual, es, en rigor, ininteligible. La lógica tira a reducirlo todo a entidades y a géneros. . . . La identidad, que es la muerte, es la aspiración del intelecto. La mente busca lo muerto, pues lo vivo se le escapa,

[31] In *Creative Evolution*, p. 270, Bergson establishes the value of intuition as a means of knowing reality.

quiere cuajar en témpanos la corriente fugitiva, quiere fijarla. Para comprender algo, hay que matarlo, enrigidecerlo en la mente. La ciencia es un cementerio de ideas muertas, aunque de ellas salga vida [*OC*, 1a, IV, 532–533].

In company with Bergson, Unamuno develops this first philosophical perspective [32] from a literary attitude. Non-being is never fulfilled in this perspective, but it is nevertheless a necessary part of the dialectic pattern of struggle. It must be clearly stated that this perspective applies to the whole of reality; thus, non-being does not threaten the individual but rather the whole. Of course the tree, the mountain, the dog, or the man of this reality all have a limited existence and all pass by, but in this first position it is merely a part of the continuous change that is existence. This flux itself does not end; it never dies, but it is constantly dying, that is, its parts are changing.

THE FORMULATION OF THE PROBLEM OF IMMORTALITY IN TERMS OF THE PERSONAL *YO*

During the same years that the first perspective was taking form, Unamuno began to develop what was to be in 1912 the second perspective. The problem is his personal immortality which cannot be approached except through the personal *yo*.[33] For, as has been shown above, the first perspective has no consideration of the personal *yo;* there can be none, for the focus is on the totality. Thus,

[32] It is very interesting to note that Bergson himself considered Unamuno to be a great thinker and only objected to the overpowering *yo* that asserts itself in its world. What the great philosopher was in agreement with is what we call Unamuno's first philosophical perspective, and what he disagreed with was the second and third. See Jacques Chevalier, "Entretiens avec Bergson," *La Table Ronde*, 137 (May, 1959), 9–28. Bergson states (p. 12) this opinion of Unamuno: "Je l'apprécie, comme j'apprécie Ortega . . . pour en revenir à Unamuno, qui est assurément un grand esprit, la seule chose que je lui reproche, c'est l'attachement qu'il avait pour son *moi*. Car le moi, l'attachement à l'esprit propre, voilà bien le grand, le principal obstacle à la moralité."

[33] The years 1896–1912 are the formative years for the second philosophical perspective resulting from a revolution in his literary attitude. But it must be remembered that the coming of a new literary attitude does not supplant the existing one; it merely expresses the Unamunian creativity through another channel, at the same time keeping the first. Of the narrative prose only *Paz en la guerra* will contain parts of both first and second attitudes. The rest of the literary achievements of this period, such as *Amor y pedagogía*, *Poesías*, some of the stories of *El espejo de la muerte*, some *relatos*, some *Paisajes del alma*, *Paisajes*, and many more, are either the development of the first literary attitude with its philosophical expression in *En torno al casticismo* or the formulation of the second attitude which will have its culmination in *Del sentimiento trágico*. These literary attitudes will be demonstrated in the subsequent chapters.

even the concept of civilization in "Civilización y cultura" (1896) is a depersonalized one. Here he applies an idealistic philosophy of force and monads to the regeneration of the individual Spaniard. However, the individual man of flesh and blood, the *yo* that is Unamuno, has not yet appeared.

There followed an attempt to recapture the faith in God, the Creator, who maintains existence; it is during these years that the residue of Unamuno's Hegelian studies formulated the metaphor of God as the Absolute Spirit that is dreaming all reality.[34] The metaphor remained with Unamuno, but the belief in God, as such, could not be sustained. Thus, Unamuno fell back upon the *yo*-will to create belief. This is what has now been called the crisis of 1897 by Unamuno's critics.[35] The result is a God who dreams reality, but who is being dreamt by all the *yos* of the world.

It is at this place in Unamuno's life that many commentators begin to study his writings and by a concentrated selective process make him a late Romantic, at best a distant echo of Kierkegaard.[36]

During the years of the end of the century, Unamuno worked on his "Meditaciones evangélicas," which were to be in two series of three each, one of which was *Nicodemo el fariseo* (1899). In this essay Unamuno meditates on the Gospel of St. John:

Respondió Jesús y le dijo: De seguro y bien de seguro te digo, que el que no naciere otra vez no puede ver el reino de Dios [*OC*, 2a, III, 129].

Both Unamuno and Nicodemo are seeking reassurance that death does not bring annihilation. But the Lord has promised the kingdom of God only to those who are born again.

¿Cómo—se dice Nicodemo—he de poder cambiar ahora y renovarme y hacerme hombre nuevo? Débome a mi pasado; aún más, no soy sino el resultado de mi vida. . . . ¿Que sin fe no he de salvarme? Pero la fe no es voluntaria; se debe a gracia, y si no la tengo, ¿qué hacer? Menester me sería hacerme otro; pero entonces no sería ya yo [*OC*, 2a, III, 130].

---

[34] Unamuno's formative years in the university in Madrid brought him in contact with Positivism and also with Hegel. However, the intellectual ambient of Madrid cannot be ignored, and this meant Krausismo in the 1880's. The universal love under which the complete man put himself in harmony with the world can be seen in Unamuno's God, who is dreaming existence. Because the idealism of Krause could not satisfy Unamuno, the tragic sentiment slowly developed until the Unamunian anthropology was complete in *Del sentimiento trágico*. For studies of Krausismo, see J. López Morillas, *El Krausismo español* (México: Fondo de cultura económica, 1958), and Luis Araquistain, *"El Krausismo en España,"* in *Cuadernos*, 44 (Paris, September-October, 1960), 3-12.

[35] The documentation of the crisis of 1897 is a valuable contribution to Unamuno scholarship by A. Sánchez Barbudo; see *Estudios sobre Unamuno y Machado*, pp. 17–29.

[36] The only serious writer who holds to this opinion is A. Sánchez Barbudo; see *Estudios sobre Unamuno y Machado*, pp. 59–62.

This is now the problem—the only problem: Unamuno's thirst for immortality, but not the empty participation in the perfect form, or a fusion with the world consciousness. Immortality must be for the individual *yo* because anything less is nothing to the *yo*. Unamuno needs faith; he must have faith in the kingdom of God promised by Christ with a spiritual rebirth. Thus, he makes an enormous effort to achieve it, hoping to find peace in faith, and end the battle that rages within him. "Id, pues, cada uno a vuestra casa, a la mía yo, y que en ella nos reciba la paz a todos" (*OC*, 2a, III, 153).

By the following year, 1900, in *La fe,* Unamuno begins formulating his "created" faith in immortality.

P.—¿Qué cosa es fe?
R.—Creer lo que no vimos.

¿Creer lo que no vimos? ¡Creer lo que no vimos, no! Sino crear lo que no vemos. Crear lo que no vemos, sí, crearlo, y vivirlo, y consumirlo, y volverlo a crear y consumirlo de nuevo, viviéndolo otra vez, para otra vez crearlo. . . y así en incesante tormento vital [*OC*, 1a, III, 227].

This is the faith of wanting to believe, of needing belief, which Unamuno has developed out of desperation, but which now will begin to form around a continuous train of thought. In this essay he continues:

Esto es fe viva, porque la vida es continua creación y consunción continua, y, por tanto, muerte incesante. ¿Crees acaso que vivirías si a cada momento no murieses? [*OC*, 1a, III, 227].

In these lines there is the genesis for the metaphysical position of personal existence as struggle. Thus, it is that faith is created by will and the *yo* exists as long as the will of the *yo* struggles against death for immortality. But, it must be understood that this *yo* is not one out of a series or a prototype for humanity; this is Unamuno's *yo*.

The metaphor of existence as the dream of God which, as has been discussed above, has certain overtones of the Hegelian world spirit is now repeated again, however, not as an affirmation but as a wish. In 1904 in *La vida de Don Quijote y Sancho* he writes:

¡La vida es sueño! ¿Será acaso también sueño, Dios mío, este tu Universo de que eres la Conciencia eterna e infinita?, ¿será un sueño tuyo?, ¿será que nos estás soñando? [*OC*, 2a, IV, 377].

But, since the threat is a personal threat to the *yo* of Unamuno, a wish cannot assure him that death will not bring annihilation. Thus, in the same essay he cries out:

¡No hay otro yo en el mundo! Cada cual de nosotros es absoluto. Si hay un Dios que ha hecho y conserva el mundo, lo ha hecho y conserva para mí. ¡No hay otro yo! Los habrá mayores y menores, mejores y peores, pero no otro yo. Yo soy algo enteramente nuevo; en mí se resume una eternidad de pasado y de mí arranca una eternidad de porvenir. ¡No hay otro yo! Esta es la única base sólida del amor entre los hombres porque tampoco hay otro tú que tú, ni otro él que él [*OC*, 2a, IV, 358].

Since it is this irreplaceable *yo* that is in constant threat of death, which may be annihilation, Unamuno's *yo* must fight the struggle against nothingness. In the following years it is becoming apparent to Unamuno that he will never be able to lose this feeling for death, nor is the first perspective of his philosophy sufficient to cope with it.

In 1910 in "Conversación segunda," recalling the metaphor of the sea as well as the one of the dreaming God, Unamuno interjects the personal note of dread for the coming of death—his death.

> Olas que sólo fueron
> sueños del mar...

—Sí, sueños del mar. El mar también sueña y son sus olas sus ensueños; sueña la eternidad, el tiempo; sueña Dios el mundo. ¡Ay el día que despierte! [*OC*, 2a, IV, 561].

This philosophical ferment leads to the second perspective and its finest expression, *Del sentimiento trágico*. It is very important to see how this problem is resolved. On the one hand, there is the complete lack of a self-sustaining faith that death does not mean personal annihilation, while, on the other hand, his *yo*-will cannot accept anything less than immortality:

Pero al ir hundiéndome en el escepticismo racional de una parte, y en la desesperación sentimental, de otra, se me encendió el hambre de Dios, y el ahogo de espíritu me hizo sentir con su falta su realidad. Y quise que haya [*sic*] Dios, que exista Dios. Y Dios no existe, sino que más bien sobre-existe, y está sustentando nuestra existencia, existiéndonos [*OC*, 1a, IV, 595–596].

Thus, the lack of God made Unamuno feel God's reality. And, therefore, he wanted there to be God; he willed that there be God, and there was God. Not a God of an independent existence, but one of a supra-existence, an existence of the will of man who is the maker of the destiny of man. If this is not yet directly stated, the next passage leaves little doubt:

. . . podemos decir que se está haciendo [Dios], y en el hombre y por el hombre. Y si cada cual de nosotros, en el empuje de su amor, en su hambre de divinidad, se imagina a Dios a su medida, y a su medida se hace Dios para él, hay un Dios colectivo, social, humano, resultante de las imagina-ciones todas humanas que le imaginan. Porque Dios es y se revela en la colectividad. Y es Dios la más rica y más personal concepción humana [*OC*, 1a, IV, 596].

Unamuno adds that all individual men live in this their God, created by their will:

Y este Dios, el Dios vivo, tu Dios, nuestro Dios, está en mí, está en ti, vive en nosotros, y nosotros vivimos, nos movemos y somos en El. Y está en nosotros por el hambre que de El tenemos, por el anhelo, haciéndose apetecer [*OC*, 1a, IV, 602].

This thought is leading to the formulation of the second perspective where authentic men are committed to the world which they personalize.[37]

La razón, la cabeza, nos dice: "¡Nada!"; la imaginación, el corazón, nos dice: "¡Todo!", y entre nada y todo, fundiéndose el todo y la nada, en nosotros, vivimos en Dios, que es todo, y vive Dios en nosotros, que sin El somos nada [*OC*, 1a, IV, 603].

Since the tragic sense of life makes the personal *yo* realize that not only is he facing possible annihilation from death but so is this universe, his Universe, it becomes imperative to will God, who is the personalization of this Universe.

Queremos no sólo salvarnos, sino salvar al mundo de la nada. Y para esto, Dios. Tal es su finalidad sentida [*OC*, 1a, IV, 607].

In the remarkable essay–short-story "La locura del doctor Montarco," of 1904, Unamuno is approaching the philosophical perspective of the personal *yo* who has the tragic sense of life:

. . . diga lo que dijere la razón, la gran alcahueta, nuestras entrañas espirituales, eso que llaman ahora el Inconciente (con letra mayúscula) nos dice que para no llegar, más tarde o más temprano, a ser nada, el camino más derecho es esforzarse por serlo todo [*OC*, 2a, III, 692].

Unamuno has applied the dialectic pattern to death—his own personal death—to reach the plane of struggle as the way to live. The approach has been toward the awareness of death through a denial of reason.

These years give Unamuno a philosophical point of view which transposes the continuing struggle from the totality to the personal living relationship of the *yo* to the world. In the essay *Mi religión*, of 1907, he writes:

Y bien, se me dirá: ¿cuál es tu religión? Y yo responderé: Mi religión es buscar la verdad en la vida y la vida en la verdad, aun a sabiendas de que no he de encontrarla mientras viva; mi religión es luchar incesante e

---

[37] Marías does not take into account the full significance of the Unamunian God as an existential commitment of the *yo* to the world. See his study *Unamuno*, pp. 101–103, 150–151. He writes: "Al mismo tiempo su afán de singularidad no le permite permanecer en una posición ortodoxa, recibida, compartida con sus prójimos." See one of the best studies of Unamuno's faith by A. González O.P., "Unamuno: Fe y descreimiento," *La Torre*, XI, 42 (April-June, 1963), 107–143.

incansablemente con el misterio; mi religión es luchar con Dios desde el romper del alba hasta el caer de la noche, como dicen que con El luchó Jacob [*OC*, 1a, III, 820].

This restatement of the problem of the *yo*'s extending world is in terms not of victory but of a continuing struggle. The entire philosophical basis begins to take form in these years. Struggle slowly reaches the position of being the end rather than the means.

Again, in 1909 Unamuno speaks in "De la correspondencia de un luchador" of the dialectic pattern that will develop into the philosophy in the second perspective.

Aunque sí, tú te imaginas luchar por la victoria y yo lucho por la lucha misma. Y como ya te oigo replicarme que la lucha es un medio y no un fin, me adelanto a decirte que nunca supe bien y cada vez sé menos la diferencia que hay de fines a medios. Y si la vida, que no es más que lucha, es un fin, según tú dices y yo no lo creo, entonces puede muy bien serlo la lucha misma [*OC*, 2a, IV, 395].

There are some Nietzschean overtones to these words of Unamuno, but not much more, for Nietzsche's struggle was a struggle *for* power, *for* the dominance of the superman.[38] Quite in contrast, Unamuno's struggle is not a struggle for any purpose, but rather his *yo* is "in-struggle" as long as he exists; in other words, existence of the *yo* is seen as a continued effort between existing and not existing and this is the end in itself: to continue to struggle. Consequently, there are two positions mentioned above and further demonstrated in this same essay of 1909:

. . . ¿volverás a preguntarme qué me propongo con todo cuanto hago? . . . Mi respuesta no puede satisfacerte, carece de eso que llamáis sentido de la realidad. . . . Tú vives entre los otros—ya sabes quiénes son los otros, los que Platón llamaba "los muchos"—y éstos, los otros, cuando ven que alguien no sigue su camino, se dicen: "¡Bah, afán de notoriedad!" [*OC*, 2a, IV, 400].

The personal struggle that is the individual existence of the *hombre de carne y hueso* has its exposition in Unamuno's fullest philosophical achievement—*Del sentimiento trágico de la vida*—written in 1912. Unamuno presents the problem in the following words:

Y hemos llegado al fondo del abismo, al irreconciliable conflicto entre la razón y el sentimiento vital. Y llegado aquí, os he dicho que hay que aceptar el conflicto como tal y vivir de él. Ahora me queda el exponeros cómo a mi sentir y hasta a mi pensar, esa desesperación puede ser base

---

[38] See F. Nietzsche, *Thus Spake Zarathustra*, trans., T. Common (London: Foulis, 1909–13); also *The Will to Power*, trans., A. M. Ludovici (London: Foulis, 1909–13).

de una vida vigorosa, de una acción eficaz, de una ética, de una estética, de una religión y hasta de una lógica [*OC*, 1a, IV, 560–561].

Thus, Unamuno's thoughts on the *yo*'s will and the dialectic pattern of continuing struggle have been brought to the point of the creation of the second philosophical perspective—the awareness of death.

THE SECOND PERSPECTIVE—THE AWARENESS OF DEATH BY THE PERSONAL *YO*

This is a philosophical position that is attained in *Del sentimiento trágico* after years of thought and inquiry; it is a radical departure from the first perspective, or from any traditional metaphysics, since any hierarchy of realities is now abandoned, as well as the consideration of a basic substance or essence of existents. The new metaphysics puts existence itself before any other consideration. The existential fact of the individual's being-there in the world becomes the basis of the entire inquiry.

The Existential Fact of Being-There

In the chapter entitled "El punto de partida" of *Del sentimiento trágico* Unamuno discusses Descartes' *Discourse on Method:*

Lo malo del discurso del método de Descartes no es la duda previa metódica; no es que empezara queriendo dudar de todo, lo cual no es más que un mero artificio; es que quiso empezar prescindiendo de sí mismo, del Descartes, del hombre real, de carne y hueso, del que no quiere morirse, para ser un mero pensador, esto es, una abstracción. . . . La verdad es *sum, ergo cogito* ("soy, luego pienso.") [*OC*, 1a, IV, 488–489].

This philosophical starting point, which puts Unamuno into the area of existentialist philosophy, carries with it the entire second perspective. For if existence precedes man's rational deliberation, he is uncompromisingly free and as such is his own maker through his will to be. To exist is simply to be there, cast in the world. The essential factor about this existence is contingency, not necessity. It is in this state that man finds himself and it is from this state that he tries to escape through the belief in a causal being. But if this belief does not remain, the individual is forced into a second look at himself and then at the world. This is what Unamuno calls "en el fondo del abismo," and in order to live with this anguish the tragic sentiment of life is realized:

Ni, pues, el anhelo vital de inmortalidad humana halla confirmación racional, ni tampoco la razón nos da aliciente y consuelo de vida y verdadera finalidad a ésta. Mas he aquí que en el fondo del abismo se encuentran la desesperación sentimental y volitiva y el escepticismo racional frente a frente, y se abrazan como hermanos. . . .

La paz entre estas dos potencias [la razón y el sentimiento] se hace imposible, y hay que vivir de su guerra. Y hacer de ésta, de la guerra misma, condición de nuestra vida espiritual [OC, 1a, IV, 546].

Thus man, the real individual man, first exists, then rationalizes his position, but the ultimate contingency of death makes some men reflect, doubt, and search for meaning to life. These men first find themselves alone in the abyss, then learn to live from this inner strife through their will as they realize they are making their own future. Unamuno states clearly, in this essay, the basis of the existential anthropology—the tragic sense of life:

Quedémonos ahora en esta vehemente sospecha de que el ansia de no morir, el hambre de inmortalidad personal, el conato con que tendemos a persistir indefinidamente en nuestro ser propio . . . eso es la base afectiva de todo conocer y el íntimo punto de partida personal de toda filosofía humana, fraguada por un hombre y para hombres. . . .

Y ese punto de partida personal y afectivo de toda filosofía y de toda religión es el sentimiento trágico de la vida. Vamos a verlo [OC, 1a, IV, 489].

The Anthropology of the Personal *Yo*

The personal *yo* is in the world and knows the world through the will:

Existe, en efecto, para nosotros todo lo que, de una o de otra manera, necesitamos conocer para existir nosotros; la existencia objetiva es, en nuestro conocer, una dependencia de nuestra propia existencia personal [*Del sentimiento trágico, OC,* 1a, IV, 480].

The rational analysis of the individual is a secondary sociological development:

Y si el individuo se mantiene por el instinto de conservación, la sociedad debe su ser y su mantenimiento al instinto de perpetuación de aquél. Y de este instinto, mejor dicho, de la sociedad, brota la razón.

La razón, lo que llamamos tal, el conocimiento reflejo y reflexivo, el que distingue al hombre, es un producto social [*Del sentimiento trágico, OC,* 1a, IV, 480–481].

Thus, if the individual *yo* wants to penetrate to the core of being, his being, he cannot depend on reason but rather on the tragic sense of life, which comes from an awareness of the impending possibility which can end all possibilities—death. Therefore some men use reason, but others, who have the tragic sense, become authentic and as such commit themselves to the world, which becomes a personalized relationship. This is accomplished by the authentic *yo* by "looking around" and reconsidering the entire complex of the living relationship with the world and with other *yos*. The authentic *yo* becomes aware that this is his relationship, and it is also in jeopardy from his death. This, together with the realization that he is an individual, free *yo*, makes him the forger of the relationship. And with the freedom comes the responsibility—the commitment which is a personalization of the entire complex.

The philosophic expression of the personalization of the living environment by the *yo* is at first an aspiration in "El secreto de la vida" (1906), but by 1912 in *Del sentimiento trágico* it becomes the result of the tragic sense:

Y si doloroso es tener que dejar de ser un día, más doloroso sería acaso seguir siendo siempre uno mismo, y no más que uno mismo, sin poder ser a la vez otro, sin poder ser a la vez todo lo demás, sin poder serlo todo [*OC*, 1a, IV, 572].

The extent of the category the-world-that-is-mine is this *serlo todo*, which means the total experience of the relationships which each individual man has with the world that he is in. Unamuno continues:

Si miras al Universo lo más cerca y lo más dentro que puedes mirarlo, que es en ti mismo; si sientes y no ya sólo contemplas las cosas todas en tu conciencia, donde todas ellas han dejado su dolorosa huella, llegarás al hondón del tedio, no ya de la vida, sino de algo más: al tedio de la existencia, al pozo de la vanidad de vanidades. Y así es como llegarás a compadecerlo todo, al amor universal [*OC*, 1a, IV, 572].

This *amor universal* is not the participation with the world-being of Hegel nor the Krausist idealism; it is the *yo*'s commitment to his world.[39] The *serlo todo* means precisely this final authentic

---

[39] Although an ethical line of thought will not be carried through by Unamuno, it can be readily seen that within this philosophy an ethics could be formulated, Bergson notwithstanding. The norm of this unwritten ethics would be: "Hagamos que la nada, si es que nos está reservada, sea una injusticia; peleemos contra el Destino, y aun sin esperanza de victoria; peleemos contra él quijotescamente," *Del sentimiento trágico, OC*, 1a, IV, 671. This awareness of death which creates the ethical thought of living so as to deserve eternal reward also can lead to an authentic consideration of others as *yos* and not as things. This is accomplished by the personal *yo*'s solitary confrontation with death. The result of this awareness is put into the dialectic of struggle by the *yo* when authentic speech makes the *yo* appear as a *yo* and not as a thing. "No hay más diálogo verdadero que el diálogo que entablas contigo mismo, y este diálogo sólo puedes entablarlo estando a solas. En la soledad, y sólo en la soledad, puedes conocerte a ti mismo como prójimo; y mientras no te conozcas a ti mismo como a prójimo, no podrás llegar a ver en tus prójimos otros yos," *Soledad*, 1905, *OC*, 2a, III, 883. For studies on the Unamunian ethics, see A. W. Levi, "The Quixotic Quest for Being," *Ethics*, LXVI (1956), 132–136; also M. Oromí, *El pensamiento filosófico de Miguel de Unamuno* (Madrid: Espasa-Calpe, 1943), pp. 169–179;

status of existential awareness of the all, which is the *yo*'s world. Each individual is now a unique, irreplaceable *yo*.

The next paragraphs point out the way to a self-realization of this complex of relationships that are within the *yo*.

Para amarlo todo, para compadecerlo todo, humano y extrahumano, viviente y no viviente, es menester que lo sientas todo dentro de ti mismo, que lo personalices todo. Porque el amor personaliza todo cuanto ama, todo cuanto compadece. Sólo compadecemos, es decir, amamos, lo que nos es semejante y en cuanto nos lo es, y tanto más cuanto más se nos asemeja, y así crece nuestra compasión, y con ella nuestro amor a las cosas, a medida que descubrimos las semejanzas que con nosotros tienen [*OC*, 1a, IV, 572].

This world exists in the *yo* and has been re-created there by the will of the *yo* in singling it out, in being aware of it, in feeling for it.

El amor personaliza cuanto ama. Sólo cabe enamorarse de una idea personalizándola. Y cuando el amor es tan grande y tan vivo, y tan fuerte y desbordante que lo ama todo, entonces lo personaliza todo y descubre que el total Todo, que el Universo, es Persona también que tiene una Conciencia, Conciencia que a su vez sufre, compadece y ama; es decir, es conciencia. Y a esta Conciencia del Universo, que el amor descubre personalizando cuanto ama, es a lo que llamamos Dios [*OC*, 1a, IV, 573].

It must be recalled that this God is a personal God of the *yo*'s creation and of the *yo*'s world-scene; this is not a transcendent concept of God, for the above lines cannot in any way be taken as a form of Pantheism or the world of Schopenhauer.[40] Unamuno concludes this thought in the following paragraph:

Dios es, pues, la personalización del Todo, es la Conciencia eterna e infinita del Universo, Conciencia presa de la materia, y luchando por libertarse de ella. Personalizamos el Todo para salvarnos de la nada, y el único misterio verdaderamente misterioso es el misterio del dolor [*OC*, 1a, IV, 573].

The "Conciencia presa de la materia" is not the Thomistic concept of the material limitations imposed on the soul; it is rather the personal effort of the individual man to personalize his world, his total living relationship with everything around him. The tragic sense of life, which opens the personal *yo* to the world for personalization in an act of commitment, is, as has been discussed,

Ferrater Mora, *Unamuno: Bosquejo de una filosofía*, pp. 83–97; and H. Benítez, *El drama religioso de Unamuno*, pp. 190–192.

40 In *Del sentimiento trágico*, Unamuno writes this analysis of Schopenhauer: "Sólo que su falta de sentido social e histórico, el no sentir a la Humanidad como una persona también, aunque colectiva, su egoísmo, en fin, le impidió sentir a Dios, le impidió individualizar y personalizar la Voluntad total y colectiva: la Voluntad del Universo," *OC*, 1a, IV, 579.

the result of an awareness of death. But it must be emphasized that this is not a passive state of inner wisdom. Quite the contrary, it is a state of emotional and intellectual struggle which rages within the authentic man. And this continuous struggle between the intellect, which can only use reason, and emotive consciousness, which can only feel the thirst to be immortal, does not put the world-relationship into these two poles, for that would be an abstraction rather than a personalization. The pattern of struggle which is the tragic sense is a positive force; its function is to make all living relationships personal ones for the *yo,* so that others will be considered to be unique individual forces that are also making their future just as the *yo* who has personalized them. Unamuno wrote the following exposition:

. . . quiero establecer que la incertidumbre, la duda, el perpetuo combate con el misterio de nuestro final destino, la desesperación mental y la falta de sólido y estable fundamento dogmático, pueden ser base de moral [p. 666].

Podemos formularla así: obra de modo que merezcas a tu propio juicio y a juicio de los demás la eternidad, que te hagas insustituíble, que no merezcas morir. O tal vez así: obra como si hubieses de morirte mañana, pero para sobrevivir y eternizarte. El fin de la moral es dar finalidad humana, personal, al Universo; descubrir la que tenga—si es que la tiene— y descubrirla obrando [p. 667].

Cada hombre es, en efecto, único e insustituíble; otro yo no puede darse; cada uno de nosotros—nuestra alma, no nuestra vida—vale por el Universo todo [p. 672].

Amar al prójimo, es querer que sea como yo, que sea otro yo, es decir, es querer yo ser él; es querer borrar la divisoria entre él y yo, suprimir el mal. Mi esfuerzo por imponerme a otro, por ser y vivir yo en él y de él, por hacerlo mío—que es lo mismo que hacerme suyo—, es lo que da sentido religioso a la colectividad, a la solidaridad humana.

El sentimiento de solidaridad parte de mí mismo; como soy sociedad, necesito adueñarme de la sociedad humana; como soy un producto social, tengo que socializarme, y de mí voy a Dios—que soy yo proyectado al Todo—y de Dios a cada uno de mis prójimos [*Del sentimiento trágico, OC,* 1a, IV, 679].

Thirteen years later Unamuno wrote *La agonía del Cristianismo* (1925) while in exile in France—a period of emotional crisis equal in depth to the one of 1897. Again the problem is the existence of the *yo,* which, when seen with the tragic sense of life, becomes an authentic view but also an unceasing struggle unto death.

Agonía, ἀγωνία, quiere decir lucha. Agoniza el que vive luchando, luchando contra la vida misma. Y contra la muerte. Es la jaculatoria de Santa Teresa de Jesús: "Muero porque no muero."

Lo que voy a exponer aquí, lector, es mi agonía, mi lucha por el cristianismo, la agonía del cristianismo en mí, su muerte y su resurrección en cada momento de mi vida íntima [OC, 1a, IV, 829].

Luchar contra la vida misma means only that the *yo* in his utter freedom is faced with the contingency of life and must struggle to make his own *yo* at every moment, since the ultimate contingency is always present.

The tragic sense of life, it must be remembered, is born in the pattern of opposition between intellect and will and results in an awareness of death that gives an authentic perspective to the personal *yo*. Thus, the existence of the authentic *yo* from the moment he finds himself in existence until his death is one continuous struggle.

Se habla de *struggle for life*, de lucha por la vida; pero esta lucha por la vida es la vida misma, la *life*, y es a la vez la lucha misma, la *struggle*. . . .

Sólo se pone uno en paz consigo mismo, como Don Quijote, para morir [OC, 1a, IV, 830].

The perspective of the personal *yo* continues throughout life to engulf the total living relationship of world and men and becomes a philosophical directive for life which is a struggle unto death.

THE THIRD PERSPECTIVE—THE RE-CREATION OF THE *YO*'S THOUGHT IN OTHER *YOS*

In *En torno al casticismo* of 1895 Unamuno considered tradition to be the ever growing sediment of human activity in the continuous river of life. In that essay the first perspective was being formulated and, consequently, the focus was on the eternal flux of reality, and men were given the rôle of being the anonymous contributors to the rich accumulation which is tradition. The individual names, which history records, were seen as mere waves on the surface of the bottomless sea.

In the years that followed, as the *yo* was taken as an existential starting point, a philosophical perspective developed around the awareness of death as the jeopardy of annihilation. Faith in the immortality of the personal *yo* was unattainable, but from the chaos of this crisis Unamuno developed the tragic sense of life. However, this second perspective did not focus at all on the work of the personal *yo*—that is, the record of accomplishments by an individual *yo*.

In this third perspective the focus is now on man's work, not as the anonymous contribution of the first perspective, but rather as the unique work of the personal *yo*. The philosophical basis lies in the idea that during a personal *yo*'s life there is another *yo* created in the minds of the other *yos*. If the personal *yo* has lived apart from his fellow man, he will die and soon be forgotten. If he has had children his flesh and blood has been reproduced, but in a few generations this also will be lost in the flow of life. If he has been well known and history has recorded his name, his name will go on, but it will soon become an empty label carrying no remembrance of the *yo* of flesh and blood that he was once. However, if Unamuno's *yo* creates through the written work a *yo* that others can re-create, then this *yo* that others create can be constantly re-created and included in the living experience of each re-creator. Thus, not only does there grow up a collective legend or image of Unamuno's *yo* that others think he is, but there is always the source of re-creation in the written word where new re-creators may go to bring his thought to life again as a part of their consciousness.

By 1904, in *La vida de Don Quijote y Sancho,* Unamuno considers the deeds of the immortal knight errant:

Ansia de inmortalidad nos lleva a amar a la mujer, y así fué como Don Quijote juntó en Dulcinea a la mujer y a la Gloria, y ya que no pudiera perpetuarse por ella en hijo de carne, buscó eternizarse por ella en hazañas de espíritu [*OC*, 2a, IV, 137].

However, Unamuno is still not ready to consider this problem from its own perspective, for he is attempting to resolve his own problem of the jeopardy of death which only the tragic sense of life will answer as the second perspective.

Del sentimiento trágico (1912) contains the seed of the third perspective in this paragraph:

¡Eso eres tú! me dicen con los Upanischadas. Y yo les digo: "Sí, yo soy eso, cuando eso es yo y todo es mío y mía la totalidad de las cosas. Y, como mía, la quiero y amo al prójimo, porque vive en mí como parte de mi conciencia, porque es como yo, es mío" [*OC*, 1a, IV, 497].

In the authentic *yo*-will which personalizes its living relationship exist other *yos* that have been encountered in life or that have been re-created from the written word, as Unamuno has done with Don Quijote. All that is needed now is for Unamuno to become aware that he also may be re-created by others through his words.

The third perspective is the awareness of a spiritual brotherhood through the written words which a personal *yo* uses to re-create the living thought of the writer. This third perspective comes to its full expression in *La agonia del Cristianismo* (1925):

Y, por mi parte, me ha ocurrido muchas veces, al encontrarme en un escrito con un hombre, no con un filósofo ni con un sabio o pensador, al encontrarme con un alma, no con una doctrina, decirme: "¡Pero éste he sido yo!" Y he revivido con Pascal en su siglo y en su ámbito, y he revivido con Kierkegaard en Copenhague, y así con otros [*OC*, 1a, IV, 837].

And this perspective of the brotherhood of living thought is not mistaken as an answer to the problem of the personal *yo*'s death, as was the case in 1904. In *La agonía* Unamuno now writes:

Y este cuerpo de muerte es el hombre carnal, fisiológico, la cosa humana y el otro, el que vive en los demás, en la historia, es el hombre histórico [*OC*, 1a, IV, 843].

Unamuno then proceeds to bring out that the basic urge in the *yo* to be re-created in his children is but a shallow compensation for the thirst to be immortal. Paternity cannot suffice, for the personal consciousness will still die.

This third perspective has had its genesis in the literary attitude which emphasizes the physical and spiritual re-creating of the *yo*. But Unamuno has made it clear in this essay that the thought of resurrection in one's children is self-delusion; the only way to face the threat of death is with the tragic sense of life of the second perspective.

The participation in the continuum of living thought, which is the third perspective, carries certain important implications: (1) the continuum of thought is an ever increasing and ever enriching body, dependent on personal *yos* for its existence and for the re-creation of the individuals from their writings. If there be no readers there will be but oblivion; thus, again the Unamunian pattern of oppositions shows itself—there must be the constant effort of re-creation by future readers to save his written words from oblivion. (2) There is also a responsibility to the writer whose written words enter into this brotherhood of thought to write the truth. What Unamuno considered to be the truth can be summed up rapidly: the truth of man is seen through the thinking of one's feelings and the feeling of one's thoughts. This becomes an esthetic theory which will be demonstrated in the following chapters, for each of the literary attitudes is a study in one phase of Unamuno's esthetics. Each attitude, in turn, has had a philosophical statement as its intellectual culmination.

In conclusion, this philosophy in all of its manifestations was born in the living experiences of the mind and of the soul of this man. After 1895 it rapidly took form and soon became a way of life which he followed religiously until his death in 1936. He wrote this résumé of his life in *Cómo se hace una novela* (1927):

Héteme aquí ante estas páginas blancas, mi porvenir, tratando de derramar mi vida a fin de continuar viviendo, de darme la vida, de arrancarme a la muerte de cada instante [*OC*, 1a, IV, 937].

CHAPTER TWO

THE LITERARY EXPRESSION OF DEATH FOR THE *YO* WHO IS PART OF THE WORLD

The death theme is as old as literature and has been a rich source of creativity in Spanish literature. And it is in line with this tradition that death is approached in this literary attitude. The subject for discussion here is the *yo* that God knows in the perspective of the totality of reality. This is the *yo* that exists outside the consciousness of the individual and outside the image of the individual created by others. Throughout this point of view there will be a constant comparison and contrast of the individual, who outside his consciousness is lost, with the world of nature that endures. Also, the contemplation of nature causes the intuitive evocation of the constantly changing duration [1] (or in Bergson's terms, *durée*) which is the whole of reality.

This *yo* that is lost in the incomprehensible non-limitations of

---

[1] See Blanco Aguinaga, *El Unamuno contemplativo*, pp. 170–203, where the attitude of this chapter is studied as "La eternidad en el paisaje." Although this chapter of our study and part of the next are to a great extent in debt to this basic study of Unamuno, we do not agree with Blanco Aguinaga's division of Unamuno's life and works into two parts—the "Unamuno agónico" and the "Unamuno contemplativo." This study of nature in the literature of Unamuno is what its author considers indicative of the Unamuno *contemplativo*, which is defined as: "Una oscura tendencia a dejarse ser, sin carne, ni hueso, ni conciencia" (p. 34), and "Cuando se abandona Unamuno a la contemplación en la idea de la paz o de la inconsciencia" (p. 35). These are two basically different metaphysical positions which are treated as one in the book. The first is the conscious yearning of the *yo* for a surrender to death, but the second does not consider the personal *yo* at all. It is rather an intuition into the totality of existence, with the focus on the whole and only incidentally on the parts. Thus, the struggle that is existence is not expressed in terms of the personal *yo* but in terms of flux and eternal motion.

infinity has a positive and a negative expression. It is either lost in the *todo* of a Spinozean God or in the *nada* of Leopardi. It must be kept in mind that this is the nonpersonal *yo* that dies and vanishes to be forgotten.

From nature two types of metaphors will be drawn: those alluding to water and trees. Water appears in the form of lakes, rivers, seas, rain, and snow, the combination of rain upon the lake being the most frequent use of nature.

As one penetrates into the literary world of Unamuno it would be well to recall the words of Ferrater Mora:

La poesía es, así, fusión entre las cosas y el hombre, objetivación del hombre al tiempo que subjetivación de la realidad.

Toda la "obra literaria" de Unamuno . . . es, por consiguiente, poesía, tanto si adopta la forma del verso como la de la prosa, la de la novela como la del ensayo, la del discurso como la de la comedia.[2]

NARRATIVE PROSE

In the prose narratives of Unamuno, as in the rest of his literary creation, the reader is aware that he is confronting a living individual who puts himself into the created work at all times. One can never forget that there is a narrator, even when the first person is not used or when the fictional characters speak in dialogue. The style of this prose can be summarized under the following elements: paradox, play on words, metaphor, repetition of images, and the syntax of spoken language. All of these elements function to give the overwhelming effect of the presence of the man, Unamuno, as well as breaking the logical necessities and limitations of the written language in favor of the emotive expression of the man. The paradox breaks the limitations of logical thought (the play on words does also, but in a more jocular tone), and it is upon this disturbance of thought that the metaphor takes hold to build the Unamunian thought. Once the metaphors have established symbols, it is merely a matter of repetition and restatement until the reader is saturated with this thought. All of this is expressed in language resembling as nearly as possible the spoken language. It is at times a stream of phrases, at other times a series of questions and answers with the constant interpolation of the conversational aside and with all the emotive emphasis that the interjection and exclamation will give.[3]

[2] Ferrater Mora, *Unamuno: Bosquejo de una filosofía*, pp. 105–106.
[3] For a study of Unamuno's ideas on this style of writing, see Blanco Aguinaga, *Unamuno, teórico del lenguaje* (México: El Colegio de México, 1954), pp. 115–

However, of all Unamuno's prose writings the ones studied in this chapter give the strongest impression of the separation of the narrator from his subject matter. This is only an impression because it is always the very essence of Unamuno's subjective intuition that plunges him into these evocations of the *yo* that is in reality. This interior thrust away from the personal awareness into a feeling for the whole of reality will be presented here, and a brief study of the mechanics will follow at the end of this section.

Paisajes del alma (1892–1936)

As can be seen from the forty-four-year span indicated above, these writings were a lifelong interest of Unamuno not limited to any phase of his intellectual development.[4] By following chronologically the course of these commentaries, two facts will become clear: (1) the evocation of nature remains throughout an intense intuition of reality, and (2) the manner of expression continually changes, becoming ever more direct and more conversational.

In 1892 Unamuno writes in "Pompeya" these thoughts on man and the world as he looks at the ruins:

La esplendidez del cielo infunde sentimiento de universal y serena indiferencia, indiferencia olímpica, no hipocondríaca, y allí, comparando Leopardi la destrucción de Pompeya a una manzana que cayendo del árbol aplasta un hormiguero, pudo decir que no tiene más cuidado del hombre que de la hormiga la Naturaleza, madre en el parto, en el querer, madrastra [*OC*, 2a, I, 863].

It is this type of comparison, so explicitly stated here, that will be worked and reworked, with the sun, light, or nature in general as so many momentary sounds and visions of the eternal vital movement that is existence. Unamuno concludes this *paisaje* with an evocation of the viable sound of the *cigarra* as the symbol of the eternal life among the ruins while the world indifferently goes on, oblivious to death: "se oye cantar a la cigarra la eternidad de la vida y lo vano de la gloria" (p. 865).

One of the most poetic prose paintings of this world of *durée* was written in 1918 by Unamuno. Its title, "Paisajes del alma,"

128; also Fernando Huarte Morton, "El ideario lingüístico de Miguel de Unamuno," *Cuadernos de la cátedra* . . . , V (1954), 31–64.

4 These Unamunian commentaries on nature were collected by García Blanco; for previous editions of the separate parts, see *OC*, 2a, I, 26–29. Critics who have studied this book are: Lázaro Montero, "Otra vez Unamuno en el paisaje," *Fénix*, II (Madrid, February, 1945), 112–115; Antonio Tovar, "*Paisajes del alma,*" *Escorial* (Madrid, 1945), 141–143; Gregorio Rabassa, "Paisajes del alma," *Revista Hispánica Moderna*, XIII (New York, 1947), 289.

was later used for the book. The initial tone is one of silence and solitude, but soon one can see that nothing is static, for everything here is striving to be. (See the study of this *paisaje* in the conclusion to this section.)

La nieve había cubierto todas las cumbres rocosas del alma, las que, ceñidas de cielo, se miran en éste como en un espejo y se ven, a las veces, reflejadas en forma de nubes pasajeras [*OC*, 2a, I, 851].

The snow, the symbol of silence and quietude, has covered the soul of God's world.

Tan sólo, de tiempo en tiempo, algún águila hambrienta avizoraba desde el cielo la blancura, por si lograba descubrir en ella rastro de presa [*OC*, 2a, I, 851].

The first sign of life was the flying eagle, but now the poet is prepared to take his view beneath the silent snow.

Pero dentro de aquellas cumbres rocosas, embozadas en la arreciente pureza de la blancura de la nieve y escoltadas de cielo, bullían aún las pavesas de lo que en la juventud de las rocas fué un volcán [*OC*, 2a, I, 851].

Therefore, it is not implied that only the valley has life and the peaks are cold, silent, and dead, for the symphony of life is just beginning in this Unamunian evocation. In the next paragraph the eternal change from mountains to valley underlines the continuous process of life.

Los arroyos que desde el valle contemplaban las cumbres estaban hechos con aguas que del derretimiento de las encumbradas nieves descendían; su alma era del alma excelsa que se arrecía de frío. Y la verdura se alimentaba de aquellas mismas aguas de las nieves. La tierra misma sobre que discurrían los arroyos, la tierra de que con sus raíces chupaban vida los árboles, era el polvo a que las rocas de las cumbres se iban reduciendo [*OC*, 2a, I, 852].

There is no place for death in this poetic intuition of reality, for all is in a constant process of change for eternity. Six years later, in 1924, Unamuno intuits the meaning of reality from nature once more in "¡Montaña, desierto, mar!"; however, the style is now closer to the spoken language.

¡Visión eterna la de Gredos! Eterna, sí; y no porque haya de durar por siempre . . . sino porque está fuera del tiempo, fuera del pasado y del futuro, en el presente inmóvil, en la eternidad viva. ¡Visión eterna la de Gredos! [*OC*, 2a, I, 937].

This stream of exclamations and paradox immediately makes logical discourse impossible. One reads, rereads, and finally the intuition that Unamuno felt as he looked upon the mountain slowly begins to emerge in the reader's mind. This is an eternal view that the mountain has given to Unamuno. It is eternal not because the material itself will remain forever, but because it is a view of the living reality that is in eternal transformation. The view is not in time, for only abstracted things are in time—the device of man to measure his own duration—but reality is outside of time in the always-now. Once Unamuno has broken away from logic with the paradox, he continues by adding more images; thus, the sea and the desert also give a view of the eternal:

. . . la visión eterna de la mar, de la mar eterna, de la mar que vió nacer y verá morir la historia, de la mar que guarda la misma sonrisa con que acogió el alba del linaje humano, la misma sonrisa con que contemplará su ocaso [*OC*, 2a, I, 938].

In "Los delfines de Santa Brígida" of 1932, already in the *ocaso* of his life, Unamuno wrote about life and death in the world he lived, as he admired the sound of water in a Madrid fountain:

Susurra la permanente transitoriedad de la cosa y la vida públicas, la queda de lo que se pasa y el paso de lo que se queda, la estadía de la corriente y el curso de lo que se está. Y en armonía con el "¡así va todo!"— "¡así viene todo!"—, susurra: "¡así se queda todo!"—. Todo, todo: revolución y reacción, progreso y tradición, rebeldía y cumplimiento, fe y razón, dogma y crítica, sueño y vela—yedras entre escombros de ruinas—, nacimiento y muerte—dos tránsitos—, todo y nada [*OC*, 2a, I, 954].

In these words (perfect examples of the Unamunian style studied above) Unamuno brings forth from the sound of a fountain the dialectic stream of thought which is his philosophical basis.

When Unamuno contemplates the running water of a river, it brings the words of Jorge Manrique into his mind: "Nuestras vidas son los rios, que van a dar en la mar" (in both "¡Montaña, desierto, mar!," 1924, and "Jueves Santo en Rioseco," 1932 [*OC*, 2a, I, 938, 1029]). But later, in 1932, the small river of Madrid, the Manzanares, brings out this striking metaphor in "Manzanares arriba, o las dos barajas de Dios":

Lo de ver quebrarse el agua entre peñascos rodados es como contemplar la rompiente del oleaje marino en una costa, o las llamaradas del fuego del hogar o los giros del humo. Juego de solitarios de la baraja de Dios. O de la naturaleza [*OC*, 2a, I, 970].

It is clear that this is an eternity, metaphorically given, with no meaning of death applicable. Since the playing cards are being continuously shuffled and reshuffled, there is a continuous change of combinations with the changing world and the changing area of human thought. A few months before writing the above *paisaje*

Unamuno ended the commentary, "Jueves Santo en Rioseco" (1932), with these words that can serve as an epilogue to this book:

Y es, lector, que alguna vez tengo que hablarte, en comentario perpetuo, no de lo de antes, ni de lo de ahora, ni de lo de después, sino de lo de siempre y de nunca, que ya volveremos a los pasos de la actualidad pasajera y a bailar al son de la guitarra simbólica [*OC,* 2a, I, 1029–30].

The basic unity of Unamunian thought is in evidence here, for the "comentario perpetuo" is his communication through the created word—his literature. (This aspect will be studied in Chapter Four.) And the reminder that all men will "bailar al son de la guitarra simbólica" is the personal awareness of death and the individual's necessity to confront it if he is to live authentically (this is the subject matter of Chapter Three). Finally, "de lo de siempre" is the eternal now that is the world of which men are parts, that is, the attitude studied in this chapter.

Paz en la guerra (1897)

Unamuno's first novel [5] is the culmination of years of reworking the historical material of the second Carlist war (1872-76) [6] in Bilbao and the Basque provinces. This novel is unique in that it is the only one written by Unamuno that has a fully developed setting in which the fictional characters are born, live, and die. One could almost say that the Basque countryside, especially around Bilbao, becomes a character itself, for at times the characters appear to be lost in its contemplation, and, what is even more striking, the narrator at certain moments of poetic intensity leaves the plot and in an evocation from the contemplation of nature intuits existence. Thus, there is much more presented than mere scenery for action. The creation of the ambient serves the function of scenery and also the basis for an evocation of reality. The latter aspect is the subject of study in this chapter. The ambient as a background for the plot to be developed by the characters will be postponed until the next chapter.

The only loss in the continuous change that is reality is the

[5] Among the many opinions and evaluations of this first novel are: Marías, *Miguel de Unamuno,* pp. 87–94; Sánchez Barbudo, *Estudios sobre Unamuno y Machado,* pp. 31–42; and Blanco Aguinaga, *El Unamuno contemplativo,* pp. 56–78. Our opinion, with the reservations already indicated, is in agreement with Blanco Aguinaga.

[6] For a detailed review of the formative period of the novel, see *OC,* 2a, II, 11–16, where García Blanco again provides the background to the writings of Unamuno.

individual consciousness; thus, death as a loss or the threat of a loss is not present in this Unamunian attitude, for nature endures in its eternal strife of existence. In this novel the author uses this attitude in juxtaposition to the personal feelings of the characters in their awareness of death.

In the following selection there is the gradual penetration into totality through nature. At first it is what is seen by the fictional character, but the narrator never leaves the contemplation to the character; rather he adopts it himself:

En los hondos senos de aquella mar, serena y tranquila entonces, en sus quietos abismos, proseguía también entre sus muchos moradores lenta y silenciosa lucha por la vida. Por todas partes cerraban el horizonte montes tras de montes, cual escalera para subir al cielo; cimas que parecían encumbrarse para mejor ver la lucha. En el fondo, allá, a lo lejos, Begoña y los alrededores de Bilbao. Una nube, en corona semicircular, velaba el valle [*OC*, 2a, II, 331].

The world that is indifferent to man's actions is the passive witness to death among men as the wreath-like cloud gives the valley the aspect of a wake. After a long description of the moment of death of one of the main characters, Ignacio, Unamuno writes: "Junto a él resonaba el fragor del combate, mientras las olas del tiempo se rompían en la eternidad" (*OC*, 2a, II, 334). Another example of this attitude of the *yo*'s loss can be seen in the following passage as Pedro Antonio responds to his wife's death and awaits his own death:

Vive en la verdadera paz de la vida, dejándose mecer indiferente en los cotidianos cuidados al día; mas reposando a la vez en la calma del desprendido de todo lo pasajero: en la eternidad; vive al día en la eternidad. Espera que esta vida profunda se le prolongue más allá de la muerte, para gozar, en un día sin noche, de luz perpetua, de claridad infinita, de descanso seguro, en firme paz, en paz imperturbable y segura, paz por dentro y por fuera, paz del todo permanente [*OC*, 2a, II, 410–411].

The *yo* being lost into the bottomless sea of totality is the result of death to the man of unassailable faith: one of the meek of the *intrahistoria*. As such a man, Pedro Antonio was awaiting the eternal participation.

Ignacio, his son, also met death without any awareness of it and with the faith of an eternal nameless peace: "En su cara quedó la expresión de una calma serena, como la de haber descansado, en cuanto venció a la vida, en la paz de la tierra, por la que no pasa un minuto" (*OC*, 2a, II, 334). After Ignacio's death the focus of the novel turns on his friend Pachico, who in a long reflective passage gives a mirror of this Unamunian attitude. The following quotation leaves the personal attitude for a moment and concentrates on nature recalling the sea once again.

Una ola muerta. . . . ¿muerta? allá venía otra, a morir también, y las aguas siempre las mismas. Por debajo del oleaje, obra del viento en el pellejo tan sólo del inmenso océano; por debajo del oleaje, contra su dirección tal vez, sin obedecerla, marchaba incesante el curso perdurable de las aguas profundas, en corro sin cesar recomenzado [*OC*, 2a, II, 361].

This view of the ocean is essentially the view of reality that Unamuno held throughout the fifty years of his literary creativity. The ocean is a changing, incessant mass, but yet there is the duration of the ever renewing change that makes it eternal to Unamuno. Just as Bergson sees the *élan vital* as the force behind the *durée,* so Unamuno will use his dialectic of *lucha*. This attitude is Unamuno's first attitude toward death. Unamuno, like his character Pachico, feels the terror of death that cries out "todo o nada," which will produce the tragic sense of life as the second attitude toward death. But by going outside of the *yo* to the vast universe where the *yo* is a minute part, both, author and character, find peace in the war of continued existence of reality. The last pages of the novel express the way by which this skirmish with death leads to the first two attitudes which are complementary—one of the totality, one of man.

Allí arriba, la contemplación serena le da resignación trascendente y eterna, madre de la irresignación temporal, del no contentarse jamás aquí abajo, del pedir siempre mayor salario, y baja decidido a provocar en los demás el descontento, primer motor de todo progreso y de todo bien [*OC*, 2a, II, 417].

In the last page of this novel Unamuno finally gives the formula of this attitude: war is to peace what time is to eternity. War is the incessant everyday force of living that is continuation itself. This flux is eternal, and for the individual who is lost outside his *yo* there is peace: "No fuera de ésta [la guerra], sino dentro de ella, en su seno mismo, hay que buscar la paz; paz en la guerra misma" (*OC,* 2a, II, 417).

Paisajes (1902)

Unamuno's early commentaries on scenery and landscape—most of which were written between 1897 and 1898—appear as a collection in *Paisajes,* published at the same time as *Amor y pedagogía*.[7]

---

[7] For a review contemporary to the work, see E. Merimée, "Reseña de *Paisajes*," *Bulletin Hispanique,* V (1903), 197–199. This book, together with some of the others considered in this chapter, has given Blanco Aguinaga the main substance for his *El Unamuno contemplativo*.

From this date on Unamuno continued to publish the commentaries on nature separately from his novels. The reason for the bifurcation will become more obvious in this study, for the Unamuno novel dominated by his personal *yo* or by the *yo* that others construct leaves no place for these delicate flights outside of the *yo* evoked by the wonders of nature.

In "Puesta del sol," of 1897, the beauty of the sunset lets the commentator forget himself and express the outside reality: "anegada la conciencia, saborea en su desmayo cierta muerte de la vida y el santo desinterés de la adoración de la Belleza" *(OC,* 2a, I, 75).

The *intrahistoria* world view that Unamuno proclaims in *En torno al casticismo* (1895) can be found in an embryonic stage in these commentaries,[8] for not only does he contemplate nature but also man as a part of this world. Beneath the exterior there is a living duration in man: he is born, he works, he reproduces, he dies, another is born, and so forth. This living cycle of man is seen as part of the constant flux of duration that is reality.

Allí está cavando, junto al río, frente a las montañas, tan inmutable aquél como éstas, con su fluir de continuo el uno y con su firme asiento las otras.

. . . . .

Es uno de los héroes, de los héroes humildes—*humiles*—, de la tierra—*humus*—; es uno de los héroes del heroísmo vulgar, cotidiano y difuso; de todos los momentos. Es su ideal la realidad misma. Viene de la piedra, por camino de siglos y siglos, que se pierde en el pasado; va al ángel, que alboreará en un porvenir inasequible [*OC,* 2a, I, 81–82].

Por tierras de Portugal y de España (1911)

Any scene, any landscape, can be transformed into an evocation of the duration of existence. In "La pesca de Espinho" fishermen have brought in their nets full of sardines and crawfish. This meditation brings out the duration that is in change; for although sun, sea, earth, man, animals, man's work, and man's tools constantly change, they nevertheless endure.

El sol muriendo en las aguas eternas y los peces en la arena, los hombres mercando su cosecha marina, el mar cantando su perdurable *fado,* los bueyes rumiando lentamente bajo sus ornamentados yugos, y allá a lo lejos, las oscuras copas de los pinos empezando a diluirse en el cielo de la extrema tarde [*OC,* 2a, I, 411].

The contrasting images of change and duration give a tone of endless fluctuation to the entire piece. Although the sun is dying,

---

[8] For a study of the concept of *intrahistoria* converted to metaphorical creation, see "La función simbólica del agua," *El Unamuno contemplativo,* pp. 221–252.

the waters are eternal and the song of the sea is duration. The ageless work of the fishermen is contrasted to "molinos de viento sobrevivientes": the fossils of another age. These images and metaphors will be used in the other attitudes, but with the addition of the personal *yo*.

El espejo de la muerte (1913)

In this collection of short stories Unamuno presents another aspect of this attitude, the *yo* that only God knows.[9] Here, Unamuno takes the narrating position of an indifferent creator who passively observes these mere parts of the milieu passing into the oblivion of death. This expression of the attitude can be found in some of his poems and in certain characters in the novels, but in these short stories it has five outstanding appearances.

In the first story, "El espejo de la muerte" (1911) which is subtitled *una historia muy vulgar,* there is only a monothematic progression toward death in a sickly twenty-three-year-old girl. The story opens with this line: "¡La pobre! Era una languidez traidora que iba ganándole el cuerpo todo de día en día" (*OC,* 2a, II, 621). Not only was she suffering "el languidecer, el palidecer, marchitarse y ajársele el cuerpo" (*OC,* 2a, II, 622), but also she was losing her fiancé. In excellent counterpoint the environment of Matilde was bursting with life: "Todo era en torno alegría y verdor" (*OC,* 2a, II, 625). But she was all bones and the mirror showed only the progression of death, and when she spoke, the sign of death was on her lips without her being aware of it. The story ends on this note:

Se pasó la noche llorando y anhelando y a la mañana siguiente no quiso mirarse al espejo. . . . a los tres meses de la fiesta se la llevaba a que la retozasen los ángeles [*OC,* 2a, II, 627].

The reason why this story creates such an overwhelming drive toward Matilde's death is the attitude of the passive narrator adopted by Unamuno. Although no specific cause of death is given, the exterior symptoms are repeated in detail by the girl herself. She was not aware that death was coming; all she knew was the day-to-day deterioration. Thus, this is the story of the death of a girl not seen from her *yo* nor as others saw her, but rather as she appeared in the world: a fleeting moment in the passing of ever changing life that almost passes without notice.

Another monothematic story of death is "Ramón Nonnato, suicida" (n.d.). This story begins with the suicide of Ramón and then reviews the life of the young man, ending with the agreement of marriage of his mother to his father—that is, at the beginning of what was to be his life. The fatalism of Ramón is immense.

Habíanle sacado a Ramón Nonnato del cadáver tibio de su madre, que murió poco antes de cuando había de darle a luz, cuarenta y dos años antes del día aquel en que se suicidó. Y es, pues, que había nacido con el suicidio en el alma [*OC*, 2a, II, 639].

And his life followed this fatal birth without the slightest deviation: "Su niñez fué un solo día largo, un día gris y frío de unos cuantos años" (*OC*, 2a, II, 638).

Again in "Soledad" (1911) a child is born and the mother dies, but here death is not the central theme and is used only at the beginning of the story to underline the continuity of life.

Soledad nació de la muerte de su madre: ya Leopardi cantó que es riesgo de muerte el nacimiento,

> nasce l'uomo a fatica
> ed è rischio di morte il nascimento,

riesgo de muerte para el que nace, riesgo de muerte para quien le da el ser [*OC*, 2a, II, 683].

There is a risk for both, but the old dies and the newborn lives; thus, life goes on. This same aspect of death is developed in another attitude—immortality in others—which will be studied in Chapter Four.

Probably one of the most complete statements of a passive creator can be seen in the story "Solitaña" (1888):

Murió; su hijo le lloró el tiempo que sus quehaceres y sus amores le dejaron libre, quedó en el aire el hueco que al morir deja un mosquito, y el alma de Solitaña voló a la montaña eterna [*OC*, 2a, I, 124].

Andanzas y visiones españolas (1922)

In the prologue to this book, Unamuno explains his separation of prose narratives into those of action by fictional characters and the others of descriptions of nature.[10] He bases the division in terms

---

[10] The most important studies of this type of Unamunian commentary are: Luis Echevarri, "El sentimiento de la naturaleza de Unamuno," *La Nación* (Buenos Aires, May 27, 1928); H. R. Romero-Flores, "El paisaje en la literatura de Unamuno, Azorín y Baroja," *Síntesis*, IV (Buenos Aires, 1930), 29-35;

of reader interest. However, Unamuno cared only to be read, not to be liked, thus this explanation is quite superficial. In terms of Unamuno's interest—his three perspectives and their literary attitudes—it is another matter. Metaphors of water, which will be studied at length as poetic expression, are used extensively throughout this book. Also, the many poems incorporated into this text will be treated in another part of this chapter. Unamuno explains their inclusion in these words:

Sin embargo, mi sentimiento rítmico, en cierto modo musical, del campo y de las cosas de viso, no me ha cabido siempre en prosa y he tenido alguna vez que verterlo en versos. De una música, si acaso la tienen, esquinada y rígida, angulosa y dura. Pero no todo ritmo se desenvuelve en curvas.[11]

With this poematic unity of prose and verse in mind, Unamuno's commentaries on nature can be appreciated in their true dimension. He states the attitude here:

"Nada hay nuevo bajo el sol," dijo Salomón. . . . Pero el pastor de Gredos, si supiese expresarse, diría: "Todo es nuevo bajo el sol" ["De vuelta de la cumbre," 1911, *OC*, 2a, I, 610].

The *durée,* the ever changing duration of the eternal struggle, is here evoked. And in another place the old towns of Castille bring to him the *intrahistoria* of their inhabitants, where death has no place, for Unamuno in this attitude does not deal with individuals:

Recorriendo estos viejos pueblos castellanos . . . es como el espíritu se siente atraído por sus raíces a lo eterno de la casta ["Hacia el Escorial," 1912, *OC*, 2a, I, 640].

A beautiful example of this interior communication with the whole of reality is again brought out with the view of mountains and with the water metaphor:

Allí arriba, en la cumbre de la Peña de Francia, sentía caer las horas, hilo a hilo, gota a gota, en la eternidad, como lluvia en el mar. . . . Ni distracción, ni di-versión, sino más bien in-tracción e in-versión ["En la Peña de Francia," 1913, *OC*, 2a, I, 712–713].

Again and again Unamuno will come back to his metaphor of the eternal *yo:*

Benjamín Jarnés, "Los intérpretes de España," *Quaderni Ibero-Americani,* II, 12 (Torino, 1952), 182–186; Jerónimo de la Calzada, "Unamuno paisajista," *Cuadernos de la cátedra* . . . , III (1952), 55–80; M. Cardis, "El paisaje en la vida y en la obra de Miguel de Unamuno," *Cuadernos de la cátedra* . . . , IV (1953), 71–83; J. Chicharro de León, "El sentimiento de la naturaleza unamuniana," *Quaderni Ibero-Americani,* III (1956), 122–127.

[11] See García Blanco, *Don Miguel de Unamuno y sus poesías,* p. 239, or in the epilogue to the first edition of *Andanzas y visiones españolas* (Madrid: Pueyo, 1922), pp. 256–285.

Y como siempre, encontraba yo no sé qué misterio, qué místico agüero en el gotear de la lluvia, en la sobrehaz de las aguas, sosegadas. ¡Sentir llover sobre una laguna! ["En Yuste," 1920, *OC*, 2a, I, 819].

The author is fully aware that since he is not expressing his *yo*'s confrontation with death, only the metaphor and the poetic evocation can reach into the *yo* of God's reality; thus he writes:

El universo visible es una metáfora del invisible, del alma, aunque nos parezca al revés. . . . La metáfora es el fundamento de la conciencia de lo eterno [*OC*, 2a, I, 842–843].

In conclusion, the prose narratives of this first attitude of Unamuno have a unique literary form dictated by the structure of the works themselves, by the language, and by Unamuno's thoughts. Unamuno's opinion that narrative prose is more restrictive than lyric verse has already been mentioned. The reasons are clear—language is such that the writer of a narrative must use the subject-verb-predicate structure and cannot deviate too far from these syntactical fetters, if he is to maintain communication with his readers. Lyric verse is another matter, for although the poet may choose a certain meter or a set form like the sonnet, the restrictions are completely exterior and do not in any way limit him from creating evocations and many subtle shades of meaning.

The Unamunian prose of this attitude is not, however, in any sense inferior to the lyric verse, for it has its own values that create a sense of continuous time so important to Unamuno's philosophy. For example, in the selection of *Paisajes del alma* which is partly reproduced above (pp. 39–40) there is a delicate variation of verb tenses from the imperfect to the present. The Spanish imperfect tense, with its sense of past action that is unfinished, is used thirty-four out of the first forty times that a verb appears. The only exceptions on the first page are in reference to the "cumbres rocosas del alma" which "se miran" and "se ven." These reflexive verbs of perception thus bring the scenery to life, but passively in self-contemplation. The heights are not called to action in the present tense again on the first page. Instead they are described and, more significantly, are placed in the unfinished time of the imperfect themselves—"también las cumbres de roca contemplaban." Then quite gradually the various components of nature begin to receive verbs in the present tense—"el arroyo, discurre, ve, sigue; las montañas ven, sienten, ansían, sueñan"—until the entire scene has come to life in the present and is in a constant striving. When the new area of the plateau is introduced, it is with the reflexive present-tense verbs, as was the case with the mountains—"el almapáramo se envuelve, se cubre." The plateau then goes on to reach the present-tense continuum of the mountain. In each scene the preterit is used only once to give the perspective of what has been finished. In the mountain scene it is: "en la juventud de las rocas fué un volcán." In the plateau scene it was "Al Cristo . . . lo irguieron . . . y pudo." Thus, the counterpoise of the only completed action—the former state which has changed in the eternal duration of change—sets off the sense of continuous time in a most effective manner. The entire evocation is in the third person with the necessary withdrawal of the narrator from the scene, as Unamuno does throughout this attitude.

Although the imperfect tense is very commonly used in Spanish as the means of setting description, it can be seen that throughout these prose narratives the description is only the beginning. It is usually the spark that sets off an intuition into this *yo* of reality. Thus, the imperfect takes on the scope of the unfinished past. Also, throughout these works the detachment of the third person is used more than any other point of view, and in some cases the impersonal *se* is used extensively. These mechanical characteristics are the means available in the Spanish language to express this attitude of Unamuno from evocations of nature.

DRAMATIC PROSE

Dialogue is the essence of dramatic prose and verse, and not the third person narrative nor the first person enunciation, although all may be present in a dramatic work. The dialogue, where a *yo* confronts another *yo* and exchanges direct utterances, represents life; it also describes when the speakers are referring to another situation.[12] This double aspect of dialogue must be insisted upon in order to include it in this attitude of Unamuno. For here Unamuno's personal *yo* is very much in evidence since he is both of the speakers. However, the conversations included in this chapter do not focus on his personal *yo*, but are rather attempting through the living exchange of language to evoke the whole of reality that does not die.[13]

[12] See "Dramatic Prose" in Chapters Three and Four for a further study of this important part of Unamuno's literature; also see W. Kayser, *Interpretación y análisis de la obra literaria* (Madrid: Gredos, 1954), pp. 533–540, 587–625.

[13] Although Unamuno's plays are not part of this attitude, there is one example of partial inclusion. In *Sombras de sueño* (1926) the sea is the symbol of the endless flux of existence and is the ever present background that underscores the dominant third attitude in that work. (See Chapter Four, pp. 147–149.)

Before examining this material it is pertinent to see what Unamuno himself said of this manner of writing:

El que dialoga, el que conversa consigo mismo, repartiéndose en dos, o en tres, o en más, o en todo un pueblo, no monologa. . . . Llevo muy en lo dentro de mis entrañas espirituales la agonía, la lucha, la lucha religiosa y la lucha civil, para poder vivir de monólogos. Job fué un hombre de contradicciones, y lo fué Pablo, y lo fué Agustín, y lo fué Pascal, y creo serlo yo [*OC*, 1a, IV, 822].

Monodiálogos (1892–1936)

This book is a collection of small works which appeared regularly throughout these years in the Spanish and Argentine press.[14] As in the narrative prose, the metaphors are taken from nature and the style becomes more direct and conversational as the years go by. Also it will be noted that the structure of the first *Monodiálogos* is all second-person *tú*, but there is no dual speaker responding. However, this structure is used less in the succeeding articles; it is replaced by the full dialogue structure where Unamuno is both speakers. At times he uses letters to set them apart (v.g., A-B, D-M), at others there is only the dash indicating change of speaker, and at still other times he converses with his fictional characters, like don Fulgencio of *Amor y pedagogía* and Augusto Pérez of *Niebla*. In the study that follows the dialogue will be examined as an expression of the dialectic.

In 1913 Unamuno writes the *monodiálogo* in this manner:

Esa selva de las almas. . . . Las raíces se tocan por debajo de la tierra, y se tocan los follajes en el cielo. Y una misma capa de agua cuando llueve y un manto mismo de luz las cubre. Y la selva es una sola y como un solo árbol. Y tú, que eres un árbol de esa selva, deja que por tu follaje se cierna la Visión, que es Viento; la Idea, que es Espíritu [*OC*, 2a, IX, 733].

As Unamuno speaks to himself he metaphorically stresses the unity of reality: "la selva es una sola y como un solo árbol." Further on, to this basis of unity he adds the continuous change of the dialectic result—struggle:

Y está siempre de parto, porque está pariendo siempre. A cada instante cae una hoja y está otra brotando, y la selva siempre verde [*OC*, 2a, IX, 734].

Thus, death has no personal meaning in this full scheme of reality; it is, however, the guarantee of life or, in philosophical terms, reality is in-struggle as being and non-being.

14 This book was published for the first time as *De esto y de aquello*, IV, collection, prologue, and notes by Manuel García Blanco (Buenos Aires: Editorial Sudamericana, 1954), pp. 27–294.

The following are two different *monodiálogos* from the years
1919 and 1920 respectively, where existence that is eternal struggle
is not only referred to, but also demonstrated in the language:

D.—¿Cómo acabará todo esto?

M.—Pues acabará volviendo a empezar, y es lo mejor que puede suceder
[*OC,* 2a, IX, 943].

B.—Y la palabra de Dios, ¿no es la idea?

A.—Más bien el pensamiento, el pensamiento histórico, contradictorio,
flúido, vivo; es la corriente que va del manantial de la cumbre al mar
[*OC,* 2a, IX, 960].

In these two dialogues the linguistic position of the speakers is
not one of exchange but of unyielding opposition. Every problem
or situation that is encountered here is split into contradictory
poles and is then fought over without resolution until the end of
the work when the problem is in the same position as it was at the
beginning. There can be no resolution to these Unamunian
monodiálogos, for this would mean the end of the struggle and,
thus, nothingness. Unamuno seeks to achieve a continued struggle
and this is accomplished by approaching everything through the
dialectic of struggle.

Once again this attitude of the totality is expressed as giving no
importance to the individual death, and in the intuition of totality
struggle is the everlasting continuity making nothingness a dialectic
opposition to being.

LYRIC VERSE

The lyric poem, whether in verse or prose, basically makes known
the sentiments and attitudes of the poematic expresser. There are
various positions that the expresser may take: (1) he can react to
his circumstance and thus give an enunciation of this private world;
(2) he can react to his circumstance and speak out in a situation
of lyric apostrophe; and (3) he can concentrate on himself and speak
out only of himself without regard to anything else. Although there
are a great many combinations and variations that can be made,
in essence these three positions are grounded in language from which
all literature must begin, and thus are the basis.[15]

The poems discussed in this chapter are all of the first or second
situation. In those of the first, some scene of nature or Spain is
being evoked through which a poetic enunciation of reality is
achieved. In the second situation, the lyric apostrophe is used in

---

[15] For the study of the lyric positions, see Kayser, *Interpretación,* pp. 541–560.

addressing something or someone else, but there is also a momentary focus on the eternal stream of reality. All of these poems share the impression of having the lyric voice fuse into this whole of reality. It seldom appears in more than a few verses, but it is important to note at these moments that the focus is not on the personal *yo,* but rather on the whole of reality. Throughout these poems the personal *yo* many times evokes death as sleep, rest, or as the end of the struggle. Reality, however, is always seen as eternal duration which is ever changing, and the *yo* of reality is lost in it as the river is lost in the sea.

Poesías (1884–1907)

Unamuno's first book of poetry contains a few poems that date from 1884, but most of them were written in 1906, a year of feverish intellectual development.[16] Referring to his state of mind during this period of poetic creation, he writes to a friend that there is a certain peace and rest that is only apparent:

Cuerpos hay que en su reposo están desenvolviendo poderosísimas fuerzas. Y no quiero escribirle de la paz como raíz y culminación a la vez de la guerra, por ser el tema melódico capital acaso de mi novela, la obra en que hasta hoy he vertido más de mi alma. En mi poesía *La flor tronchada* volví al mismo tema.[17]

"La flor tronchada" is a poem of 1899 that was rewritten for *Poesías;* it is in *silvas* of hendecasyllabic and octosyllabic verses with rhyme only in the last two of each strophe. The leitmotif of the poem is repeated in a five-verse chorus:

> Padre del Amor, Sol de las almas
> que destruyendo crea
> y creando destruye,
> Labrador Soberano de los mundos
> que lleva la mancera del Destino [*P,* 94].

After an introductory metaphor of plowing, the entire poem follows in the second position of lyric apostrophe as the eternal Creator is being addressed. The ever changing duration which is existence is seen clearly in the leitmotif and in its variations in the poem.

---

[16] An evaluation of this book by Rubén Darío appears as the prologue to *Teresa;* this was a reprint from an article, "Unamuno poeta," *La Nación* (Buenos Aires, March, 1909). Also see M. Alvar, "Motivos de unidad y evolución en la lírica de Unamuno," *Cuadernos de la cátedra* . . . , III (1952), 19–40; and F. Sevilla Benito, "La fe en don Miguel de Unamuno," *Crisis,* I, 1 (Madrid, 1954), 361–385, which treats death and immortality in the "salmos" of this book.

[17] For this letter to Bernardo G. Cándamo, see García Blanco, *Don Miguel de Unamuno y sus poesías,* pp. 19–20.

The basic situation of this poem is one of a farmer who plows a flower under as he prepares the field for the seeds. From this metaphor, existence is readily established, since the flowers of life, both human and botanical, have to pass away and make way for the seeds of life in the continuous flux.

> Lucha es la vida y el arado es arma,
> arma la reja de la odiada idea.
> Para luchar, por tanto con porfía,
> sin odio y sin blandura [*P*, 94–95].

Hence, the flower, the traditional symbol of the finite limitation of life, is used to create an eternal *durée* of flux. Death has no place in this view of reality since the only true loss is the individual consciousness, and this is of no concern to Unamuno in this attitude. He writes about this poem to Ruiz Contreras:

> Si tengo algo que decir, y sé decirlo, ello
> irá al Espíritu colectivo a que me debo,
> puesto que de El venimos todos. Y si un día
> se incorpora mi labor al legado de los siglos,
> de tal modo que se borre como gota en el mar,
> y mi nombre se olvida, ¡bien olvidado estará![18]

Also of 1899 is "Al sueño," written in the same verse form as "La flor tronchada" and also in the position of lyric apostrophe where sleep is being invoked. This poem gives an intuition into eternity: "Eres tú de la paz eterna y honda" (*P*, 98).

In "La elegía eterna" of 1900 Unamuno presents one of his finest poetic insights into the Unamunian-Bergsonian thought on reality:

> Una vez más la queja,
> una vez más el sempiterno canto
>   que nunca acaba,
> de cómo todo se hunde y nada queda,
> que el tiempo pasa
>   ¡irreparable!
>
>   .   .   .   .
>
> ¡Irreparable!, sí, nunca lo olvides.
> ¿Vida? La vida es un morir contínuo,
>   es como el río
> en que unas mismas aguas
>   jamás se asientan
> y es siempre el mismo [*P*, 194].

In the later stanzas of this poem the personal consciousness makes an appearance seeking eternal repose in death. This aspect of death to the *yo* will be taken up in detail in the next chapter.

---

[18] See García Blanco, *Don Miguel de Unamuno y sus poesías*, p. 18.

Probably the best-known poem in this book is "Salamanca," first written in 1904 and reworked off and on until its final publication in 1907. It is in a Sapphic strophe of three hendecasyllabic verses and one pentasyllabic verse, always ending in *verso llano*. The tone throughout the thirty-one strophes is classic, as the ode structure would indicate. It is primarily in the position of a lyric apostrophe as the august image of the city of Salamanca is addressed. Not only is Fray Luis de León mentioned in the poem, but there is a conscious effort to evoke the classic serenity of the sixteenth-century poet's odes. The opening strophe immediately sets this tone:

> Alto soto de torres que al ponerse
> tras las encinas que el celaje esmaltan
> dora á los rayos de su lumbre el padre
> Sol de Castilla [*P*, 29].

However, it is in the fourteenth stanza that the Unamunian attitude on eternity and death comes out:

> [Cervantes quiso] Volver á verte en el reposo
> quieta
> soñar contigo el sueño de la vida
> soñar la vida que perdura siempre
> sin morir nunca [*P*, 31].

The metaphor of the dream of life by man, and the dream of reality that here Salamanca dreams, is one that will be seen throughout Unamuno's poetry. And, again in stanza nineteen, eternal life is seen in the stones of the city: "Pregona eternidad tu alma de piedra" (*P*, 32). In contrast to the serene repose of the city itself, there is the flux of life within it.

A great many of the poems of this collection were written during 1906. Among these are "El mar de encinas," "El aventurero sueña," and "El regazo de la ciudad," which are representative of this first attitude.

In "El mar de encinas" the position of lyric enunciation is developed as the scene from the Castillian countryside is described; its place as part of the whole is evoked. The verse form is the same as in "Salamanca." In this poem the passing of man through this almost timeless sea of trees gives the enunciation the perspective of the eternal in contrast to the temporal situation of life. Thus, this scene is a mirror of the divine, that is, reality.

In "El aventurero sueña" the verse form is the Unamunian combination of five, seven, and eleven syllable verses with the rhythm-breaking pentasyllabic verse in an e/o assonance throughout the poem, giving the redundant litany tone that Unamuno used so often.[19]

> Soñó la vida en la llanura inmensa
> bajo el cielo bruñido
> como un espejo,
> la soñó inacabable y reposada
> llevando al mundo todo
> dentro del pecho [*P*, 44].

The short poem "El regazo de la ciudad" is, like "Salamanca," a lyric apostrophe directed at the city. The verse form is hepta-syllabic and hendecasyllabic verses with no rhyme. This poem is written in the same vein of the last pages of *Paz en la guerra*, where nature is merely used as the portal through which Unamuno enters into the contemplation of the struggle: the dreamt existence of the unity that is peace. The death of man is just touched upon in the second stanza when the lyric voice, in a sigh, tells the city that it is in the hours of silence that one can hear the voice of death with which eternity calls man to oblivion: "dejan oir la voz con que nos llama/la eternidad á la abismal congoja." The last lines can especially be singled out as typical of the Unamunian attitude of totality:

> Es, mi ciudad dorada, tu regazo
> un regazo de amor todo amargura,
> de paz todo combate
> y de sosiego en inquietud basado [*P*, 47].

Here, symbolically, the city's *regazo* of love is now all bitterness, its peace is now all combat, and is formed of the serenity which is based on restlessness. There is love for the whole of reality that is eternal, but only bitterness for the individual consciousness that must end; similarly, for the whole there is an apparent peace, but it is made up of a continuous struggle.

Poems from 1907 to 1928

During this twenty-one-year span Unamuno published several books of poetry, among which were *Rosario de sonetos líricos* (1911), *Rimas de dentro* (1923), *De Fuerteventura a París* (1925), and *Romancero del destierro* (1928).[20] Also a few poems were included

---

[19] For a study of this aspect of Unamuno's poetry, see Ernesto Veres D'Ocon, "El estilo enumerativo en la poesía de Unamuno," *Cuadernos de literatura*, 1 (Madrid, 1949), 115–144.

[20] The studies of this part of Unamuno's poetry are: F. Sarmiento, "Considerations Toward a Revaluation of Unamuno: The Poetry," *Bulletin of Spanish*

in *Andanzas y visiones españolas* (1922). Since only one or two poems from each of these books is expressive of the Unamunian attitude of totality, the books will not be treated as units in this chapter.

Although "El hombre aquel que allí habla en la esquina" was written in 1907, it was not published until 1923. It is written in hendecasyllabic and heptasyllabic verses with one pentasyllabic verse. The rhyme throughout the sixteen-verse poem is an a/o assonance. The scene in this rather rare poem is the observation of the gestures made by a man in the street. Unamuno begins to observe subjectively but then abruptly stops (the pentasyllable) and adds: "¿Y quién soy yo para medir los grados/de importancia?" The second half of the poem then brings out the contemplation of man and the resting place for all in the dead waters. It will be recalled that several of the stories from *El espejo de la muerte,* of this same period, brought out the same reaction to human life in the perspective of the totality:

> Mientras así bracea,
> de sí mismo se olvida, y con los años
> su agitación, mi calma,
> irán a descansar al mismo lago
> de aguas muertas estériles [*AP,* 300].

Thus, if only for a moment, Unamuno leaves his *yo* and his world to consider the relative insignificance of man.

"Ruit Hora," a sonnet of 1910, is another example of the reality that is change without end:

> Querer guardar los ríos en lagunas
> resulta siempre una imposible empresa;
> no son sepulcros las abiertas cunas
>
> en que la vida se eternice presa,
> y no pudiendo detener las lunas
> con ellas va en el giro que no cesa [*RSL,* 34–35].

The lyric enunciation of a stream which is in constant change is established in the first quartet. An image of sea life is the transition to the second quartet which introduces the favorite Unamunian metaphor for reality—the sea. The sea always serves the purpose of giving a sense of unity to this never ending, struggling thrust that he feels is reality. The first tercet clarifies that the sea is not immobile still life but rather an open cradle of everlasting birth

Studies, XX (1943), 35–48, 84–107; J. Ibarra, "La poesía y la muerte," *Arriba* (Madrid, November 5, 1943); Julio de la Calzada, "Notas sobre la muerte: temas unamunianos," *Boletín de edificación* . . . , 18 (París, 1953).

and death. And the last tercet finally presents reality as movement that does not end.

Unamuno wrote four sonnets in 1920 that must be considered among his finest, both for the depth of thought and the poetic imagery that he creates. Unfortunately they were lost until 1955, when they were brought out by García Blanco. Of these, the second one, entitled "Polvo de otoño," contains an excellent expression of the Unamunian attitude of this chapter. In a delicate lyric enuncia-tion the death of the individuals is portrayed as leaves on their way downriver in the continuous current that is existence:

> Es ocaso de otoño; dulcemente
> va al río—una ola sola, llana y lenta—
> llevándose la manta amarillenta
> de las hojas que el viento del poniente
> arranca de los chopos; contra el puente
> presa el agua entre piedras se lamenta
> y el sol al enterrarse la ensangrienta
> de luz; el cielo pésame en la frente.
>   Las horas todas son una sola hora,
> hora amarilla y tierna, hora de ocaso,
> tinta en sangre que presto se evapora;
> abierto al cielo el corazón es vaso
> donde la noche su rocío llora
> cuando nos abre, al fin, el postrer paso [PI, 414].

Only the first four and one-half verses of this sonnet express the attitude of the whole of reality, but, as has been often stated in these pages, all three attitudes are expressions of a basic unity: the man himself, Miguel de Unamuno. In the first half-line the situa-tion of the poem is briefly and directly stated: it is an autumn sunset with all of the traditional connotations of the coming of death. The next five verses smoothly flow in describing the move-ment of the river. Not only does this expression begin with the adverb *dulcemente,* but also the internal rhyme is very strong in these lines—in the second verse: "una ola sola, llana y lenta"; in the third: "manta amarillenta"; and, in the fourth: "viento de poniente"—all of this giving the impression of flowing continuity. However, the fifth line not only begins with the verb "arranca" with its sharp connotations, but the enjambment breaks the thought at midverse. The tranquil view of the totality is over; some of the individual strife involved is beginning to appear as the red tones of the setting sun make the waters bloody. Then, again in the eighth verse, the verse is broken with an enjambment and the *yo* enters the poem. The first tercet puts the *yo* in the context of eternal time where the blood in the stream will soon evaporate. And the last tercet gives the *yo* the way to prepare for the last step, which is death, by opening its heart to the sky and receiving the tears of the night, as man loves his fellow man.

One of the most acclaimed poems of Unamuno has been "Aldebarán," which was written and published in 1909 and republished in 1923. The verse form is the Unamunian *silva*, which is a free variation of eleven-, seven-, and five-syllable verses. Only the first twenty-six lines of the poem's one hundred and fifty-six present the Unamunian attitude of eternity. In fact, as has been recently stated by Diego Catalán Menéndez Pidal,[21] it is because of the combination of Unamunian attitudes in one creation that this poem has achieved its remarkable lyric enunciation of the *yo* and reality face to face. The entire poem is a lyric apostrophe of increasing intensity as the distant star is being invoked.

The introductory verses give this poetic insight into an eternal totality:

> Rubí encendido en la divina frente,
> Aldebarán,
> lumbrera de misterio,
> perla de luz en sangre,
> ¿cuántos días de Dios viste a la tierra
> mota de polvo
> rodar por los vacíos
> rodar la tierra?
> ¿Viste brotar al Sol recién nacido?
> ¿Le viste acaso, cual diamante en fuego,
> soltarse del anillo . . . [*AP,* 307]?

The earth is a mere speck of dust; the sun has just been born with the planets under its watchful eye; new worlds are being born and old worlds are disappearing. It is with questions directed at "Aldebarán" that this view is created. These questions have no answers and are not intended to question as much as to create the general atmosphere of unknowing penetration.[22]

---

[21] " 'Aldebarán' de Unamuno," *Cuadernos de la cátedra* . . . , IV (1953), 43–70.

[22] See J. Marías, *Miguel de Unamuno,* p. 134, where he writes: "mediante el empleo constante de las interrogaciones. Es la expresión poética de la problematicidad." Also see Diego Catalán, " 'Aldebarán' de Unamuno," *Cuadernos de la cátedra* . . . , IV, 56: "Unamuno, en cambio, rehuye el formular directamente la pregunta personal, limitándose a expresar este ¿para qué? del Universo, de Aldebarán. La razón es obvia: En todo el comienzo ha buscado colocar a Aldebarán casi fuera del espacio y el tiempo, en contraste con el pobre yo, perdido acá en esta mota de polvo que brilla un instante para sumirse después definitivamente en la eterna tiniebla; le basta, pues, ahora con sugerir el para nada de ese casi eterno Aldebarán."

In the same line of thought is the last tercet of a sonnet of 1924 written in Fuerteventura:

> Arraigado en las piedras, gris y enjuto,
> como pasó el abuelo pasa el nieto
> sin hojas, dando sólo flor y fruta [*FP*, 39].

In 1927 during Unamuno's stay in Hendaya he wrote many short poems of a searching meditative tone. Among these is the eight-verse poem without rhyme or set verse form:

> Arroyuelo sin nombre ni historia
>
> .   .   .   .
>
> Al nacer en la cumbre, en el cielo,
> con la mar te sueñas [*RD*, 79].

The familiar Unamunian symbols appear again in this poem: the stream as the unending current of existence, the oak tree as the individual, and the sea as the total image with which the river dreams itself. The first lines set the symbol in the perspective of the individuals participating in the stream of being "in-struggle." This theme of participation ends with the also familiar Unamunian interrogation: "¿Quién llama a tus aguas?" But the second part develops the nature of the stream itself. It is born in the mountain from the snows, and as it is in this process of birth it is making itself, that is, dreaming itself with the sea. The stream is making itself with the sea, for the sea rests on the sky and the sky is the source of the stream. Thus, there is a continuous cycle of creation and re-creation in an eternal flux. This metaphor of the self-propelling stream as the continuity of existence is very close to the metaphors used by Henri Bergson to present his thought on reality as the *durée*.

In the poem beginning with "Y pasan días sin que pase nada" Unamuno presents the theme of the transformation of dust to stone: "el polvo cuando posa se hace lodo/y luego piedra que sirve de arcada" (*RD*, 89).

Consequently, in this attitude, the never ending transformations of nature are used by the poet to banish the impact of death. The individual changes in the ever changing flux cannot be given any importance, since that could only be accomplished by taking them out of the stream and focusing on their individuality.

Cancionero (1928–36)

From February 26, 1928, until December 28, 1936 (three days before his death), Unamuno kept a poetic diary—his *Cancionero*.[23]

[23] The critics of this posthumous publication are: Guillermo de Torre, "El

It accumulated 1,755 poems of the most diverse themes: political preoccupations, landscape evocations, philological play on words, and philosophical intuitions. They share in common the intimate personal tone and the spontaneity of the poetic creation.

Fragments of this poetic diary appeared for years in anthologies and periodicals in the Hispanic world. But it was not until 1953 that Federico de Onís published it with the greatest scholarly devotion to the author's manuscript.

Among these poems are a great many expressive of Unamuno's attitude of the totality of existence. The poet himself has explained in verse the moods of this attitude toward reality:

> Una tarde de aquellas en que se olvida el alma...
>
> .   .   .   .
>
> Una tarde de aquellas en que todo era puesta
> del sol, de la montaña, del cielo y de la mar,
> y en la caída roja se congregaban, nubes,
> águilas de evangelio dejando de volar...
> Una tarde de aquellas... pero es la misma tarde [C, 112].

Unamuno wrote this on July 30, 1928, but it can also serve to explain his literary attitude in the previous years.

The poems that follow are in chronological order, and although each is a poem in itself, together they are a poetic intuition of existence.

March 25, 1928:

> Si cada día que pasa—nos dejase su canción,
> nuestra canción cantaría:—Todo es nuevo bajo el sol [C, 35].

Everything is new for nothing is static in the totality of flux and struggle.

The place of the individual *yo* in this attitude is that of indistinct drops in an eternal ocean. In this poem, as in many of 1928, Unamuno uses the Alexandrine verse with rhyme in the longer poems.[24]

Good Friday, April 6, 1928:

> Seréis sueños nebulosos—del Universo soñado;
> en su presente de siempre—Dios os soñará pasados.
> Y riendo risa santa—sin cesar iréis pasando;
> sin saber que pasa todo—y sin saberos pasados [C, 43].

Man is both dawn and sunset at the same time, for he is a being

---

Cancionero póstumo de Unamuno," *Sur*, 222 (Buenos Aires, 1953), 48–64; José Luis Cano, "El Cancionero de Unamuno," *Insula*, IX, 98 (February 15, 1954).

24 For a study of this verse form in Unamuno's poetry see Francisco Maldonado de Guevara, "Unamuno y el verso alejandrino," *Revista de Literatura*, IV (Madrid, 1953), 383–386.

in-struggle as all beings are in the passing movement of an eternal time.

April 21, 1928:

> Misterio eterno del tiempo,—¿volverá a ser lo que fué?
> re-muérese el Occidente,—¿es que fué lo que ha de ser?
> Renaciendo está el Oriente,—¿no es morir el renacer?
> el Mediodía durando—va mientras el Sol le dé.
> Nace, dura, muere, vive,—y el hombre sueña que es;
> ni es ni está sino que pasa,—orto y ocaso a la vez [C, 57].

In the next poem the mystery of time is seen again through the familiar metaphor of the lake.

May 16, 1928:

> Los ayeres derretidos—en un solo y mismo ayer
> hacen el lago sin fondo—del hoy, nuestro único haber [C, 67].

In the following penetrating metaphor of existence the expression of Unamuno's theory of knowledge can be found.

January 4, 1929:

> Hoy es la eterna anécdota de cada día,
> la cotidiana,
> de noche se me hará categoría,
> me anudará el mañana
> al que lo fué: el ayer;
> flores que fueron sueñan bajo el verde,
> nada se pierde,
> el padecer es la flor del hacer.
> En padecer el corazón se salva,
> retorna a revivir;
> la luz del alba
> devora la sombra del porvenir [C, 192].

Since existence is a never ending stream, forever jetting forth, there are no isolated moments. Therefore man's rational attempt at understanding this reality of flux only ends in abstractions taken out of reality. There are generally three abstractions: *el hoy, el mañana,* and *el ayer.* Thus, the poet can say *el hoy* is the anecdote of every day, that is, the intellectual isolation and commentary on reality. By nightfall this abstraction will be processed into a category and will become *el ayer,* which, as memory, will serve to project into *el mañana* of the next day. The function of reason is not denied its rôle; however, it cannot enable man to know reality. The knowing of the flux is achieved only through intuition and is expressed in metaphor. And this is accomplished by the poet in lines 6 to 12. Here, there is no abstraction but instead a lyric enunciation of reality.

Similar metaphorical expression is in the following quartet where a point is infinite and a moment is eternal, for thought has been broken up and there is in its place intuition from the all to the nothingness locked together in everlasting struggle.

October 12, 1929:

> Ay infinitud del punto!
> eternidad del momento!
> el Todo a la Nada junto
> y deshecho el pensamiento! [*C*, 354].

The rhymed octosyllables that follow express the position of lyric apostrophe, as the lyric voice speaks to the dog rose that has been crushed in a downpour. The last four lines remind the flower that death is only a change in the endless repetition of life.

June 22, 1930:

> Mira, el chaparrón te lleva
> al arroyo y a morir
> hecha tierra; a rosa nueva,
> mantillo así, has de nutrir [*C*, 397–398].

The depersonalizing literary attitude of Unamuno takes him into the contemplation of the whole of reality. This he sees not through reason but through intuition as the never ending struggle. And death is only a surface view, just as peace is only a surface view of nature.

The literary elements which have been involved in this first attitude have been metaphor, imagery, and symbols expressed in prose and verse, and to a very slight extent plot and characters. The latter appear in this chapter only in the short stories of *El espejo de la muerte*.

The literature in this chapter is representative of the Unamunian attitude that looks toward the whole of reality rather than the parts or an individual part. It is an attitude that attains a concentration not on the *yo* and the circumstance that is relative to it, but on the totality, where man is an insignificant speck. It is clear that this insight into reality is gained through Unamuno's personal intuition. Both the metaphysical position and the manner of securing it must be emphasized at this point so that confusion will not result as the next attitude is presented in the following chapter. This literary creation has been traced throughout Unamuno's life, demonstrating that this was not an inspirational flash that passed rapidly through his consciousness only to be forgotten. On the contrary, the literature of the eternal flux, where death is meaningless, is an active living frame of creative intuition which covers his entire mature life—1884 to 1936.

Since this attitude was the first active force in the thought of Unamuno, it is to be expected that the first intellectual expression would come soon after its inception. The philosophical perspective that uses intuition rather than reason and sees existence as an endless change is most clearly stated in *En torno al casticismo* (1895), as has been studied in the previous chapter.

As the years progress into the twentieth century, other creative frames of mind or attitudes come into Unamuno's spirit. Each of these, in turn, finds a place in his mind as a philosophical perspective. His philosophy is the intellectual culmination coming from the trajectory of the creative insights of the attitude. Thus, in the chapters that follow, the other two coexisting attitudes will be demonstrated.

CHAPTER THREE

THE LITERARY EXPRESSION OF
DEATH FOR THE *YO* AND
HIS WORLD

The second philosophical perspective—the personal *yo* that engulfs his circumstance—is expressed in a literary attitude of intimate personalization of everything in the circumstance by the Unamunian *yo*.

As has been discussed in Chapter One, this perspective has two aspects: (1) the existential fact that the *yo* is there in the world with things and others around it, and (2) the ontological fact that the *yo,* when it becomes aware of death in its full meaning of a personal approaching possibility that can end all possibilities, "looks around" and begins to personalize his total experience in an ever widening scope with the realization that this world is completely dependent on him: "La existencia objetiva es, en nuestro conocer, una dependencia total de nuestra propia existencia personal" (*Del sentimiento trágico* [*OC,* 1a, IV, 480]). On the levels of personality, the *yo* one thinks he is corresponds to the existential fact of being-there, while the *yo* that wants to be is the ever expanding *yo* that has the awareness of death, or in Unamuno's words "el sentimiento trágico de la vida."

Ferrater Mora has pointed out that being and wishing to be are really one in Unamuno's thought;[1] it is quite true, for in Unamuno's philosophy the highest level of his anthropology is the awareness of death as a way of life. Thus, although there is a personal *yo*

---

[1] Ferrater Mora writes: "Unamuno believes the result of an effort . . . to such an extent that there is no fundamental difference between being and wishing to be," "On Unamuno's Idea of Reality," p. 520. See the study of this observation in Chapter One, pp. 8, 10–13.

cast in the world to make its own future, not all *yos* have the capacity to sense this freedom of the will. Some are only aware that they are in the world, but they have no sense of their unique individuality. Others, who have felt an awareness of death, have had their *yo* opened to the world in a commitment to it. They have realized that they are the makers of their own destiny, and as such, also the makers of their own world. This is the tragic sense of life which opens the personal *yo* and makes it authentic. However, it will be noted that the crucial moment comes for the personal *yo* when he feels the presence of death in his life's trajectory. If this awareness does come, it is then that the choice must be made: either a decision for the world by continued struggle or the resignation to the inevitable end.

The literary attitude from which these ideas developed presents the confrontation of death from the two basic human situations: the authentic, which can lead either negatively to the choice of suicide or positively to the courage to continue the struggle to be, and the unauthentic, which sees death as an event in others, not as the jeopardy of the individual *yo*. Both situations will be expressed through the fictional characters of the narratives, the antagonists of the dramas, and the lyric voice of the poetry.

This second literary attitude developed along with the philosophical perspective originating the thoughts that culminated in Unamuno's philosophy. Thus, in the literary creations, the full implications of the philosophy will not appear until after 1910. The years 1910 to 1912, as has been discussed in the first chapter, mark the culmination of the second philosophical perspective in *Del sentimiento trágico*.

Not only the characters, but often also the structure of the works themselves is indicative of the Unamunian counterpoint of oppositions that permeated his entire philosophy.[2] Unamuno's style becomes more intense in this attitude as the years progress.[3] Since

[2] Structure is understood as the aspect of form which deals with the construction of the literary work as a unit. In general, there are two facets of structure—the external of chapters, acts, or stanzas, and the internal of the allocation of time and space within the work itself. Quite often the external structure has a direct bearing on the internal limitations of the created world; thus, the study of structure must begin with the exterior and move on to the interior.

[3] Style refers to all the elements of meaning and sound in language that are used in the creative process of literature. Beginning with the most basic phonemic level of sonority, passing to the consideration of the morphemic quality of the words, and the location of words in the sentence or verse as well as the construction of the sentence or verse, one encounters the primary unit of style—

description and setting become more and more scarce, the main part of the narrative is taken up with the presentation of the authentic and the unauthentic *yos*, as is also the case in the drama. The poetry is almost completely an exposition of an authentic *yo*.

NARRATIVE PROSE

The theory behind this second literary attitude for the narrative creation was given by Unamuno himself:

[Las novelas ejemplares son] ejemplo de vida y de realidad. ¡De realidad! ¡De realidad, sí! Sus agonistas, es decir, luchadores—o si queréis los llamaremos personajes—, son reales, realísimos, y con la realidad más íntima, con la que se dan ellos mismos, en puro querer ser o en puro querer no ser, y no con la que le den los lectores. . . .

¿Qué es lo más íntimo, lo más creativo, lo más real de un hombre? . . .

[el yo] que uno quiere ser, es en él, en su seno, el creador, y es el real de verdad [Prólogo, *Tres novelas ejemplares y un prólogo*, 1920, *OC*, 2a, IX, 415–416].

And if one would ask Unamuno "What about the others who are there in the world but who have no will," he would answer:

Y ahora os digo que esos personajes crepusculares . . . que ni quieren ser ni quieren no ser, sino que se dejan llevar y traer . . . no son en su mayoría personas, y que no tienen realidad íntima [Prólogo, *Tres novelas ejemplares y un prólogo*, *OC*, 2a, IX, 420].

And since the fictional characters are for Unamuno the example of men of flesh and blood, this will-awareness of the *yo* is born from the same experience—the tragic sense in the literary creation and in life. Thus, the *yo* that wants to be is not only the sustaining force in the individual but because it is such, it is also the basis for the creation of the fictional character which to Unamuno is the created example of man.

Therefore Unamuno develops four types of characters:

1. Those with the tragic sense of life
   (a) those who will to be = *voluntad*
   (b) those who will to be not = *noluntad*

---

words as part of the linguistic form in the singular expression of man's thoughts or emotions. The supra-sentence linguistic forms must be studied from the aspect of the arrangement of the units within them. This brings the examination to the consideration of patterns of tone, thought, and secondary meaning induced into the work by the figurative language but not obvious until forming a pattern. Finally, the culmination of style in the literary work is the interaction of all these elements within a given structure to create a new world of esthetic experience.

2. Those who never leave the primary existential state of being-there

    (c) those who Do Not will to be = *abulia*

    (d) those who Do Not will not to be = *abulia*

To the above ideas Unamuno adds the following thought, which emphasizes the intimate relation of his philosophy to his literary creation:

¿Qué? ¿Os parece un lío? Pues si esto os parece un lío y no sois capaces, no ya sólo de comprenderlo, mas de sentirlo y de sentirlo apasionada y trágicamente, no llegaréis nunca a crear criaturas reales, y por tanto no llegaréis a gozar de ninguna novela, ni de la de vuestra vida [Prólogo, *Tres novelas ejemplares y un prólogo, OC*, 2a, IX, 417].

"Relatos novelescos" (1886–1932)

The dispersed short narratives of Unamuno [4] often anticipate longer, more polished narratives and dramas.[5] There is some indication that the earlier short narrative was usually the result of a literary theme or idea that would come to Unamuno and which he would put into writing as soon as possible.[6] Subsequently it was from this storehouse of themes, plots, and characters, or merely literary ideas, that the greater literary achievements were developed. A few of these anticipations—those relative to this second literary attitude—can be pointed out here. "Nerón tiple o el calvario de un inglés" of 1890 will be reworked as "¿Por qué ser así?," which appeared in 1913 in *El espejo de la muerte*; "Sueño" of 1897 presented the terror of nothingness which was incorporated into the novel *Paz en la guerra* of the same year;[7] "Don Martín, o de la

---

[4] These short narratives gathered by García Blanco which otherwise would be inaccessible were first published as a collection in *De esto y de aquello*, II (Buenos Aires: Sudamericana, 1951), 383–545.

[5] See García Blanco's prologue in Unamuno's *OC*, 2a, IX, 10–23.

[6] See *OC*, 2a, II, 32–33, where Unamuno himself writes of this direct expression from intuition to prose. Also of interest to the creative process of this prose is López Morilla's study, "Unamuno y sus criaturas . . . ," *Intelectuales y espirituales. Ensayos de literatura y filosofía* (Madrid: Revista de Occidente, 1961), pp. 11–39.

[7] The dread of nothingness is a personal emotion of Unamuno which he used repeatedly in his writings; these two narratives of 1897 are the first literary appearances. This personal terror dates back to Unamuno's childhood, which he has mentioned in many letters and commentaries. For example, in a letter of 1902 to Jiménez Ilundain he wrote: "¡Sí, temo mucho, muchísimo morirme; tiemblo ante la imagen de la muerte!" in Benítez, *El drama religioso de Unamuno*, p. 377. Also see *Recuerdos de niñez y de mocedad* (1908), *OC*, 2a, I, 269–272.

gloria," 1900, became "Una visita al viejo poeta," also in *El espejo de la muerte,* 1913; "El que se enterró" of 1908 was reworked in the drama *El otro* of 1926;[8] the *relato* "La redención del suicidio," 1901, was used in the novel *Amor y pedagogía* of 1902.

In some of the narratives death appears only as the culmination of life, as a long awaited rest, while in others the shock of the spectacle of death creates a lifelong fear. Also death as suicide is sometimes the solution to the problems of living. But the most important use of death in these short narratives is in its imaginative anticipation and the living awareness of it that results.

"El dios pavor" (1892) is the story of a young girl's increasing terror that leads to insanity. In it the spectacle of death creates the psychological shock which builds up into blind terror. First, her drunken father died in bed next to her; years later, the sudden shout of her aunt, for whom she worked, frightened her into dropping her infant nephew to his death. Thus, when her own son falls from her arms, her mind snaps and all she can say is: "¡Yo no he sido...ha sido sin querer!," as she stares into space. The girl was never conscious of death as a personal limitation; she only feared what she saw as death in others. The unauthentic situation of all those around her is expressed in the "ha sido sin querer," for she has lived without truly willing it.

In "Abuelo y nieto" (1902) both the grandfather and the grandson die at the end of the narration. Since the birth of the grandson the daughter-in-law had been forcing the old man out until he left the house to live from whatever he could beg on the roads. However, he feels the need of returning to die in the house where he was born. To the old man death is a welcome rest from the disillusionment of life. The irony is that the infant also dies. Again, in this narrative, death is a negative factor since the individuals do not realize its towering presence as the completion of the project that began with birth.

"El que se enterró" (1908) presents the action which will be used in *El otro*'s first act. But the difference is that in the narrative the *yo* is re-created, he buries his other *yo,* and then becomes an authentic individual who lives life with the awareness of death. On the contrary, the *yo* of the drama never recovers from the shock; he loses his individuality and becomes *el otro.*

The short narrative "El secreto de un sino" (1913) is a grotesque

---

[8] For the study of the genesis of this theme, see Chapter Four, pp. 133–134, 150–152.

tragicomedy of a timid little man with no will who was led to suicide by his only friend. The protagonist Noguera cannot be liked by anyone during his life. No matter how congenial he tries to be, he is always rejected. The secret of the antagonism toward him is the nauseating bad breath that he is plagued with. But Perálvarez, a nihilistic pessimist, proves to be the exception; he befriends poor Noguera. After some time of association with Perálvarez, Noguera has a deep-seated hatred of humanity. The narration ends with this comical turn, which is also tragic:

A los pocos días el pobre Noguera, loco de desesperación, convencido de que su alma, y no su cuerpo, era ya incurable, se mataba pegándose un tiro por las narices arriba, sin haber antes averiguado por qué Perálvarez, que fué quien más le suicidó, carecía de olfato [OC, 2a, IX, 217].

This is one of the most tragic characters in Unamuno's early narratives. This man never emerged from his shell to encounter life; he was poisoned while still inside of it. Death appeared to him only as an escape from the immutable antagonism he had encountered.

"La sombra sin cuerpo," which is subtitled "fragmento de una novela en preparación," is a very short narrative published in Buenos Aires in 1921. There is no information available as to the date of the writing or of Unamuno's intentions. However, in theme it must also be related to the drama El otro of 1926. Unamuno probably intended to develop this theme into a novel, but instead, worked out the drama that will be studied in the next chapter. Here, it is the death of the father that starts the protagonist's mind working as to the separation of shadow and body.

Paz en la guerra (1897)

This novel is set in Bilbao from the years 1812 to 1876, the lifetime of Pedro Antonio Iturriondo. In Spain this is a period of a long, hard, and generally futile struggle toward representative government. And in the Basque provinces it is, more specifically, the struggle of the conservative Carlists allied with the Church against the liberals of the constitutional monarchy or the ill-fated first Spanish Republic. Two generations of men fight and die for the immediate cause of the pretender and the more ambiguous defense of absolute monarchy under the blessing of God and the Church.

The novel begins with a description of the life of Pedro Antonio from his birth, in 1812 in the provinces, to his marriage with Josefa

Ignacia and the establishment of the couple in his uncle's *choco-latería* in Bilbao in 1840. Before his marriage Pedro Antonio took part in the first Carlist war of 1833–40; it was this experience that was to supply him and his friends with a never ending source of conversation at their *tertulia*. The opening part of the first chapter ends with the birth of a son, Ignacio, in 1849.

The focus changes quite abruptly from the Carlist Pedro Antonio to the coexisting opposition in Bilbao, the liberal José María de Arana and his family. The older son, Don Juan, "un liberal al modo de Bastiat," [9] is the same age as Pedro Antonio, and he too has a son, Juancito, and a daughter, Rafaela.

The sons of the two factions become close friends during their younger days only to be separated later as each is swept into the irreflective, blind, and stupid pattern set by their elders. In striking contrast to Ignacio, or any of his friends, is Francisco Zabalbide, known as Pachico, who appears late in this first chapter and upsets Ignacio's set pattern of thinking. Pachico was a young man to whom death had become an ever present reality. At this point in the novel he is not yet an authentic *yo*, although he has begun to realize his individuality:

¿Yo? Yo con mote como si fuese un insecto seco y hueco, clavado en una caja de entomología, y con una etiqueta que diga: género tal, especie tal... Un partido es una necedad...

        —Entonces tú, ¿qué eres?
        —¿Yo? Francisco Zabalbide [*OC,* 2a, II, 135–136].

The second chapter follows Ignacio as he joins the Carlist army for the war (1872–74), through the period of training and leading up to the battle for Bilbao. This chapter is the rather simple review of the preparations for war; it is much shorter and uncomplicated in its scope and development.

In counterbalance, the third chapter is also short and is dedicated entirely to the confinement of the Arana family as Bilbao is under siege. During this time both the mother Micaela and the uncle Miguel die.

In the fourth chapter, the shortest in the novel, the action moves back to the battlefield and concentrates on the furor of the senseless killing. The fighting is followed from the situation of Ignacio until

---

[9] Bastiat was a political economist very fashionable at that time among the liberals who believed religiously in the social doctrine of the survival of the fittest.

he is killed. He does not die heroically, but rather absurdly as he peeks out of his trench with the curiosity of a child.

The fifth and last chapter takes up the plight of the old Carlist Pedro Antonio and his wife Josefa as they return to the city, disillusioned and impoverished, having lost their only son in battle and their life's earnings in backing the Carlist cause. Josefa soon dies and the old man resigns himself to his situation as he awaits death, which he is sure will reunite him with his wife and son. He meets his son's friend Pachico on the street and speaks with him; they recall Ignacio, then the old man goes his way, moved by the sincerity of the youth. The novel ends as Pachico approaches life with an authenticity which has come from his confrontation with death.

The structure of this novel has been one of an intricate counterpoint between the two youths, Ignacio and Pachico. The first chapter, which creates the human and material ambient of the novel, also sets off the aimless, will-less nature of Ignacio against the strong and expressive will of Pachico. The second and third chapters show the two sides of the same type of person—the irreflective man who is never aware of his individuality. The unauthentic considerations of death can thus be seen in two very different circumstances: with the soldier preparing for battle and with the family whose members die. Subsequently, Chapter Four has the appearance of death on the battlefield. Finally, the last chapter returns to Pachico, who is the only one to gain from the war—he has become an authentic individual who feels a commitment to the world.

This novel contains a gallery of fictional characters who were carefully created over a ten-year span by Unamuno. He has stated that he wanted to present a group of men, thrown together into the historical frame of these years, in their environment and their living relationship with each other: "Esto no es una novela; es un pueblo" (Prólogo a la edición de 1923, OC, 2a, II, 74).

The consideration given to death by these characters indicates the presence or absence of a self-awareness of their individuality. Once this self-realization has been effected, the yo must choose between the world or suicide. In this novel only Pachico has this choice.

Death appears in the following situations: (1) as indifferent talk about death; (2) as the inescapable confrontation with the act of death by the man of faith, and by the emotional spectator; (3) as an existential awareness of death.

(1) The most unauthentic and common reference is the indifferent consideration of death as an event in another's life. For example, Juancito Arana thinks to himself about his father: "¡Bah! Si así no fuese, no habría hecho acaso la fortunita que has de heredar un día, cuando él muera" (*OC*, 2a, II, 115). It is also in the mass consideration of death: "¡Mueran los frailes! era la canción de los '60" (p. 117), and in the mottos of the various factions: "Constitución o muerte, / será nuestra divisa; / si algún traidor la pisa / la muerte sufrirá..." (p. 121).

All of these references to death treat it as an event that happens; they do not consider the individual who is to die as a unique irreplaceable *yo*. Among the Unamunian characters who speak in this way are the members of Pedro Antonio's *tertulia*. Don Juan Arana and his son also speak in this manner, but in their case they will also be confronted with the act of death in the family.

(2) When death comes to another person who is intimate with the spectator, the consideration of death is inescapable, but there are different reactions depending on the individual *yo* who must face this presence of the act of death.

Pedro Antonio Iturriondo was a man of unfaltering faith. He was one of the timid anonymous men who are the layers of sediment of the *intrahistoria*. Such men are never aware of their individuality: "De haber oído hablar a su tío . . . sacó Pedro Antonio lo poco que sabía de la nación en que la suerte le puso, y él se dejaba vivir" (*OC*, 2a, II, 76). They speak, act, and live without knowing or questioning the course of their life: "Fluía su existencia como corriente de río manso, con rumor no oído y de que no se daría cuenta hasta que se interrumpiera" (p. 78). When death appears at the end of his son's life, Pedro Antonio is disturbed and cast into confusion:

Allí duerme para siempre, muerto..., muerto ¿por qué? ¡Por la causa! ¿Por la causa? ¿Y por qué causa? "La causa por que murió mi hijo" [*OC*, 2a, II, 409].

But, after regaining his emotional control, he lets himself sink away into the nameless continuity which is the eternal flux as expressed in the first literary attitude. This type of resignation has been discussed in the previous chapter.

The unauthentic evasion of death as a personal threat is never broken by characters such as Don Juan Arana, Juancito, and Rafaela. When they are forced to face death, there is the human emotional reaction and perhaps, even for a time, a new consideration of life, but since death has not been made a personal threat it can soon be forgotten.

Rafaela reacts to her mother's death:

Lloraba de miedo, sin saber de qué. . . . Cuando Rafaela vió sacar la caja, vínole a la mente, involuntariamente, aquello de:
Encima de la caja, carabí;
encima de la caja, carabí,
un pajarito va, carabí, hurí, hurá [OC, 2a, II, 279].

Death strikes fear in Rafaela, to which she responds almost subconsciously by repeating the rhyme with which she calmed her emotions in her childhood days.[10] The pauses in the song bring out the basis for this fear as being the broken mother-daughter relationship. She asks herself who will sit by her side, who will be her companion (if she only had a sister), whose hair will she comb, and so forth. This is only the human pattern of habits which are interrupted, and as such it is only a matter of time before new habits are substituted for the old and the impressions of death are forgotten: "Aparecía el 'morir habemos' cual realidad viva, que fué poco a poco disipándose, hasta volver a su estado normal de fórmula abstracta y muerta" (p. 283).

(3) However there are the authentic yos, those men who are aware of the jeopardy of death and who consequently look to the world as their world, to which they are committed. In this novel only Pachico has this sense of death:

Era un terror loco a la nada, a hallarse solo en el tiempo vacío, terror loco que sacudiéndole el corazón en palpitaciones, le hacía soñar que, falto de aire, ahogado, caía continuamente y sin descanso en el vacío eterno, con terrible caída [OC, 2a, II, 134].

This terror before death's possible annihilation was the way to open the personal yo to his world. When the personal yo comes to the realization that from this struggle of the tragic sense of life an entire way of life can arise, then the anthropology of the authentic individual will have been established.

Pachico feels at times that there must be an end to the interminable struggle that this awareness of death as a personal jeopardy brings into his soul. At times like these he goes up into the mountains where Ignacio had first taken him. There the contemplation of the landscape evokes an intuition of the eternal waters of reality.

[10] For the source of this rhyme see Unamuno's *Recuerdos* . . . , *OC*, 2a, I, 246, and for the last mention of similar ones see *Cancionero*, poem number 300, p. 111. Also see nursery rhymes in *Amor y pedagogía* (*OC*, 2a, II, 466).

However, he returns to the city and to his personal *yo*, which is in jeopardy of death at all times. And it is at this crucial moment that he makes the existential choice. He chooses the world; he decides to struggle against ignorance and for his fellow men because, as an authentic *yo*, he feels a commitment to this, his world. Pachico, who in the first part of the novel had just attained the realization of his individuality but who still looked on his fellow men as things, has now come out of the war with the authentic realization that each individual *yo* is a unique occurrence that cannot be replaced.

In this novel Unamuno has not yet developed the tragic sense of life as the anthropology of the *yo*, but it is in its formative stages. What can be seen at this point is the clear distinction made between Ignacio: "La muerte seguía pareciéndole idea abstracta," and Pachico: "Era un terror loco a la nada," and the consequences of each. The basis of this literary attitude is in the awareness of death as a personal jeopardy to the *yo*. The narrator himself, in excellent counterpoint, describes this attitude amidst the killing of battle:

Al morir los pobres se apagaban sus recuerdos, la visión de su serena campiña, y de su cielo; sus amores, sus esperanzas, su mundo; el mundo todo se les desvanecía; al morir ellos morían mundos, mundos enteros, y morían sin haberse conocido [*OC*, 2a, II, 326].

In conclusion, this first novel of Unamuno contains the first literary attitude, studied in the previous chapter, where the fictional characters lose the personal *yo* and become drops in the endless flux of the sea. But, also, in this literary world the personal *yos* of many individuals have spoken of death themselves or have had to face death. In this, the second literary attitude, there have been two basic responses to death. The first is the commonplace unauthentic evasion of death; to these characters, death has no meaning in their lives since they are not aware of it. Pedro Antonio was never aware of his individuality. He was a timid believer. Just as he followed his uncle's political opinions, he also believed in the faith to which he was born. He never doubted for a moment that death would reunite him with his son and wife. It never occurred to him to doubt since he never had the capacity to doubt— that is, he lacked an individual mind. Rafaela, as well as Ignacio, avoided thinking of death; when circumstances forced them, they responded with their emotions. Thus, as soon as they could, they forgot.

But, the second response is the authentic one. Pachico becomes aware of death, his own death, as the impending jeopardy that can be annihilation. The result of this awareness of death is to make him want to give the truth to his fellow men and to fight ignorance, that is, a sense of commitment to his world. This position is seen as a solid basis for action in this novel. But Unamuno does not explain how. He cannot, for he has not yet found the culmination of this attitude, which will be the tragic sense accepted by the personal *yo* as the dialectical basis for becoming all of one's world.

Amor y pedagogía (1902)

In this second novel Unamuno begins a new and more highly concentrated prose style.[11] It has been suggested that this change was due to the influence of Carlyle, whose works Unamuno translated and studied during this period.[12] Unamuno himself merely states that this novel was written in a new style: "Relatos dramáticos acezantes, de realidades íntimas, entrañadas, sin bambalinas ni realismos en que suele faltar la verdadera, la eterna realidad, la realidad de la personalidad" [Prólogo a la segunda edición, 1934, *OC*, 2a, II, 429].

In effect, this new style is the concentration on the personal individual view of the fictional character without giving this view any exterior support by the narrator. Unamuno also gave this profound statement of self-analysis:

En esta novela que ahora vuelvo a prologar está en germen—y más que en germen—lo más y lo mejor de lo que he revelado después en mis otras novelas: *Abel Sánchez, La tía Tula, Nada menos que todo un hombre, Niebla,* y, por último, *San Manuel Bueno, mártir y tres historias más* [*OC*, 2a, II, 429].

[11] There have been innumerable mentions of this novel by all the critics that review the works of Unamuno, but few have concerned themselves with a close examination of the novel itself. For a critical review, see Guillermo de Torre, "Estilo en Unamuno," newspaper *Luz* (September 7, 1934). Julián Marías in his *Unamuno* briefly studies it, pp. 94–96. More recently D. L. Fabian has studied it in connection with the "Prometeo" theme and Pérez de Ayala's novel in "Action and Idea in *Amor y pedagogía* and *Prometeo,*" *Hispania*, XLI, 1 (1958), 30–34.

[12] Carlos Clavería studies the relation of Carlyle's style to Unamuno's change in style of these years. Clavería certainly proves two factors: (1) Unamuno worked on Carlyle during this period more than at any other time, and (2) Unamuno used many terms and names which were borrowed from Carlyle. However, there are so many differences between the styles of these two writers that similarity might be explained as one dictated by the comic grotesque satire which Unamuno saw in Carlyle and adapted to his style and to his thoughts and insights on the use of reason and emotions in confronting life and death. Also, see P. G. Earle, *Unamuno and English Literature*, pp. 114–119.

The study of *Amor y pedagogía* in this chapter and in the next will demonstrate what Unamuno was referring to, for in this novel of 1902 lies not only the development of his second literary attitude but also the genesis of the third. He refers to the second attitude in these words:

"Sé tú, tú mismo, único e insustituible"—le decía mi don Fulgencio al pobre conejillo Apolodoro. Luego desarrollé yo, su autor, en mi obra—novela también—*Del sentimiento trágico de la vida,* ese mismo tema [*OC,* 2a, II, 433].

The book is divided into four parts: the prologue, the novel itself with fifteen chapters, an epilogue, and *Apuntes para un tratado de cocotología.*

The prologue sets a humorous and at times sarcastic tone as the author addresses himself in the third person in the vein of a narrowminded critic.

The novel itself, whose plot Unamuno altered slightly from the general outline he had in 1900, presents death, always in a humorous tone, through these exaggerated caricature-like characters: Avito—the father of the genius to be; Marina—the mother; Don Fulgencio—the teacher; Menaguti—the poet; and Apolodoro or Luis, depending on who calls to him, his father or his mother—the genius to be.

There are three situations for the presentation of death in this linear-structured novel of Apolodoro's life: (1) the intimate thoughts about death of the genius to be, (2) the talk of death with don Fulgencio as the teacher lectures Apolodoro, and (3) the act of death, first of his sister Rosa and then of Apolodoro himself.

(1) Apolodoro's thoughts move into the mystery of death. Sleep always escapes from him, although he attempts, every night, to trap it. He wonders whether death will come in the same way:

¿Sucederá lo mismo con la muerte?, piensa, y pónese a imaginar qué será eso de la muerte, aun cuando asegura su padre que no es más ni menos que la cesación de la vida; la cosa más sencilla que cabe [*OC,* 2a, II, 510].

Thus, by using the ridiculous, Unamuno has presented the philosophical comparison of sleep and death as a grotesque farce rather than as a personal tragedy. The world of this character is an incompatible bifurcation—logical abstractions and uncontrollable emotions—which he has received from the two sources of his father—la forma—and his mother—la materia.

Essentially, it is because the empirical Positivists create a falsification of life that Unamuno has created this ridiculous abstraction. This novel is an answer to the logical limitations of the intellect.

Here Unamuno is saying: if you do not live, love, and die in that logical rigidity, why do you try to explain life and man through it. By applying the systems of the Comtian sociologists to life, Unamuno has created Apolodoro's world.[13]

He continues the tragic-grotesque maze in Apolodoro's mind as a direct application of logical systemization to life:

Y toda esta ciencia, cuando yo muera y mi cerebro se descomponga bajo tierra, ¿no se reducirá a algo? ¿En qué forma persistirá? Porque nada se pierde, todo se trasforma... Equivalencia de fuerzas... ley de la conservación de la energía... [OC, 2a, II, 528].

It is in this frame of mind that the question of human existence appears to this caricature of an *agonista*. Logic and reason merely sink him further into the abyss.

When this caricature is confronted by the human problems of life and death, he searches for meaning and finds only abstractions. He goes to his tutor seeking an answer. The effect of this conversation with don Fulgencio will be seen in Apolodoro's thoughts as the novel of his life progresses. Here is the answer of the logical system builder:

(2) The dialogue of Apolodoro and don Fulgencio:

—Tú sabes que nada se pierde...

—Ley de la conservación de la energía... trasformación de las fuerzas...— murmura Apolodoro.

.   .   .   .

—Todo cuanto nos entra por los sentidos en nosotros queda, en el insondable mar de lo subconciente . . . resucitaremos todos en nuestros descendientes. . . . Los que no tenemos hijos nos reproducimos en nuestras obras, que son nuestros hijos; en cada una de ellas va nuestro espíritu todo y el que la recibe nos recibe por entero [OC, 2a, II, 545–546].

Unamuno has in this dialogue created the *comedia tragi-grotesca* he sought, for the presentation of the problem is the intimate tragedy of the man who has lost the faith of immortality and who is aware of death as the jeopardy that can mean annihilation. But the answer to the problem by don Fulgencio is a grotesque ridicule

[13] Comtian sociology was the attempt to create through the methods of the natural sciences a science of man which Comte named sociology. He even went so far as to create a positive religion to go along with the science of man and lead the inferior men of emotions to the good of society. There can be no doubt as to what Unamuno was satirizing with the following lines: "[Carrascal] anda por mecánica, digiere por química y se hace cortar el traje por geometría proyectiva" (p. 437); "mientras sonríe la Pedagogía sociológica desde la región de las ideas puras" (p. 450); "Y hay en ella [la casa] su altar, su rastro de culto, hay un ladrillo en que está grabada la palabra *Ciencia*, y sobre él una ruedecita montada sobre su eje" (p. 459).

of the entire spectrum of empirical Positivism and neo-idealism. Thus, Unamuno's burlesque is merely the use of the abstract logical systems to answer the personal, illogical, emotive dread of annihilation, with the result, as has been shown, in the ridiculous absurdities enumerated by the abstract philosopher. Two factors remain clear: first, that this caricature of a man, Apolodoro, has been given an awareness of his individuality and of his will, together with the awareness of death; and second, that don Fulgencio has not been able to assure him against death, but he has suggested possible escape routes—both absurd: the re-creation of the personal *yo* inside of the subconscious of future generations of offspring and the personal *yo*, like a monad, being able to come to life through literary creation.[14]

The effect of this conversation on Apolodoro can be seen by turning again to his intimate thoughts: "Me mato...si no, ¿cómo voy a presentarme ante Menaguti? Pero antes tengo que asegurarme esa inmortalidad, por si es verdad, pues ¿quién sabe?" (p. 546).

The scientistic pedagogy of Apolodoro's father has led him to the tragic conception of his failure in life. He cannot cope with this confusing mass of feelings, senses, and emotions since he is oriented toward an abstraction. The only phenomenon he is aware of is his own *yo*, which does not want to die. The poet Menaguti has told him that he could find meaning in life only by dedicating himself to art. But now that both his love, Clarita, and his creation, a short story, have failed him, he feels abject disillusion and seeks to remove himself from the unbearable struggle of life, but at the same time he does not want to die utterly. Thus, this is a character of *noluntad*, that is, of the "querer no ser." He recalls these lines of Leopardi: "Fratelli, a un tempo stesso Amore e Morte / Ingenerò la sorte." And then the words of don Fulgencio come back: "Mas antes, Apolodoro, haz hijos, haz hijos; busca la inmortalidad en ellos..., por si acaso...!" (p. 547).

Inside the contorted mind of Apolodoro the world becomes more absurd and ridiculous as he attempts to put the living into the scientistic abstractions with which he observes life. Unamuno uses various grotesque images throughout the novel to demonstrate the ridiculous made sublime.[15] All of this world continues to accumu-

---

[14] The falseness of these solutions lies in that they are the rational attempts to solve the sensitive and spiritual problems. See the next chapter, where these same two solutions are approached through intuitional feeling.

[15] See my study of this aspect of Unamuno's prose, *"Amor y pedagogía* y lo grotesco," *Cuadernos de la cátedra* . . . , XIII (1963), 53–62.

late in Apolodoro's mind, and as it does, he reaches the point of near insanity. But he knows enough to realize that it is his father's logical abstractions put to practice that have made him so inadequate. He confronts his father with this accusation, but Avito responds only by crying out: "No andaremos bien mientras no se propague el hombre por brotes o por escisión, ya que ha de propagarse para la civilización y la ciencia" (pp. 549–550). Apolodoro continues to advance in his inability to cope with life; he thinks:

Si no me quiere Clarita y no sé hacer cuentos, ¿para qué vivir? La Muerte lo mismo que el Amor le dice: ¡Haz hijos! La Muerte, ¿es distinta del Amor? Para la ameba, morir es reproducirse [OC, 2a, II, 550].

The death of Apolodoro's sister, Rosa, is the last crisis that affects the aborted genius. Again Unamuno applies the intellectual limitations of science to a life situation, with the result of another grotesque scene. The scene presents the girl dying and the father, Avito, lecturing on the physiological and pathological aspects of the case.

(3) The death scene of Rosa:

Marina reza y llora en silencio, en sueños, hacia dentro; Apolodoro piensa en su dimisión y en la inmortalidad. Y don Avito, ante lo irremediable, da una lección:
—Va a concluir el proceso vital . . . [OC, 2a, II, 556].

After this experience, Apolodoro is in a mad rage to give a child to a woman in order to immortalize himself like the amoeba. He finally convinces the maid, Petra, and in the darkness, calling her Clarita, gives her the seed of a child. In a few days when he comes out of his rage he feels only pity for Petra and disgust toward himself. As he continues to meditate he pours forth a ridiculous mixture of pseudoscientific phrases and pent-up emotions. Finally, Apolodoro locks himself in his room and prepares to commit suicide by hanging himself from the ceiling. The novel ends with Avito's first human cry as he discovers the hanging body of his son:[16] "¡Madre!—gimió desde sus honduras insondables el pobre pedagogo, y cayó desfallecido en brazos de la mujer. El amor había vencido" (p. 561).

However, in the epilogue to the novel, Unamuno takes the complete array of characters and explores the effect which Apolodoro's death had on them. None have really been affected for none of

---

[16] This cry of anguish is also indicative of Unamuno's personal life entering into his created world. For documentation, see OC, 2a, II, 26. The "hijo mío" of the wife or the "madre" of the husband can also be found in La esfinge and Abel Sánchez.

them have learned to live with the awareness of death. As soon as Avito finds out that he is to be a grandfather to the son borne by Petra he resumes his abstractions.[17] And don Fulgencio, to whom the death of Apolodoro should have meant more, is submerged even deeper into his grotesque abstracted world. The last part of the book is the satire of the scientific method applied to life, as in the Comtian sociology. Here don Fulgencio has written a treatise for the making of paper birds. In the appendix to the *Tratado* Unamuno gives the culmination of the use of reason to life: the completely false world created by don Fulgencio as the view of a sunset upon the sea by a paper bird.

In conclusion, this book has given the application of the scientific method to life. The ridiculous artificial world is strictly, however, the making of the fictional characters, since they have been given no exterior setting. But since they were characters, individual living *yos,* although some did not realize it, life came to them as they acted and reacted to each other in the situations of living. The result is the grotesque farce, both tragic and humorous. Apolodoro is a tragic *agonista* and his suicide, because of his *noluntad,* is pathetic. The figures of don Avito and don Fulgencio are ridiculous adaptations of an abstraction—scientism as life. Thus, through humorous, sometimes sarcastic, satire, Unamuno has developed the theme that the truth of man and life, that the meaning of existence, cannot be grasped through logic and reason but only by the emotive intuition of the spirit. The ultimate question throughout has been the meaning of death; there has been no answer since only reason has been used in the search. Two assurances for immortality of the personal *yo*—children and literary creation—have been based on reason.

The problem of the existence and possible annihilation of the personal *yo* has been authentically presented; it has only been the method which has led the characters to the ridiculous artificial abstractions in which they lived.

El canto de las aguas eternas (1909)

This short narrative is a metaphorical expression of life, the meaning of life, death, the state of death to the *yo,* and the eternal flux

[17] Avito Carrascal reappears in *Niebla* as a saddened but enlightened man (*OC,* 2a, II, 868–871): "—Sí, yo por aquí [rezando en la iglesia]; enseña mucho la vida, y más la muerte; enseñan más, mucho más que la ciencia" (p. 868).

of reality.[18] There is also the image of an eternal paradise, much closer to the Moslem heaven than to the Christian beatific vision, which is the goal of man whose life is: "el angosto camino, tallado a pico en la desnuda roca, va serpenteando sobre el abismo" (OC, 2a, IV, 497).

Among the walkers of this road is a man called Maquetas; he is singing a song, that is, making his life so that he cannot hear the sound of the eternal flux: "el torrente que corre invisible en el fondo de la sima." Along the road of life there are many stopping places, that is, situations of life into which man enters; now, as Maquetas approaches one of these, a young beautiful girl beckons to him to stop and rest, to sleep on her lap.

—¿Y qué es lo que canta [el agua que corre ahí abajo, a nuestra espalda]?
—Canta la canción del eterno descanso. Pero ahora descansa tú. . . .
La muchacha le da con sus labios un beso en los labios. . . . Pierde el sentido. Sueña que va cayendo sin fin por la insondable sima [OC, 2a, IV, 498–499].

When Maquetas awakens he realizes that it is late in life and that he must hurry if he is to get to the long-awaited castle of paradise before night falls. He rushes rapidly down the road, but the night encloses around him and he is forced to crawl in the bitter cold of the absolute darkness. Finally he loses his senses and he stops. The yo is now in a limbo of death which is neither in the eternal waters nor in the castle of paradise when he begins to re-create the story of life once more, this time giving an idea of the sensual heaven he seeks.

Había hace tiempo—sigue pensando—un hombre que se llamaba Maquetas, gran caminante, que iba por jornadas a un castillo donde le esperaba una buena comida junto al fogón, y después de la comida un buen lecho de descanso y en el lecho una buena compañera. Y allí, en el castillo, había de vivir días inacabables, oyendo historias sin término, solozándose con la mujer, en una juventud perpetua [OC, 2a, IV, 500–501].

As Unamuno goes through the metaphor the second time, he explains and gives meaning to all of its facets. Thus, the road of life is being walked by the living, and each inn and stop along the way represents the different stages of an individual's life. Since Maquetas is seeking the paradise of the castle, he follows the road singing the story of his existence without knowing it. An old man

[18] El canto de las aguas eternas lies hidden among the essays of Mi religión y otros ensayos breves (1910). The usual source of information on the background of the Unamunian writings, García Blanco, is silent in this case; however, both the tone and the theme indicate that it was written some years before it was published in 1909.

stops him and asks for the meaning of life, but Maquetas does not
care to know. Again the narration tells of the meeting with the
beautiful girl and the kiss: "le dió la muchacha un beso, el beso
de la muerte." And as the sun of life set behind the towers of the
castle, Maquetas felt himself to be surrounded by darkness. It was
a sensation of sinking into a solid mass of darkness and cold. He
was overcome by an almost complete silence which was broken only
by the song of the eternal waters from the abyss. In life the song
of the waters had been inaudible because it was in the company of
all of the sounds of life, but here, in this profound silence of darkness and cold, in this silence of death, the song of eternity moved
unceasingly.

The narration is suspended and the thoughts of Maquetas appear
once more:

Y Maquetas se repitió una, y otra, y otra, y otra vez el cuento de aquel
Maquetas, y siguió repitiéndoselo, y así seguirá en tanto que sigan cantando
las aguas del invisible torrente de la sima, y estas aguas cantarán siempre,
siempre, siempre sin ayer y sin mañana siempre, siempre, siempre... [*OC*,
2a, IV, 502].

The symbolism of the protagonist's name is clear; it is taken from
maqueta, that is, mock-up. And this is precisely what he is—a scale
model representation of *un hombre de carne y hueso*. He is a
demonstrative medium that brings out the vast metaphor of Unamuno's reality: the eternal waters, the relations of man, and the
re-creation of man. This is not to say that all three literary attitudes are present in this short prose work, but only anticipated.
The fundamental element that must be noted is that it is Maquetas,
the mock-up of a *yo*, who experiences the struggle of life as he
attempts to reach the material happiness of the castle. Thus, it is
the model of the unauthentic man, himself, who is constantly re-
appearing in existence as he tells his story over and over. Maquetas,
in his story, meets death and experiences the sinking into the limbo
of personal nothingness. The personal consciousness is lost there,
but from this darkness emerges the next traveler, also as unaware
as his predecessor.

El espejo de la muerte (1913)

The twenty-seven short stories that comprise this book were all
written earlier and published in the Hispanic press. Among these
narratives there are ten which are the further development of the
second literary attitude: the personal *yo* before his world and his

death. The earlier creations (1891–1900) are the negative rejection of the unauthentic man who has no realization of his individuality nor of death. In "La beca," "¡Viva la introyección!," "¿Por qué ser así?," "El diamante de Villasola," and "Juan Manso," Unamuno creates the empty man of the *no querer ser* and the *no querer no ser*. Even when death comes to others who are near this man, he is oblivious, for he has neither will nor individuality. Consequently, death is never known by these negative men. Death is a reality only to the authentic man; thus, in this first phase it is a meaningless event seen in others. In the case of "Juan Manso," which is subtitled "Cuento de muertos," because it depicts the living dead, Unamuno turns the focus on a little man. He appears to be timid only because he hates everyone and is empty inside. This is a *yo* who has only a shell existence. Other narratives—"Una visita al viejo poeta" and "El abejorro"—move toward the authentic self-realization of the *yo*. However, the last three representative narratives treated here, all of 1912, give the positive expression of the attitude: "El sencillo don Rafael, cazador y tresillista," "Cruce de caminos," "El amor que asalta."

In "La beca" (n.d.) Unamuno creates one of his *abúlicos* who has no awareness of himself nor of those around him as personal *yos*. Don Agustín rationalizes to himself: " 'Pero ¿por qué seré así, Dios mío?', se preguntaba, y seguía siendo así, como era, ya que sólo de tal modo podía ser él el que era" (*OC*, 2a, II, 699). He was a man who met failure at every turn due to his almost entire lack of will. After every defeat he planned new projects, but the time was never right for them or he simply did not have the will to put them into reality. Thus, he and his wife put all their expectations into one hope—a scholarship for their son on which they could all live: "Es nuestra única esperanza—decía la madre."

The son is burdened with the responsibilities of the family and he receives the scholarship, but only at the cost of his health. The situation continues from day to day; the boy needs rest and fresh air, but the demands of the family force him to continue:

> —¡Dejar los libros!—exclamó don Agustín.
> ¿Y con qué comemos?
> —Trabaje usted [dijo el médico].
> —Pues si busco y no encuentro; si...
> —Pues si se les muere, por su cuenta...
> . . . Y se lo comieron, con ayuda de la tisis [*OC*, 2a, II, 704].

After the son's death the mother could only feel the loss of a provider for the family. And don Agustín gave this epitaph to his son:

"—Sí, muy triste—murmuró el padre, pensando que en una temporada no podría ir al café."

The narrator ends the short story with the pessimistic tone that humanity is composed of these will-less *mansos*, who consider themselves to be without any voice in their life and therefore must depend on someone else, be it the government or, as in this case, their children.

The same type of negative attack is launched in "¡Viva la introyección!," where the mass-man who follows like a sheep is depicted.

The negative focus of "La beca" is used again in "¿Por qué ser así?" (1898) which was first part of a longer story, "Nerón tiple o el calvario de un inglés" (1890):

Pero, ¡Dios mío!—se decía—, ¿por qué soy así? ¿Por qué soy como soy? Todo se me vuelven propósitos de energía que se me disipan en nieblas así que afronto la realidad [*OC,* 2a, II, 712].

"El diamante de Villasola" (1898) has the theme of *Amor y pedagogía* without the sarcastic humor. The *maestro* is probably the first characterization of what will later be don Avito Carrascal in the novel. The teacher of the town considers his students only as means to an end: the abstraction of the system itself. When a brilliant student finally comes his way, he can only think of the system: "¡Aquél sí que era ejemplar para sus ensayos y para poner a prueba su destreza!" (*OC,* 2a, II, 718).

The result in this narrative is not suicide, as with Apolodoro, but rather frustration and disillusionment as the boy encounters life treating his fellow men as things.

"Juan Manso," which is subtitled *cuento de muertos* (1892), is the clearest example of this phase of Unamuno's literary creation. Juan is the man who does not want to differ in the slightest manner from the social group. He is the *yo que no quiere ser.*

—Yo no soy nada. . . .
No le valió, sin embargo, su mansedumbre y al cabo se murió, que fué el único acto comprometedor que efectuó en su vida [*OC,* 2a, II, 722].

From this extreme of the unauthentic man, the first step toward an authentic awareness of the *yo* and his world is to question the "why" of human activity. In "Una visita al viejo poeta" (1899), Unamuno takes this first step into the character of the old poet. At the height of his fame the poet had retired from public life. Now, in an interview, he recalls his secluded life:

He renunciado a aquel yo ficticio y abstracto que me sumía en la soledad de mi propio vacío. Busqué a Dios a través de él; pero como ese mi yo era una idea abstracta, un yo frío y difuso, de rechazo, jamás di con más Dios que con su proyección al infinito, con una niebla fría y difusa también; con un Dios lógico, mudo, ciego y sordo [*OC*, 2a, II, 750].

The poet has not found the key to an authentic way of life; he has fled from the unauthentic but he has not found the authentic.

Again in "El abejorro," 1900, there is the feeling of anguish before the question: to what end is human behavior directed? What is good and what is bad? "Sin esa pregunta, nadie creería en la muerte" (*OC*, 2a, II, 756).

In 1912 Unamuno wrote "El sencillo don Rafael, cazador y tresillista." Don Rafael is a strong-willed character who has felt the necessity of having faith in order to live and who has accepted the approach of death as the source of meaning to life. Don Rafael lived alone, having lost his family years before; his life was empty, but it was his life and he was aware of it. To this man was left a newborn child—abandoned on his doorstep. He responded with decision and firmness. He would adopt the child and give him a home. His doctor was able to get a wet nurse for the infant; she was an unwed mother whose child had been born dead. In response to the objections of the housekeeper about appearances, don Rafael answered with an expression of the freedom of will of the protagonist of *Nada menos que todo un hombre:* "Soy libre. . . . No me cabe la culpa de que haya nacido, pero tendré el mérito de hacerle vivir" (*OC*, 2a, II, 630–631). The young girl nursed the child and don Rafael accepted her as an individual, with no prejudice because of her past. After an illness of the child during which he obliged the nurse to remain with them in his house, he proposed marriage to her. She accepted, and that night they began the continuation of the family.

By giving chance a place, don Rafael accepts his position of being free to accept or reject what it might bring; thus, in essence, he, the man don Rafael, is the maker of his destiny.

Two other stories of 1912 which had appeared as "Don Rafael . . .," with the subtitle *cuentos del azar,* also bring out the freedom of the will of the *yo.* In "Cruce de caminos" and "El amor que asalta" the characters are brought together by pure chance, but they consciously choose each other from that moment unto death. Death comes to the old man in "Cruce de caminos" when his adopted granddaughter finds a love to fill her life—all the man awaited before death. In "El amor que asalta" the fulfillment of

love, which the man and woman choose, brings death from a
heart attack. Thus, in both stories the characters choose love which
gives life meaning and purpose before death.

Niebla (1914)

This has been the most popular outside of Spain of Unamuno's
novels.[19] Three important factors for this acceptance are: (1) Unamuno achieves a technique which places multiple independent
points of view in one interaction, anticipating Kafka,[20] and makes
each a personal *yo* with his own world; (2) he develops the problem
of the existence of the *yo* with the fictional characters and him, their
creator, in existential correspondence, in anticipation of Pirandello,[21] and (3) like Kierkegaard, Unamuno again presents the personal *yo* in the process of existence going from the unauthentic
passive, sleep-walking *yo,* to the active expression of the *yo* made
authentic through his will. Thus, by the time his novel was translated, Unamuno had a ready-made public throughout Europe and
America due largely to the fact that there were parallel European
giants of literature who had received their inspiration from the
same sources: Kierkegaard, Leopardi, and Dostoevski.

The first two factors mentioned above do not concern this chapter directly and will have to be postponed for later consideration.
However, the third point is not only the key to the entire literary

[19] *Niebla* has been translated into Hungarian (1922), Italian (two editions:
1922, 1955), French (1926), German (two editions: 1926, 1933), Dutch (1928),
English (1928), Polish (1928), Swedish (1928), Rumanian (1929), Serbo-croatian
(1929), and Lett (1935).

[20] Unamuno's *Niebla* of 1914 is two years earlier than Kafka's *Der Verwandlung*
(Metamorphosis), where there is a similar technique of using the absurd and the
grotesque to give the characters' isolated view of the world.

[21] The similarities between Unamuno and Pirandello have been studied in
numerous articles. See E. Bay, "Unamuno and Pirandello," *The New York*
Herald Tribune (January 21, 1923); Luis Leal, "Unamuno and Pirandello,"
Italica, XXIX (1952), 193–199; Manuel García Blanco, "Italia y Unamuno,"
Archivum, IV (Oviedo, 1954), 182–219; G. Vicari, "Unamuno e Pirandello,"
Settimana Illustrata (Rome, May 21, 1955); R. Brummer, "Autor und Geschöpf bei
Unamuno und Pirandello," *Wissenschaftliche Zeitschrift,* V (Jena, 1955–56),
241–248; F. Sedwick, "Unamuno and Pirandello Revisited," *Italica,* XXXIII
(1956), 40–51.

Unamuno himself in an article of 1923 clarified the parallel paths that he and
Pirandello followed without knowing of each other's work. If this article,
published in Argentina, had been accessible, much scholarly speculation would
have been resolved earlier. "Pirandello y yo" has been recently published in
OC, 2a, X, 544–548.

attitude being studied in these pages, but it is also a masterpiece of character development.

The bittersweet tone of this novel is established through the tragicomic use of paradox and arbitrary reflection by the characters in a grotesque inner reality of the *yo* in his world.

Augusto Pérez is presented standing in his doorway:

Extendió el brazo derecho, con la mano palma abajo y abierta, y dirigiendo los ojos al cielo, quedóse un momento parado en esta actitud estatuaria y augusta. No era que tomaba posesión del mundo exterior, sino era que observaba si llovía. Y al recibir en el dorso de la mano el frescor del lento orvallo frunció el sobrecejo. Y no era tampoco que le molestase la llovizna, sino el tener que abrir el paraguas. ¡Estaba tan elegante, tan esbelto, plegado y dentro de su funda! Un paraguas cerrado es tan elegante como es feo un paraguas abierto [*OC*, 2a, II, 804].

By using an arbitrary turn of the mind, Unamuno immediately gets the reader into the private point of view of don Augusto Pérez, who is a fictional character but a unique one, an irreplaceable one. The direct thoughts of the character follow on the matter of opening the umbrella. Unamuno will use this technique throughout the novel: first giving the general scope of the character's point of view and then following with the very personal thoughts of the character himself. Augusto does not know where he is going; thus he thinks: "Esperaré a que pase un perro—se dijo—, y tomaré la dirección inicial que él tome" (*OC*, 2a, II, 805). This character is established as a passive creature without the slightest indication of a will nor any awareness of his individuality. What, in fact, he does follow down the street is the magnetism of the beautiful eyes of a girl, Eugenia. However, he is not aware that he is following her until he reaches her doorstep. As Augusto walks, the personal point of view is developed: "Para trabajo el de ese pobre paralítico que va ahí medio arrastrándose... Pero ¿y qué sé yo? ¡Perdone, hermano!—esto se lo dijo en voz alta—. ¿Hermano? ¿Hermano en qué? ¡En parálisis!" (p. 805). In this manner he arrives at Eugenia's doorstep and only there does he realize that he has followed her. Since the house manager sees him, he feels obliged to ask about the girl whom he has scarcely noticed. Once he has taken this initial step a trajectory is established that he will follow. The more he converses with himself the more he is convinced that he is in love with her, that she is in love with him, that they will have children, and so forth. Thus, this man, who is no more than a leaf in the wind, is drawn into a life situation purely by chance and the pen of Unamuno. Since his mother had died he had lived alone in his house

with two old servants. In his present frame of mind, his house was
not a home to him, but rather he regarded it as an ashtray. The
ashtray symbol is explained in the life Augusto had lived with his
mother after his father's death—those days, all the same, were in
that house like the ashes of a cigar. But now his life had meaning.
He had somewhere to go and something to do: win Eugenia from
her fiancé. "¡Lucharemos! . . . Ya tiene mi vida una finalidad:
ya tengo una conquista que llevar a cabo" (p. 814).

In the course of the novel there is the personal *yo* of Augusto as
he looks at his life and its experiences, but there is also the ever
present limitation of time. At first it is the narrator that keeps
reminding the reader of the temporality of this life. The days, the
hours, are all stated. At this point in his life Augusto begins to
become aware of his senseless drifting as he becomes aware of his
temporality. But he still feels that he is at the mercy of chance as
he flounders in life: "El mundo es un caleidoscopio" (p. 822). He
cannot meet life for he has never made a decision; he tells himself:
"Si viviera mi madre encontraría solución a esto" (p. 828).

Augusto finally enters Eugenia's home when he returns the bird
cage that happened to fall as he passed by. With this event Augusto
begins to consider his active part in the temporal existence he calls
his life. He speaks to his dog, Orfeo:

Cuando el hombre se queda a solas y cierra los ojos al porvenir, al ensueño,
se le revela el abismo pavoroso de la eternidad. La eternidad no es porvenir. Cuando morimos nos da la muerte media vuelta en nuestra órbita y
emprendemos la marcha hacia atrás, hacia el pasado, hacia lo que fué. Y
así, sin término, devanando la madeja de nuestro destino, deshaciendo todo
el infinito que en una eternidad nos ha hecho, caminando a la nada, sin
llegar nunca a ella, pues que ella nunca fué [*OC*, 2a, II, 836–837].

Thus, death is seen not as an event, but rather as an approaching force that is the counterpart of being. Death is at every moment
negating being, moving toward non-being which is not a point nor
a conclusion; it is a direction, a negating direction. It is not reached
because of the counterpart which is being. Just as man is making
his future he is also unmaking his existence in that he is approaching death. Thus, at the same time the personal *yo* is weaving his
destiny, the possibility of annihilation of the personal consciousness
is bringing the *yo* closer to his destiny and unweaving life. This is
the struggle of man.

Augusto is duped by Eugenia and Mauricio, her fiancé, into
thinking that she will marry him so that they can get money out of

him. When he is informed of the *fait accompli* in a letter from
Eugenia, he is deeply disturbed and goes to his friend Víctor Goti
for advice. Augusto, now fully aware of his *yo,* tells Víctor:

—¡Es que me ha hecho padre, Víctor!

—¿Cómo? ¿Que te ha hecho padre?

—¡Sí, de mí mismo! Con esto creo haber nacido de veras. Y para sufrir,
para morir.

—Sí, el segundo nacimiento, el verdadero, es nacer por el dolor a la
conciencia de la muerte incesante, de que estamos siempre muriendo [*OC,*
2a, II, 969].

Augusto is now an authentic *yo* who feels that he is his own maker
in that he is aware that every action he takes or does not take is a
choice taken by himself.

He reaches the decision that his life is and has been meaningless
and that the only way out is to commit suicide. But before doing
away with himself, he goes to visit a certain Miguel de Unamuno,
who knows about death and suicide. The meeting of creator and
fictional character is narrated. Unamuno tells Augusto that he
cannot kill himself because he, Unamuno, his creator, was going
to do away with him. But Augusto reminds Unamuno, the creator,
that he, like Cervantes, existed only through his creations of fictional
characters. Unamuno becomes angry and tells the impertinent
Augusto that he will die very soon:

—¡Sí, voy a hacer que mueras!

—¡Ah, eso nunca!, ¡nunca!, ¡nunca!—gritó [*OC,* 2a, II, 979].

Unamuno insists that he has written it and it will come to pass;
Augusto will die. He dies in bed, as Unamuno, his creator, willed.
However, before succumbing, Augusto achieves full consciousness
of his existence as a fictional character.

Nada menos que todo un hombre (1916)

This very powerful short novel of Unamuno has the simplicity of
a Greek tragedy.[22] This characteristic was recognized by Julio de
Hoyos, who adapted the novel into a drama in 1925, and by Pirandello, who presented it in Italy as *Un vero uomo* in 1928.[23]

[22] The novel *Nada menos que todo un hombre* was written in 1916, but it was
not published until 1920 in the volume *Tres novelas ejemplares y un prólogo.*
The other novels are *Dos madres* and *El marqués de Lumbría,* which will be
examined in the next chapter.

[23] For the study of the dramatic adaptation by Julio de Hoyos and the changes
involved, see *OC,* 2a, XII, 109–115. For information on Pirandello's presentation,
see p. 114.

Alejandro Gómez is a true Unamunian Oedipus. Alejandro was fully aware of his individuality and knew that he, the *yo*-will, was the maker of his own destiny. He accepted the full responsibility for his actions and had little use for the *señoritos* who were not capable of the same acceptance of man's utter freedom to forge his life and to accept without reproach whatever consequences may result. His answer to the query of who he was always came out the same: "un hombre, nada menos que todo un hombre."

Alejandro saw the beautiful Julia Yáñez, bought the right to marry her from her father, and then won her through his personality. Julia was overwhelmed and could not keep from repeating "éste sí que es un hombre." However, she wanted more than to be the most precious possession of this iron-willed man; she wanted to be loved. Every day she understood less this seemingly emotionless man. The question of his capacity to love her began to grow into an obsession. She reached the point where she had to know at any cost whether Alejandro loved her, the woman of flesh and blood. The cost she paid was an abortive love affair with a count, a spineless leech, whom Alejandro considered to be like a pet cat to her. When she confessed her betrayal, Alejandro responded by placing her in an asylum until she recognized that she had suffered from delusions. The scene where the doctors and the count confronted Julia to pronounce her unbalanced has the greatest dramatic tension. Finally she gave in to Alejandro and he brought her back and ordered the count to come to dinner. Now, full of loving admiration for her husband and scornful disdain for the weak count, Julia responded with her husband's strength of will after he had left the two alone at the table:

Usted puede venir acá cuando quiera, y ahora que estoy ya, gracias a Dios y a Alejandro, completamente curada, curada del todo, señor conde, sería de mal efecto que usted suspendiera sus visitas [*OC,* 2a, IX, 513–514].

Julia's frail health took a turn toward death, and for the first time Alejandro was forced to come face to face with the possibility of death. During her illness Julia had true moments of insanity when she called out to her husband in the most passionate and ardent words. He now began to give himself emotionally to her and to fight against death with everything he had: his wealth, his life, his *yo*. As Alejandro cried out in search of God "¡Sálvamela! ¡Sálvamela y pídeme todo, todo, todo: mi fortuna toda, mi sangre toda; yo todo..., todo yo!," she finally found the answer she had been seeking.

Death claimed Julia, and Alejandro reviewed his life as he witnessed this death that was taking his wife and his future from him. He wrote his will, kissed his son goodbye, and then returned to the bedroom and opened his veins as he frantically kissed his wife's corpse.

Thus, the novel presents a strong-willed man who realizes he is his own maker but reaches the level of authenticity only when death is claiming his beloved wife. His final assertion of will is the *noluntad* of suicide. Alejandro never had any sense of humanity for he had not reached the sense of commitment to the world that comes only with the awareness of death.

Abel Sánchez. Una historia de pasión (1917)

This novel is an intense psychological probe into the subtleties and complexities of the human consciousness: the impassioned psyche of Joaquín Monegro.[24] It is the tragic plot of a man who struggles with his passions throughout his life, searching for the inner freedom which can only come with the awareness by the personal *yo* that he is the maker of his own future. The tragedy lies in that this personal *yo* who is aware of his individuality never achieves the victory over himself for which he yearned with such fervor. During his life Joaquín Monegro is constantly pursued and dominated by his demoniac alter ego, a blind hatred which is fed by envy for Abel Sánchez. The theme is biblical: the fratricide of Cain which grew out of his envy for Abel, God's favorite.

Unamuno uses the literary convention of the manuscript which has been left by the author and is later put in order with a commentary by the discoverer. This technique gives Unamuno the oppor-

---

[24] This novel has been the subject of psychoanalysis by M. Cabaleiro Goas, *Werther, Mischkin y Joaquín Monegro vistos por un psiquiatra. Trilogía patográfica* (Barcelona: Editorial Apolo, 1951), pp. 217–310. This study makes the basic error of taking a piece of imaginative literature and examining it as if it were a case history of its author. A psychological study, at best, might be able to analyze the mind of the fictional character as he is constructed in the world of the novel. But to assume the same rational correlation (fictional character to his world) as existing between the author and his environment is just short of being absurd. The novel is a closed world where characters and ambient exist to the limited extent which the author gives them, and no matter how well a character is developed he is not a man. Thus, Unamuno's ideas and sentiments are openly expressed in the novel, but there is much more to the man Unamuno than is in *Abel Sánchez*. For an excellent study of the theory of personality in fiction, see Paul Ilie, "Unamuno, Gorgy and the Cain Myth," *Hispanic Review*, XXIX, 4 (October, 1961), 310–323.

tunity to present the internal psychological struggle of Joaquín in a first person narrative and also to render in the third person the emotional ambient and situation in which the antagonist found himself. The novel opens with these words:

Al morir Joaquín Monegro encontróse entre sus papeles una especie de memoria de la sombría pasión que le hubo devorado en vida [*OC*, 2a, II, 1001].

After Abel, already everyone's favorite, also wins Helena's love, Joaquín is beset with envy and hatred. He writes of this uncontrollable emotional state in his confession:

Fuí a ella [la boda] como quien va a la muerte. Y lo que me ocurrió fué más mortal que la muerte misma; fué peor, mucho peor que morirse. Ojalá me hubiese entonces muerto allí [*OC*, 2a, IX, 1023].

Death at that moment would have been an escape but not an answer. Joaquín awaits with growing anxiety to hear the exchange of vows between Abel and Helena. But after he hears the *sís*, he reacts in this manner: "Me sentí peor que un monstruo, me sentí como si no existiera, como si no fuese nada más que un pedazo de hielo" (p. 1023).

Abel's paintings began to bring him glory and fame during his lifetime, increasing Joaquín's burning envy. Their professional paths cross when Joaquín, a physician, attends a woman whose portrait Abel has painted. The immortality which Abel has given her in the work of art so blinds Joaquín that he does not treat her properly and she dies. He writes in his diary: "¡Yo la dejé morir y él la resucita!" (p. 1032).

The basis for Joaquín's black passion is his inability to love himself. Since he has only contempt for himself he cannot feel anything approximating love toward his fellow man: "¿Para qué querrá vivir?—decíase de algunos—. Hasta le haría un favor dejándole morir. . . . La humanidad es lo más cochino que hay" (pp. 1032–33).

The hatred that Joaquín feels toward himself and the world thus finds its focus on his friend Abel, who is almost his brother. When Abel has a son, Joaquín writes: "sentí que el odio se me enconaba." But instead of fleeing from Abel, Joaquín seeks him out. He is aware that he is unable to love because of the hatred that lives within him; thus he tries to cure it by confronting what he thinks is the cause.

While on a professional visit to see Abelín, Abel's son, they discuss the research Abel was doing for a new painting which was to be the murder of Abel by Cain. Seeing how much Joaquín becomes interested in the project, Abel gives him Lord Byron's *Cain* to read. This book has an enormous effect on Joaquín, who now begins to believe in this alter ego, a demon of hate.

Hasta que leí y releí el *Caín* byroniano, yo, que tantos hombres había visto agonizar y morir, no pensé en la muerte, no la descubrí. . . . Y empecé a creer en el Infierno y que la muerte es un ser, es el Demonio, es el Odio hecho persona, es el Dios del alma [*OC*, 2a, II, 1044–45].

With the thought of this personal demon, Joaquín begins the struggle to free himself from it. A moment of dramatic intensity comes when Joaquín gives a speech at a testimonial dinner for Abel. He arrives pale and nervous; the other men expect an acid dissection of Abel's art, but Abel insists that his lifelong friend will not attack him. Joaquín's speech is a masterpiece of impassioned oratory:

"El es nuestro, de todos, él es mío sobre todo, y yo gozando su obra, la hago tan mía como él la hizo suya creándola. Y me consuelo de verme sujeto a mi medianía..."

Su voz lloraba a las veces. El público estaba subyugado, vislumbrando oscuramente la lucha gigantesca de aquel alma con su demonio [*OC*, 2a, II, 1051].

However, this heroic act does not cure Joaquín, for even as he is attaining the closest ties of friendship, his demon speaks to him: "Y al abrazarse le dijo a Joaquín su demonio: 'Si pudieras ahora ahogarlo en tus brazos!'" (p. 1052). He turns to religion in an attempt to kill the demon of hatred that resides in his mind, but even as he is praying to the Virgin before a picture of the Madonna, for which Helena had been Abel's model, he thinks: "¡Así se muera! ¡Así te la deje libre!" (p. 1056).

Everything Joaquín tries fails to free him from the alter ego that is now stronger than ever before. His daughter Joaquina is going to enter a convent to pray for the salvation of her father's soul, but he convinces her that she can cure him with her love by giving him grandchildren. She marries Abelín, who has become almost a son to Joaquín since he has been an assistant in his practice. Abelín has never felt close to his father; he is much closer to the temperament and interests of Joaquín. The married couple lives with Joaquín and Antonia, and for a time Joaquín seems to find the inner unity he has so long desired. When the child is born and named after him—Joaquín, Joaquín Sánchez Monegro—he thinks that his daughter's love has finally conquered his demon and cured his spiritual leprosy. But each day it becomes

more evident that the child prefers Abel to Joaquín. Finally, in a
burst of rage, Joaquín tells Abel to leave the area and allow him
to find peace in his old age. Abel refuses, knowing he has only a
short time to live. Joaquín rushes to Abel and puts his hands on
his throat; the emotion kills Abel and he falls dead in Joaquín's
arms. In a state of semidelusion Joaquín stutters his fault to the
grandchild, who has come upon the scene: "—¡Muerto, sí! Y le he
matado yo, yo; ha matado a Abel Caín, tu abuelo Caín" *(OC,* 2a,
II, 1115).

But the death of the object of a lifetime of envy and hatred does
not cure Joaquín, for, as has already been indicated, the basis of
the alter ego is the self-hatred of the agonizing *yo* who was never
able to win in the struggle with his own passions. Only his death
brings an end to this struggle. Joaquín dies, and, as if to purge
himself, he calls the entire family to his bedside and confesses his
demon and asks only to be forgiven and to die.

Joaquín Monegro was never able to achieve the inner freedom of
being aware that he was his own maker throughout his life, due
largely to the obsession that he developed of the alter ego of hatred.

San Manuel Bueno, mártir (1930)

Unamuno's last novel was written upon his return to Spain from
exile in France, but was not published until 1933. Thus, the return
to the prose narrative in this novel and others, during these years
of the second Spanish Republic (1931–36), marks the last period
of devoted literary creation in Unamuno's life. These facts would
indicate not only a mature literary production but also the culmination of artistic achievement that a period of meditation brings.
Unamuno accomplishes precisely that culmination of the second
literary attitude in this novel—*San Manuel Bueno, mártir.*

The first person narrator throughout the novel is Angela Carballino, who is writing the life of the town priest don Manuel Bueno:
"San Manuel Bueno . . . que fué mi verdadero padre espiritual,
el padre de mi espíritu, del mío, el de Angela Carballino" *(OC,* 1a,
II, 1196).

The novel presents its subject—don Manuel—not from his own
point of view nor from a detached narrator's view, but from the
personal *yo* of a narrator who has known him intimately. This technique allows Unamuno to present an authentic *yo* from outside the
inner fire of the *lucha.* The exterior indications of don Manuel's

struggle with death and his authentic expansion of the *yo* in commitment to his world begin to appear in the narration as slight variations in the behavior of the man. Angela first gives the image of
the man who has dedicated his life to making the townspeople
treat each other as unique, irreplaceable individuals and at the same
time to have an overwhelming faith in God and in immortality.
Yet amid his enormous success in preserving and strengthening the
faith of his flock, the astute Angela notes a curious personal trait
—the first indication of the inner struggle. All of the townspeople
go to mass even if it be only to see and hear the man don Manuel,
who is their spiritual father. He has instituted the practice of re-
citing the Credo. The prayer arises not as a chorus but as one simple
and united voice, and at the peak of this mountain of divine invocation is don Manuel, but he himself can never finish the prayer:

Y al llegar a lo de "creo en la resurrección de la carne y la vida perdurable"
la voz de Don Manuel se zambullía, como en un lago, en la del pueblo todo,
y era que él se callaba [*OC*, 1a, II, 1201].

He does not pray those words himself, but he insists that his spiritual
sons pray them and believe them. This is the paradox that begins
to take shape in Angela's observations and thoughts of don Manuel.
He is like a Moses who guides his people to the promised land but
cannot enter it himself. Every act of his daily life is entirely devoted to his people—to make them better men and women and to
bolster their faith; this is his living mission. Therefore, those that
are out of his reach move him to greater action. Angela writes:
"Un niño que nace muerto o que se muere recién nacido y un
suicidio—me dijo una vez—son para mí de los más terribles mis-
terios: ¡un niño en cruz!" (*OC*, 1a, II, 1203). Here again the personal *yo* of don Manuel shines out, even if Angela cannot capture
the full significance of it. A child born dead as well as the suicide
victim are beyond hope and beyond don Manuel's help. He cannot
face death for them. He would say: "que estén todos contentos de
vivir" (p. 1204). He has told Angela: "Yo no debo vivir solo; yo
no debo morir solo. Debo vivir para mi pueblo, morir para mi
pueblo" (p. 1206). He does not say *no puedo,* but *no debo,* that is,
this is his obligation, his commitment.

The narrator continues almost unwittingly to describe this living
paradox of a man. When she asked him whether hell existed, he
answered immediately: "Not for you." There is no hell, because
don Manuel has lived it for her and the other townspeople.

Don Manuel's inner struggle is the tragic sense of life that he carries in his own *yo*. He is living the hell of strife for all his people. His constant driving antagonist is a desire of *noluntad* to commit suicide. It is this negating force that he fights in an assertion of inner freedom at every moment of his existence.

When Angela's dying mother asks to be reassured that she will see God, don Manuel answers in words that could be taken directly from *Del sentimiento trágico:* "Dios, hija mía, está aquí como en todas partes, y le verá usted desde aquí, desde aquí. Y a todos nosotros en El, y a El en nosotros" (p. 1212). For God is the collective desire of man to be immortal.

Lázaro, Angela's brother, returns from America and is drawn to don Manuel through their basic affinity as authentic *yos* who know the tragic sense of life. Don Manuel converts him and makes him his Joshua to continue the deliverance of his people. He accomplishes the conversion in this pragmatic argument: "¿La verdad? La verdad, Lázaro, es acaso algo terrible, algo intolerable, algo mortal; la gente sencilla no podría vivir con ella" (p. 1215). But how can men live without the truth? That is don Manuel's mission: to give them an awareness of themselves without having to carry the burden of the truth:

Yo estoy para hacer vivir a las almas de mis feligreses, para hacerles felices, para hacerles que se sueñen inmortales y no para matarles [*OC*, 1a, II, 1215].

In his intimate relationship with Lázaro, don Manuel confesses the struggle that he must continually fight:

¡Mi vida, Lázaro, es una especie de suicidio continuo, un combate contra el suicidio, que es igual; pero que vivan ellos, que vivan los nuestros! . . . Sigamos, pues, Lázaro, suicidándonos en nuestra obra y en nuestro pueblo, y que sueñe éste su vida como el lago sueña el cielo [*OC*, 1a, II, 1219].

The dialectic of struggle is in the *yo* himself, don Manuel; he has to choose between the continued effort of the commitment to his world or the surrender, losing the individual consciousness in the totality, through suicide; that is, the question is to be all or nothing. The metaphor of the totality which annihilates the individual is sensed by don Manuel: "¿Has visto, Lázaro, misterio mayor que el de la nieve cayendo en el lago y muriendo en él mientras cubre con su toca a la montaña?" (pp. 1219–20).

The *nada* and the *todo*, in mortal combat in the *yo*, are the basis of the tragic sense of life, but yet this man does not want his people to suffer this anguish; he wants to suffer it for them and to give them the fruits of being authentic *yos*. Just as Christ took the burden of man's sins and died to redeem them, so does don Manuel want to suffer the tortures of the tragic sense in order to give a true life to his people. This is the true essence of his martyrdom. He indicates his purpose to Angela when he is near death himself: "No hay más vida eterna que ésta..., que la sueñen eterna..., eterna de unos pocos años..." . . . "Reza, hija mía, reza por nosotros.". . . "...y reza también por Nuestro Señor Jesucristo..." [OC, 1a, II, 1222].

Don Manuel Bueno now becomes San Manuel Bueno, mártir; he dies as he had lived: ministering to his people. He asks to be taken to the church to give his farewell and there leaves with them his moral imperative to do good to each other and live as brothers with the solace of faith, for, as Calderón said, even in dreams doing good is not lost. To Lázaro he leaves the essence of the tragic sense of life: live every moment in such a way that it would be an injustice if there be no life after death.

Angela ends the narrative believing that it was the design of the Almighty to have these men, San Manuel and Lázaro, believe that they did not believe. And Unamuno ends the novel explaining that this manuscript has come into his hands and that undoubtedly this was an intimate confession of the man San Manuel as seen by his disciple Angela.

DRAMATIC PROSE

The dramatic prose of the second literary attitude is closer to being theatre than the first one, but the capabilities of the stage are still not fully utilized. In these writings Unamuno presents his own dramatic situation and not that of the characters. This expression is very well suited to his creation of the monodiálogo, where he is both speakers. However, in theatre Unamuno cannot follow the same pattern of speaking to his audience in the dialectic of conversation if he is to create real, fully developed characters or, as he would say, "hombres de carne y hueso." This basic conflict with the art form must have been realized by Unamuno after the first dramas, for his later dramatic writings give the dramatic situation to the characters; all of the latter will be studied in the next chapter as expressions of the third literary attitude.

This second attitude with its focus on the yo's intimate struggle to be in the face of death is presented through dialogue which is the dialectic of struggle in representation. Each character in the drama, or speaker in the monodiálogo, is not a yo but a half yo whose struggle is effected not within himself but in the exchange with another half yo.

There is little doubt that Unamuno's first approach to the art of writing for the theatre was in the period when the second literary attitude was being formulated. In "El desinterés intelectual" (1911) don Miguel writes:

Y hay, señora, muchos escritos que aunque no parecen dramas, lo son; son verdaderos dramas que se desarrollan, en el escenario de nuestra conciencia, donde muchedumbre de personajes luchan y discuten entre sí [*OC*, 2a, X, 223–224].

Therefore, Unamuno's contributions of this second attitude were dramas, dramas intended primarily for the personal stage of the individual's conscience and only secondarily for the theatre. By studying the *monodiálogo* first, one can more clearly see the intimate relation to this dramatic expression of the Unamunian *yo* of *La esfinge* (1898, 1909), *La venda* (1899, 1913), and *Fedra* (1910, 1921). (The first date in each listing represents the first writing and the last the actual publication.)

Monodiálogos (1892–1936)

This collection which consists of eighty-four articles is represented in this chapter by the following seven, many of which foreshadow longer literary works in later years.[25]

In 1892—three years before Unamuno wrote *En torno al casticismo* and a full eight before he began to work on *Amor y pedagogía,* while he was still translating Spencer—he had already begun to question the use of reason and logic in finding the reality of man. The tone is humorous in "Elecciones y convicciones" as don Miguel argues with don Cándido, but it is not yet the grotesque tragicomedy of *Amor y pedagogía.* Don Cándido fears that he is thinking too much, and thinking in excess can only lead to death; he asserts that what is needed are good solid principles which man can follow without thinking. Don Miguel has been making fun of these rationalizations and has now told Cándido that the struggle of thinking is worth more than the conclusion of thought, that is, the idea.

"De la vocación" (1900) has the tone and structure of a Socratic dialogue. The two speakers are quick to agree that what is needed is a new sense of authenticity by the individual man. They see the unauthentic man as being lost in the routine of everyday life, to

---

[25] For a study of the personal *yo* in the *Monodiálogos*, see D. Catalán Menéndez Pidal, "Personalidad y sinceridad en un monodiálogo de Unamuno," *Studia philologica,* I (Madrid: Gredos, 1960), 333–347.

the point that he lives out of pure habit, and he treats his fellow
men as if they were things, merely means to the particular end at
hand. The speakers do not arrive at a formulation of how the individual man can be taken out of this vegetative existence, but the
important aspect of this "monodialogue" is that it clearly presents
the problem of man in terms which will be resolved in *Del sentimiento trágico* (1912). There is evidence that Unamuno first intended to put his philosophy into dramatic dialogues but later
decided on the essay.[26]

"¡Vae Victoribus!" was written in 1913 during the culmination of
the second philosophical perspective. In this "monodialogue" the
attitude is presented in parts as the living passionate expression of
the dialectic exchange of speakers. In this writing Unamuno is
once more using don Quixote as the symbol of the authentic man:

— . . . me suele doler España como si fuese parte de mí, siéndolo yo de
ella. Pues si nos duele el cuerpo todo, ¿no ha de dolerse cada parte de él?
—Pues a mí—me replicó—empezó por dolerme España, como a ti, y
ahora me duele el universo mundo todo, y hasta me duele Dios. Quizás
esto te suene a enorme desatino. Voy a explicártelo.

. . . . .

—Hay quien ha llamado soberbio a Don Quijote. ¡Es más, hay quien se
ha atrevido a sostener que lo que le llevó a la Cruz a nuestro Divino Maestro no fué más que soberbia!
—¡Qué honor para un cristiano a quien le motejen de soberbio!—
exclamó [*OC*, 2a, IX, 780–785].

The authentic life is, of course, the result of the facing of death
by the personal *yo*. This awareness of death, which is the tragic
sense of life, leads to the commitment to the world by the *yo* and
the subsequent personalization of it as has been repeated in the
above *monodiálogo*. The dual symbol of Christ and Don Quixote,
which is clearly established in this creation of 1913, will be seen in
much of the poetry and has already been studied in *San Manuel
Bueno, mártir*.

The awareness of death brings with it the full realization by the
yo that he is the maker of his own future. It is because of this
sense of being alone that the crisis results in the *yo*. In "La vida

[26] Unamuno wrote to his friend Jiménez Ilundain in 1899 the following:
"Ahora estoy metido en una obra de largo aliento, en que acaso emplee años.
Son unos diálogos filosóficos de plan vastísimo, en que vierto toda mi filosofía con
la mayor sinceridad posible" in H. Benítez, *El drama religioso de Unamuno*,
pp. 293–294. As this correspondence continued, Unamuno indicated that this
long-range project would be called "Tratado del amor de Dios," which subsequently became *Del sentimiento trágico*; see Benítez, pp. 391, 425.

y la obra" (1919) Unamuno again comments on the basic freedom of man.

B.—No; no hay más obra que la vida para cada uno. Vivir, cuando es más que vegetar; vivir pública y civilmente, es obrar. Y a lo que hay que aspirar es a la vida duradera y definitiva. . . . El [hombre auténtico] hace su obra, pues que hace su vida y se hace a sí mismo [*OC*, 2a, IX, 938].

This response has brought out the mission of the authentic man— the Quixotic endeavor to free men who are galley slaves in order to make them individuals with an awareness of the *yo* as the maker of his universe.

The *chusma* has been called the herd, the masses, and the no-man by various philosophers, but Unamuno presents the unauthentic man first in the tragicomic character of don Fulgencio of *Amor y pedagogía* and later, in 1924, in the false man of "Una vida tranquila."

The no-man is never threatened by death, for only men die. The no-man is not any one man but rather all men in a composite abstraction that does not exist except through the unauthentic state of many individuals. The speech, the thinking, and even the actions are impersonal and false when done by the no-man. This can be seen even when the act itself is meaningful, for the interpretation of the act has no effect on the mind of the unauthentic doer. If an individual can become aware of his utter freedom before death, he would then come out of this state.

Unamuno also presented the positive side of the second perspective in these *monodiálogos* as the authentic man committed to his world. In an article entitled "Monodiálogo" (1922), Unamuno presents the prototype of these writings as well as their finest creation of the individual *yo*'s responsibility to his personalized world.

Both speakers are named Miguel and both share the same life. They are in a fraternal struggle and can never be united into a single dogmatic position since they are in continuous contradiction. However, both Miguels sense that the awareness of death has brought them to the self-realization of their will and their struggle to be. One calls this authentic awareness freedom, the other refers to it as responsibility. It is the inner freedom of the *yo* both as his own maker and as the responsibility for making his world; thus, they arrive at the existential sense of the commitment to the world: "Libertad no es más que responsabilidad. Es libre el que se siente libre, y se siente libre el que se siente responsable" (*OC*, 2a, IX, 984).

By 1932 a final, direct, dialogued statement of this existential position is given in "Pan y toros" as B answers A regarding the tragedy of man: "¡Qué pocos viven, lo que se llama vivir, la vida pública! ¡Qué pocos viven el papel que en ella les toca llenar!" (*OC,* 2a, IX, 1017).

La esfinge (1898)

Unamuno wrote this drama in 1898, as indicated in a letter to Angel Ganivet, where the theme is presented as follows:

> Ahora estoy metido de hoz y de coz en un drama, que se llamará *Gloria o paz* o algo parecido. Es la lucha de una conciencia entre la atracción de la gloria, de vivir en la historia, de trasmitir el nombre a la posteridad, y el encanto de la paz, del sosiego, de vivir en la eternidad. Es un hombre que quiere creer y no puede; obsesionado por la nada de ultratumba, a quien persigue de continuo el espectro de la muerte [*OC,* 2a, XII, 11].

As described in this letter, the original plot, which was essentially the same in the final form of 1909, centered on the inner fears and doubts of Angel, a political leader. He is encouraged by his wife and a group of friends to take control of the revolutionary party. However, at the moment of greatest acclaim, he shocks his backers by resigning from the leadership. Abandoned by wife and friends, he seeks refuge in the house of the only remaining friend. He hopes to find peace and solitude in his retreat from public life. On the day of the revolution an angry mob descends on his hiding place, accusing him of having betrayed the cause. In an effort to contain them, he is shot and dies in the arms of his wife, who has returned in an attempt to save him from the mob.

Unamuno goes on to explain that this drama is based on a personal anguish which he felt the previous year. It can be concluded that the plot was developed in order to put this personal dramatic situation into a creative expression. Unamuno feels that the plot development is the most important aspect of his drama, for the succession of events forces the man—Angel—into a personal intimate crisis. But, in fact, it is the plot that is weak and the crisis which is the achievement of the drama. The deep roots of the personal *yo*'s struggle are not carried by the dialogue. The other characters do not serve any other purpose than to be the receptors of Angel's crisis; they do not contribute to the dramatic situation. In fact, it is doubtful if this second literary attitude can be made into good theatre because of its concentration on the expression of the personal *yo*. Unamuno seems to anticipate this result in the above-quoted letter, where he states: "Temo que me resulte en exceso lírico."

The drama of the personal *yo* before death is found in the following situations. As the play progresses, Angel's alter ego—Felipe— presents this Unamunian philosophy:

—[Ama a tu prójimo] ¡Como a ti mismo! Si no sabes amarte, ¿cómo has de amar a los demás?

.   .   .   .

—Sí, sé que no soy nada, pero quiero serlo todo. Serlo todo para gozar de la paz del todo. ¡Paz! [*OC*, 2a, XII, 229].

By the end of the first act, Angel has decided to give up all his political ambitions. The only thought that matters to him is the gaining of inner peace. The vision of death strikes terror in his heart and drives him to near insanity as he battles with his passions. His choice to abandon the revolution has been one of escape from the world and, he hopes, from himself into a state of eternal sleep. The personal agony comes to a climax as Angel monologues:

¡Quién pudiera sorberse [toma un vaso de agua de un trago] así al Espíritu universal! ¡Dios mío! ¡Anégame, ahógame! ¡Que sienta mi vida derretirse en tu seno! [*OC*, 2a, XII, 250].

He wants to lose his *yo* in the *todo,* thus finding some meaning for the absurd situation that life represents in the face of death.

Angel is convinced that his wife Eufemia only wants him to continue in the revolutionary party so that she will receive her share of the glory of victory and thus insure her name in history. He feels that she blames him because she has been childless, denying her that path to continued existence. It must be pointed out that all of these thoughts are the fabrication of Angel's mind; she never expresses them nor does her thinking move in that direction, for it is his struggle and his tragedy. After having listened to her husband's accusation, Eufemia gives the play one of its finest moments of dramatic situation.[27] She gets up, indignantly confronts Angel, and tears off the shrouds from his *yo:*

—Como vives lleno de ti mismo, crees que en muriéndote tú se acaba el mundo, y la muerte significa para ti la nada... [*OC*, 2a, II, 255].

Angel is at an impasse; since he is his own maker and the maker of his world, it will end with him. Beyond death he senses only nothingness awaiting him, but he wants immortality. He

[27] The character of Eufemia seems to be the only departure of importance that Unamuno took from his original outline, for she begins to take on a personality of her own by the third act, rather than remaining a mere exterior force moving Angel to his ruin.

feels the dread of death as he realizes that he is alone without support in existence before the impending end.

In the abyss of this personal hell—now in the third act—Angel begins to realize that in choosing himself and his freedom, he is also choosing his world and is thus committed to it. When his friends return to save him from the mob that is marching on his refuge, he refuses to escape. His dread of death disappears and a new-found courage asserts itself in his speech and his actions: "En él [pensamiento de la muerte] se diferencia del animal el hombre. Cuanto más se piensa en la muerte, más hombre se es..." (*OC*, 2a, XII, 298). The authentic Angel has now accepted the responsibility of his commitment:

> —¡A salvarlos!
> —¿Y si te pierdes?
> —¡No es posible perderse salvando a los demás!
> [*OC*, 2a, XII, 302].

Angel steps out onto the balcony with the courage to be and to die and speaks to the mob:

—No, no callaré mientras tenga vida en el pecho...; no debo callarme porque soy palabra...; callarme es morir, y no quiero morirme, no moriré... Sois unos cobardes... (El tumulto crece; arrecian las pedradas y suena un tiro. Angel se desvanece y se apoya) [*OC*, 2a, XII, 304–305].

Angel is taken into the room by his friends. He dies in Eufemia's arms as she calls out to him "hijo mío" and as he gazes upon the figure of Christ: "es el divino abrazo del amor y la muerte. . . . Señor, acuérdate de mí en tu reino..." (p. 311).

Certainly, the play has an intense drama in the *yo* of Angel, but the situation of the rest of his world lacks the viability to create a situation for the theatre.

La venda (1899)

This drama was written soon after *La esfinge* was finished. It was a custom with Unamuno to begin another work immediately after finishing the prototype of a literary genre.[28] In the following year Unamuno used the same material of this play for a *relato* with the same title.

La venda is a symbolic one-act play which was published in 1913

[28] See García Blanco's comments on this characteristic in his prologue to *Teatro completo* (Madrid: Aguilar, 1959), p. 61; and also in his study *Don Miguel de Unamuno y sus poesías*, p. 74. For Unamuno's personal views on the matter, see his correspondence to Jiménez Ilundain in H. Benítez, *El drama religioso de Unamuno*, p. 416.

but was not staged until 1921. The plot is simple: María, who has gained her sight in the last two days, runs out onto the street upon hearing that her father is dying. She had been born blind and had learned to move throughout the city with the utmost of confidence and facility. The world of sight is strange and foreign to her as she sees the streets for the first time. She is so thoroughly confused that she cannot find her way. Finally, María stops two strangers and asks them for a handkerchief to use as a blindfold; with it and a stick she immediately finds her way. She arrives in time to solace her dying father, but refuses to take the blindfold off. Marta, her practical, rational sister, tears off the blindfold for the sake of truth. The old man sees his daughter with sight for the first time and dies. The sight of her father's death is deeply imprinted in her mind. She closes her eyes and asks to see no more.

Unamuno himself has indicated that María is the symbol of faith in man's life. Man is born with faith, lives with it, and learns to move through the obstacles of living with it, serenely and without question. However, science brings the sight of rational thought through which man begins to doubt until the blind faith is destroyed. But man cannot find his way through life with logic and reason; thus, it becomes necessary to re-create faith through the will of the *yo*. The conclusion is striking as reason tells man that death is the finality of human existence, but the blindfold created by the will asserts a blind faith in immortality.

This drama has been one of the most successful of all of Unamuno's theatre. Its success may be due to the fact that, within the short space of the one-act play, there are two levels of reality which are fully developed: (1) the basic one of the dramatic situation of the blind girl, and (2) the symbolic one of the lost faith of the personal *yo*. The former works out the dramatic conflict of the two sisters, Marta and María, in facing the reality of life, and the latter places the philosophical problem of death in the contrapositions of reason and faith. Reason can only see death as the physiological end of life, while faith blindly hopes for immortality.

Fedra (1910)

In his modern version of the Greek classic, Unamuno presents the anguish of the personal *yo* in the basic human situations of love and death. Unamuno describes his *Fedra* as being made up of lyric intensity with no dramatic oratory.

The passion is intense and without diversion in Fedra's death scene. Her faith is restored as she believes that she will find immortality by cleansing herself of the evil of having desired her husband's son and then having accused him of her own intentions. The tragedy ends as she dies offstage and Pedro and Hipólito are reunited. Pedro states: "¡Después de todo, ha sido una santa mártir! ¡Ha sabido morir!," and Hipólito adds: "¡Sepamos vivir, padre!" (*OC*, 2a, XII, 472).

LYRIC VERSE

In poetry Unamuno finds the fullest expression of the *yo*'s imaginative anticipation of death. The basic lyric inspiration, which is at the roots of all poetic writing, was fundamentally the approach Unamuno adopted throughout the second literary attitude. This point of departure has led such able Unamuno scholars as Ferrater Mora [29] and Julián Marías [30] to say that he was primarily a poet. Yet the opinion of respected critics like Arturo Barea cannot go unheeded: "His rough-tongued poems with their blend of fervor and contemplation brought indeed a new note into Spanish lyrical poetry at the turn of the century, but their poetic form was never strong enough to absorb the sentiments and thoughts that inspired them."[31] This critic is willing to give Unamuno the status of a poet in the broader sense of the word as meaning a man who projected himself into all of his work. However, in the narrower connotation—poet as the writer of poetry in verse form—Barea says of Unamuno: "If he sometimes failed as an artist, it was because he handled his tools clumsily." Notwithstanding Barea, the opinions of two of the greatest poets of the Spanish language come up in defense of Unamuno—Rubén Darío in 1909 [32] and Antonio Machado in 1921.[33]

[29] See Chapter Two, p. 38, for the entire statement of the poematic unity of Unamuno's writing.

[30] Julián Marías writes in *Unamuno*, p. 130: "[Unamuno] pide densidad a la poesía, pide que se piense el sentimiento y se sienta el pensamiento. Todo esto, que se ha solido entender de un modo trivial, ha hecho pensar a muchos que la poesía de Unamuno era de ideas, entendiendo por esta expresión que consistía en decir en verso lo que podía y tal vez debía decir en prosa. Pero es una total incomprensión de la poesía de Unamuno."

[31] Arturo Barea, *Unamuno* (New Haven: Yale University Press, 1952), p. 37. This short impression of Unamuno was published nine years after Marías' study, but the opinion is the same as that which Marías was attacking.

[32] See "Unamuno poeta" of 1909, published as the prologue to Unamuno's *Teresa* (Madrid: Renacimiento, 1924), pp. 5–13.

[33] See José Ramón Arana, *Cartas de Antonio Machado a Miguel de Unamuno* (México: Ediciones Monegros, 1957), pp. 9–25.

A slight digression from the examination of the second attitude of death must be taken here to establish two factors of vital importance to the topic: (1) the place of poetry within the scope of the *yo*'s awareness of death, and (2) the poetic process of Unamuno.

First, philosophers from Kierkegaard to Heidegger, who have been concerned with death, have consistently stated that the awareness of death is an extra-rational process. Heidegger [34] and Sartre [35] today realize that only literature can truly approach death without distorting it into an abstraction. And of all literature the expression with the most freedom from rational discourse is lyric poetry with its multiplicity of shades of meanings, metaphorical implications, tone patterns, and rhythmic mood-creating techniques.

Second, Unamuno's way of knowing the reality of man is fundamentally emotive and subjective and only in its culmination takes the form of ideas, thoughts, themes, and so forth. In other words, Unamuno knows man through himself in the personal intuition of the phenomena of man in terms of metaphors, symbols, and images, that is, poetic introspection. It is only when he takes this knowing process out of his experience that it comes to be an intellectual factor. Thus, to say that Unamuno could not put his ideas into poetry is a gross misunderstanding of the man and of the poetry. This is like saying that the fruit cannot make a good tree when it is the tree that has produced the fruit—a philosophical idea. It is quite another matter to say that the tree, the poetic experience, is not the same as the others around it.

Consequently, it was in poetry that Unamuno found the greatest freedom of expression. And since the knowing process of Unamuno was first poetic and only secondarily intellectual, the artificialities of verse were never accepted by him. Thus, all of his poems, even the longer ones like *El Cristo de Velázquez*, have no prosaic unification but are rather a series of poetic experiences of the man put into the rhythm of verse and the meaning of language in a most direct manner. This poetic world that Unamuno builds, far from being an intellectual fabrication of the mind, is a lyrical inspiration of the emotions. Verse is not a form into which ideas are forced; it is to Unamuno the rhythm of song and the outburst of the lyric enunciation or the lyric apostrophe. Emotions find expression in

[34] In the essays of *Existence and Being,* Heidegger's quest for philosophical truth has led him to poetry, especially Hölderlin. See "Remembrance of the Poet," pp. 243–269, "Hölderlin and the Essence of Poetry," pp. 270–291, and "On the Essence of Truth," pp. 292–324.

[35] See Sartre's *The Psychology of the Imagination,* trans., Max Schoen (New York: Philosophical Library, 1948), pp. 3–77.

the contradiction, the paradox, and the metaphor. This poetic creation is the pure lyric without a tinge of the prosaic harness of logical discourse.

The poetry of Unamuno will be studied in the chronological order of its creation, not of its publication, since in many cases there was a long period between one and the other.

Poesías (1884–1906)

In this first collection of Unamuno's poetry, the above-stated process of poetic creation, which Unamuno used throughout his life, can be clearly demonstrated in the poems of the second attitude of death.

In 1907 Unamuno wrote to the Uruguayan philosopher Carlos Vaz Ferreira: "He llegado, a posteriori, claro está—yo hago los versos a oído, y no a ojo—a su teoría [la nueva forma de Silva]" (PI, 28). And in Mi religión of 1910 he wrote:

Esos salmos de mis Poesías, con otras varias composiciones que allí hay, son mi religión, y mi religión cantada y no expuesta lógica y razonadamente [OC, 1a, III, 823].

Now, turning to the poetry itself, one can better appreciate the various feelings about death that lead to an authentic awareness of the impending possible annihilation. "Salmo II" is one of a group of poems written in 1906 for the collection published as Poesías in the next year.

In the first seven verses, faith without doubt is established as the negative force which chains God to impious anthropomorphism of rational thought: "Fe soberbia, impía, / la que no duda, / la que encadena Dios á nuestra idea." And in lines 8 to 17, death appears as the truth of man's life: "Eres, Verdad, la muerte." This is not a fearful view of death nor the unauthentic non-awareness of death, but it is rather the solace for the faith that doubts—an eternal repose for the battle-weary yo. In the typical Unamunian manner of dialectical oppositions, doubt is seen as the force that inserts viability into faith, just as death makes life authentic through struggle: "La vida es duda, / y la fe sin la duda es sólo muerte. / Y es la muerte el sustento de la vida, / y de la fe la duda."

Beginning with verse twenty-six the poem takes on the biblical tone of the psalm as the lyric yo invokes the unknown deity. The lines that follow are an impassioned plea for the continued dialectical force of doubt in life and pure faith only after death: "Mien-

tras viva, Señor, la duda dame, / fe pura cuando muera." The poem
continues in a constant reformulation of oppositions that are each
the guarantee of the other. Thus, to live authentically is to doubt,
that is, to struggle with the awareness of death unto death. And it
is through the struggle that there is the feeling, not the knowledge,
that there should be an assurance of an immortal participation; this
feeling is the faith of doubt in the eternal God. The invocation of
God is moving, but the repose of the *yo* in the eternal sleep is not
questioned. Is this really a continuation of the *yo*? This question
is in the spirit of the poetic tone, but it is not yet posed. The poem
ends in an affirmation of faith: "Creo, Señor en tí, sin conocerte."

The phrasing of a staccato rhythm that Unamuno was to use in
many of his finest poems (see *Romancero* for a study) is used for the
first time in this section of the "Salmos" in "Libértate, Señor." This
poem has the tone of an invocation to God from the beginning;
it is divided into four parts: (1) the *yo* in search of himself as he
enters into his own world: "dime quién soy"; (2) the full dimensions of the *yo*'s world with other *yos* as he seeks his freedom, which
is tied in commitment to his world: "Tu palabra no muere...,
nunca muere... / nunca puede morir! / Follaje de la vida, / raíces
de la muerte..."; (3) the seeking of repose for the weary embattled
yo: "Déjame descansar en tu reposo"; and (4) finally a unified plea
for the freedom of the *yo*'s world. This intense poetic feeling for
man and his predicament can be sensed not only through the
accumulation of images and the incessant repetition of the rhythm,
but also in the profoundly moving tone:

> 104 liberta-los, Señor!
> Mientras quede algo esclavo
> no será mi alma libre,
> ni Tú, Señor
> ni Tú que en ella vives...
> serás Tú mismo esclavo...
> liberta-me
>   .   .   .
>
> liberta-te! [*P*, 123].

Of the one hundred poems of this book, the majority could be
included in this chapter as expressions of the second attitude.
Among these are such intense lyric achievements as "Alborada espiritual," "Nubes de misterio," "Muere en el mar el ave que voló del
buque," and the sonnet "Muerte." A detailed study of all of this
poetic creation is a long study in itself and must here be deferred.

However, the few poems presented above may be considered exemplary of the attitude and the book *Poesías*.

There is one more poem that can be mentioned, "Es de noche, en mi estudio," a most remarkable imaginative anticipation of death. The solemn intensity of the sensing of one's death increases from line to line until the thirst for immortality is uncovered. But the remarkable aspect of this poem lies in the verse "más bien presentimiento misterioso," for don Miguel de Unamuno died in the same room with his books, as he anticipates in the poem, exactly thirty years later—December 31, 1936.[36]

Rimas de dentro (1908–11)

This collection contains one of Unamuno's greatest poetic achievements—"Aldebarán." This poem has been studied by Diego Catalán Menéndez Pidal,[37] whose interpretation clearly establishes the meaning of this poem as a part of what has been seen to be Unamuno's second literary attitude. The poem was written some time before 1909, in the Unamunian *lira* (a free combination of eleven-, seven-, and five-syllable verses), with an extent of one hundred and fifty-six verses, divided into three parts (1–62, 63–147, 148–156). The first part presents the totality of existence, and not until line 47 does the questioning *yo* appear (see Chapter Two, p. 59). The second part brings together two seemingly unrelated spirits: Leopardi's feeling of the immense totality that is indifferent to man and Fray Luis de León's love of the individual in the union with God's universe. However, the indifference of Leopardi's universe of God has been personalized by the *yo*. Thus, in the Unamunian poetic sense the world that is threatened by death is the *yo*. The very short third part is the lyrical cry of the tragic sense of life.

---

[36] The only witness to Unamuno's death was Bartolomé Aragón Gómez, who published his experience as a preface to his book on economics, *Síntesis de economía corporativa* (Salamanca: Librería "La Facultad," 1937), pp. 13–16. The following is Aragón's account of Unamuno's last moments: " 'Me encuentro mejor que nunca.' Estas fueron, precisamente, las palabras con las que contestó al autor de este agudo libro el 31 de diciembre de 1936, a las cuatro y media de la tarde. Tras ellas sentóse a la camilla para comenzar el último de sus monólogos. . . . [Aragón] 'La verdad es que a veces pienso si no habrá vuelto Dios la espalda a España disponiendo de sus mejores hijos.' D. Miguel descargó un recio puñetazo sobre la camilla y exclamó: '¡Eso no puede ser, Aragón! Dios no puede volverle la espalda a España. España se salvará porque tiene que salvarse.' . . . con la última palabra dió el último suspiro."

[37] *Cuadernos de la cátedra . . .*, IV (1953), 43–70.

114 ¿Y cuando tú te mueras?
    ¿Cuando tu luz al cabo
    se derrita una vez en las tinieblas?
    ¿Cuando frío y oscuro
    el espacio sudario
    ruedes sin fin para fin ninguno?

         .   .   .

137 ¿No lo es aún hoy, Aldebarán ardiente?
    ¿No eres acaso, estrella misteriosa,
    gota de sangre viva
    en las venas de Dios?
    ¿No es su cuerpo el espacio tenebroso?
142 Y cuando tú te mueras,
    ¿qué hará de ti ese cuerpo?
    ¿Adónde, Dios, por su salud luchando,
    te habrá de segregar, estrella muerta,
    Aldebarán?
    ¿A qué tremendo muladar de mundos?
    ¡Sobre mi tumba, Aldebarán, derrama
    tu luz de sangre,
    y si un día volvemos a la Tierra,
    te encuentre inmoble, Aldebarán, callando
    del eterno misterio la palabra!
    ¡Si la verdad suprema nos ciñese
    volveríamos todos a la nada!
    De eternidad es tu silencio prenda,
    ¡Aldebarán! [*AP*, 312–313].

The tone of lines 114 and 147 is one of increasing anguish as the *yo*, feeling the annihilation of death, questions the star. This exact tone appears in *Del sentimiento trágico,* from which an insight into this poetic version can be gathered:

Porque de este amor o compasión a ti mismo, de esta intensa desesperación, porque así como antes de nacer no fuiste, así tampoco después de morir serás, pasas a compadecer—esto es, a amar—a todos tus semejantes y hermanos en aparencialidad, miserables sombras que desfilan de su nada a su nada, chispas de conciencia que brillan un momento en las infinitas y eternas tinieblas. Y de los demás hombres, tus semejantes, pasando por los que más semejantes te son, por tus convivientes, vas a compadecer a todos los que viven, y hasta a lo que acaso no vive, pero existe. Aquella lejana estrella que brilla allí arriba durante la noche, se apagará algún día y se hará polvo, y dejará de brillar y de existir. Y como ella, el cielo todo estrellado. ¡Pobre cielo! [*OC*, 1a, IV, 571–572].

The awareness of man's utter freedom, of his being alone there-in-the-world, brings the tragic sense of life. Thus, from despair love is born. As the *yo*, in deep compassion, is driven to the personalization of "Aldebarán," he feels the corresponding commitment of love to all men and to all the universe. Again, turning to *Del sentimiento trágico,* the following explanation is given by Unamuno himself:

Si llego a compadecer y amar a la pobre estrella que desaparecerá del cielo un día, es porque el amor, la compasión, me hace sentir en ella una conciencia, más o menos oscura, que la hace sufrir por no ser más que estrella, y por tener que dejarlo de ser un día. Pues toda conciencia lo es de muerte y de dolor [*OC,* 1a, IV, 572].

After pausing to engulf the universe, the *yo* now reaching into religious imagery goes on in the questioning of the star (lines 137–140). The *yo* inquires of the burning star if it not be a drop of living blood in the veins of God. But being one with the Universal Spirit, that is, God, is not enough for the *yo*. The individual, personal consciousness must be preserved.

The last part of the poem (lines 148–156) is an intense plea by the *yo* to be eternal, but death will come and the star's light of blood will shine on the *yo's* grave. To be part of the eternal all is not enough, for the individual is lost in nothingness together with his world. The star is no longer being questioned, but rather it is being implored as the *yo* is seeking a way out. There is no way out. Death is a mystery where the all can be nothingness, unless the *yo* is the all. Thus, the *yo* must live with the mystery and the doubt of death. This is the *yo* that has committed himself to his entire world.

Rosario de sonetos líricos (1910–11)

Unamuno considered the sonnet to be a sigh made immortal, but it was not any sigh which might have been felt by another or at another time; it had to be the personal feeling at the moment of the writing. Consequently, he was careful to note down the day, month, year, place, and at times even the hour of the day which corresponded to the poetic experience. This collection is chronological in its order, as are many of Unamuno's poetic books, having the exterior form of an intimate diary or confession.

All of the one hundred and twenty-eight sonnets that comprise the book were written between September, 1910, and February, 1911. This was the period of intense philosophical activity for the second perspective. The feelings and intuitions of the imaginative anticipation of death were being transformed into thought, for example, the "Tratado del amor a Dios" which became *Del sentimiento trágico.* Therefore, the poems of this *Rosario* are the lyrical beads of poetic testimony to the formation of a philosophy. However, their intrinsic value as poetry lies in their being the lucid expression of this intimate human truth—man in confrontation with his mortality—within the demanding form of the sonnet. These poems are not philosophy, but only the seeds for a philosophy, that is, they are the lyrical outburst of a man who was first a poet and second a philosopher. Of the one hundred and twenty-eight sonnets from the *Rosario,* six will be presented here as representative of the personal *yo* under the shadow of death.

"La vida de la muerte"

Oír llover no más, sentirme vivo;
el universo convertido en bruma
y encima mi conciencia como espuma
en que el pausado gotear recibo.

. . . . .

á merced de los vientos de la suerte;
este vivir, que es el vivir desnudo,
¿no es acaso la vida de la muerte? [*RSL,* 14–15].

The *yo* confesses himself in lyric introspection as the experience of rain is used once more to create the metaphor of existence. Death appears immanent to all life, and the *yo* who stops to consider it barely feels alive as he receives everything as rain upon a pool. The *yo* is motionless with the summary of his existence: the memory. There is only emptiness on the brink of nothingness. The *yo* feels the utter loneliness of being cast into the world with absolute freedom and without support. The unprotected *yo* feels the threat of death since he is at the mercy of chance in the naked position of existence. Self-awareness slowly comes into his grasp—could it not be that this naked vulnerability is in reality the life that is to be shaped out of the shadow of death.

"El fin de la vida"

. . . . .

12 que es el cuerpo algo más que vil enjalma
de la mente; para el canto es lira,
y es fin de la vida hacerse un alma [*RSL,* 22–23].

This sonnet aspires to give the beautiful neo-platonic poetic tradition of the separation of the immortal soul from the finite body. However, the disturbing factor is that in this poem man does not have both body and soul. The lyric enunciation puts man in the position of having to make his soul. The last line of the sonnet is left in the ambiguous position of having two different meanings: (1) the finality of life for man is to become a soul, and (2) the purpose of life is for man to make oneself a soul. The basic difference lies, outside of the poem, in the reader. For if he have faith in an immortal soul, the first interpretation follows clearly since the immortality is expected to come at the completion of life. But if the reader have doubts, then it is the second meaning that strikes him. Here, he sees the imperative to make, to create, a soul, and as Unamuno said in *Del sentimiento trágico,* the created faith is made by living life in such a way that he deserve immortality and nothing short of it.

> "Ni mártir ni verdugo"
>
> Busco guerra en la paz, paz en la guerra,
> el sosiego en la acción y en el sosiego
> la acción que labra el soterraño fuego
> que en sus entrañas bajo nieve encierra
>
> nuestro pecho. Rodando por la tierra
> al azar claro del destino ciego
> vida en el juego y en la vida juego
> buscando voy. Pues nada más me aterra
>
> que tener que ser águila ó tortuga,
> condenado á volar ó bajo el yugo
> del broquel propio á que no cabe fuga,
>
> y pues á Dios entre una y otra plugo
> dar á escoger á quien sudor enjuga
> ni mártir quiero ser ni ser verdugo [*RSL,* 58–59].

This is one of Unamuno's more *conceptista* poems, but in essence the yearning for the immortality of the personal *yo* underlies the opposition of thoughts. The first quartet creates the image of life as the dialectic of struggle. The *yo* searches for war in peace and for peace in war because the struggle to be—that is authentic living —is war, a war unto death caused by death. Yet, the never-ending battle is in the heart of peace itself, which is the existing totality, or, in this second attitude, the existing *yo*. The *yo* is the definite, unique, and irreplaceable unity of his personal consciousness; this *yo*'s war is also his action and his repose. The action is the fight against *esto y aquello,* into which the *yo* is forced by the doubt and agony that burns within him. Nevertheless, there is the calm of building a way of life from the struggle that must not end. Thus, beneath the exterior of the calm individual, there is the torrent of fire that makes him at every moment what he is.

The second quartet places the *yo* and his struggle in the world— cast there alone without any support. The enjambment moves the poem from one stanza to the other without transition. It is also in the first tercet where the *yo* reaffirms his need to be all and yet be himself. He is terrified with having to choose between flight into totality or utter annihilation as the end of life. Therefore, he concludes, he cannot be either the mystic martyr who yearns to be one with the all of God, or the executioner of his consciousness anticipating the nothingness of Leopardi. The *yo* must be all and be himself at once; in other words, he has the thirst to be God.

"Redención"

. . .

12 No por tus obras tus tesoros midas
   si no que el alma, de fé pura en pago,
   se levanta merced á sus caídas [*RSL*, 68–69].

"Redención" carries the significance of self-redemption, for it is the battle cry of the *yo* to other *yos* in lyric apostrophe to get up after a fall, not to surrender to the struggle that is life, not to give in to sadness and pessimism of the futility of man's acts. For the *yo* should not judge himself in terms of how much he has accomplished, but rather in the light of how well he has fought the battle. It is the struggle that counts and not the outcome.

"Soledad"

. . .

9 La vida es soledad, sola naciste
   y sola morirás, sola so tierra
   sentirás sobre tí la queja triste

   de otra alma que en el yermo sola yerra,
   que al valle del dolor sola viniste
   á recabar tu soledad con guerra [*RSL*, 172–173].

This poem restates the utter freedom of the *yo* there-in-the-world. Especially in the tercets, the lyric apostrophe strikes a note of meditation as the *yo* invokes the sad soul in the predicament which man comes upon alone in his existence. Life is solitude which can be won completely with the struggle. This is the message of the battle-weary *yo*.

"Irresignación"

No me resignaré, no, que mi lote
bregar es sin espera de victoria
y sucumbir en busca de gloria
de palizas cual las de Don Quijote.

Mientras mi terco anhelo no se agote
defenderé aun la absurda, la ilusoria
creencia que da vida, no á la noria
del saber triste con esclavo trote

> regar haré. Que esa agua de la ciencia
> al ánimo nos mete cual calambre
> la desesperación, pues la creencia
>
> vital borrando, nos amarga el hambre
> de no morir y seca la existencia
> desenterrando su inmortal raigambre [*RSL*, 208–209].

This sonnet with its *quijotismo* is in sharp contrast to the previous one. This is a reaffirmation of faith in the uncompromising struggle to form life out of the feeling for the approaching death. Science and reason cannot reach an authentic knowing of the reality of life —the reality that man is his own maker and, thus, unique. Even if there be no hope of victory, the struggle must be fought. The lyric enunciation of the quartets changes from *yo* to *nosotros* in the tercets as the *yo* becomes involved in the belief of his world.

Other representative poems of this second attitude are "Sueño final" and "Ateísmo." The former sonnet recalls the ancient image of death and sleep as twin brothers. The latter evokes the Unamunian-created God, later to be brought out in *Del sentimiento trágico* in these verses: "...Dios es el deseo / que tenemos de serlo y no se alcanza."

The study of *Rosario de sonetos líricos* will be completed in the next chapter since the poetic formulation of the third attitude has here some of its finest expressions.

El Cristo de Velázquez (1913–20)

Many critics and poets have considered this long poem—2,538 verses—to be Unamuno's greatest literary achievement.[38] Whatever place may be given to it, this was certainly his most carefully made lyric poem. He began writing it shortly after finishing *Del sentimiento trágico,* not completing it until October, 1920. In 1913 he wrote to the Portuguese poet Teixeira de Pascoaes:

A mí me ha dado ahora por formular la fe de mi pueblo, su cristología realista, y... lo estoy haciendo en verso. Es un poema que se titulará *Ante el Cristo de Velázquez,* y del que llevo escritos más de setecientos endecasílabos. Quiero hacer una cosa cristiana, bíblica y... española. Veremos [28 VII 1913].[39]

During the ensuing seven years he constantly added to it, revised, and reworked it with the realization that the poem was becoming not only the lyric expression of Spanish faith, but also his

---

[38] A study of the rhythm of this poem has been connected to Unamuno's interest in Milton's *Paradise Lost* by Calvin Cannon, "The Miltonic Rhythm of Unamuno's *El Cristo de Velázquez,*" *Hispania,* XLIV (March, 1961), 95–98.

[39] See *Don Miguel de Unamuno y sus poesías,* p. 209.

most fervent religious sentiment, in no small measure inspired by the Pauline image of Christ and Fray Luis de León's inspired intellectual devotion to the Lord Saviour.

The poem is written in unrhymed hendecasyllables and is divided into four parts of unequal length. The poem begins by establishing the theme of Christ the Saviour as the guarantee of personal immortality. The brush of Velázquez is to Unamuno the miracle that has created the esthetic experience in the painting. Through line and color the artist has created the supreme *auto sacramental,* which is the death of God that gave life to man.

The entire poem is a series of variations on the central theme. There is no attempt to give any transition from one poetic insight to the next. Although such connective elements might add to the unity, they would also bring the verse down from the lyrical heights of poetic intensity. There is very little in this poem of the description of epic poetry. Most of it is cast into a lyric apostrophe as the *yo* questions, implores, entreats, and addresses the overwhelming image of Christ the Saviour. The unity of the poem is the concentration on the theme. Each of the variations is a poem in itself and is set into each of four tone patterns. The first tone is one of religious depth as the names and attributes of Christ are brought forth like so many beads on a rosary in a manner similar to Fray Luis de León's *Nombres de Cristo.* The sources of the attributes are all from the scriptures which Unamuno had gathered from his biblical readings. Yet, through this diversity, there is a definite pattern established as the God-man brings the promise of life everlasting. Of all the variations, two stand out as the peculiar creations of Unamuno: "La vida es sueño" and "Paz en la guerra," but they remain biblical in scope. In the latter poem's lyric speech with Christ, Unamuno draws from the four gospels as well as from the book of Genesis.

The structure is a simple one as the painting of Christ is meditated upon by the observer and commentator—the *yo*—through whom the biblical tradition of the Messiah runs.

In the second part, the tone pattern of the lyric apostrophe changes from the meaning of the Saviour's death to the act of death itself.

The first poem, "Soledad," emphasizes Christ's complete lack of support as He faced death: "Tú, solo, abandonado," and then returns to the theme—Christ died to save the individual from the *nada.* In poem after poem, a different aspect of the dying Christ on the cross is touched upon. As the tone increases in intensity up to the ascent of Calvary so does the promise of life everlasting: "la sonrisa del Cielo, que es el nido / donde nuestra esperanza irá a parar."

The third part turns to the pictorial representation in the painting and focuses on one fragment after another, creating a mosaic of religious fervor. This imagery creates a powerful sense of the divine presence which can be compared to the effect of the colored stained-glass creations of religious art. The poetic depth of the poems can best be sensed and not described; for example, in the poem of the divine ears, the poet writes: "Son dos rosas / que se abren al rocío del lamento / fugaz de nuestra nada; son dos conchas / marinas que recogen los sollozos / de la noche" (CV, 105).

These poems complete the painting as a mosaic with the contemplation of the background of the figure of Christ, who is now the Saviour of the yo and also of his Universe.

The fourth and last part reaches the intense meaning of the fulfillment of the promise of immortality to the yo who has been beseeching the God-man: "fuiste Muerte de la muerte al fin!"

De Fuerteventura a París (1924)

Like the Rosario de sonetos líricos, this is a chronological diary of the lyrical experiences of Unamuno. It is made up of one hundred and three sonnets; the first sixty-six, written in Fuerteventura from February 21 to July 26, 1924, contain two themes: Unamuno's attack on his political persecutors and the awareness of the immensity of the ocean. The poems of the former theme contain a minimum of lyrical expression and a maximum of Quevedesque satire.

A second book was written in Paris from November 10 to December 21, 1924. The thirty-seven sonnets included in this part are of a greater poetic intensity and not as easily grouped into themes. In the more inspired creations, three influences can be discerned: the New Testament, Leopardi, and Dante.[40] Of this poetic activity, Unamuno wrote:

Así resulta este mi nuevo rosario de sonetos un diario íntimo de la vida íntima de mi destierro. En ellos se refleja toda la agonía—agonía quiere decir lucha—de mi alma de español y cristiano [FP, 9].

[40] Unamuno's constant readings during his exile prove to be the books he refers to in all this poetry. He has said that he only took three books with him when he was taken to Fuerteventura: the New Testament in the original Greek, Leopardi's poems, and Dante's La Divina Commedia. See Don Miguel de Unamuno y sus poesías, p. 285.

The second as well as the first attitudes of Unamuno's literature are given forceful expression in this poetry, for the influences can be seen coming to a culmination of spiritual forces working in opposition. A good example of this are the two sonnets Unamuno wrote on December 20, 1924 (Sonnets C and CI, pp. 159–160). The first reaches for faith as the *yo,* in the last verse, speaks out to God, yearning for Him. In contrast, the second sonnet presents only the annihilation of personal consciousness in either the *nada* or the *todo,* which are the same if there is no personal immortality, that is, they are both an indifferent continuity.

Romancero del destierro (1925–27)

This book of poems, which was published in Buenos Aires, contains eighteen *romances* of political satire and thirty-seven poems of great intensity and depth of meaning. The difference between the *romances* and the other poems is striking not only in theme but also in the level of poetic insight. The *romances* were written in Hendaya in the early part of 1927. The other poems were started in Paris in 1925 and continued through the following year in Hendaya. Among these poems there are two that are poetic moments of the greatest intensity in the expression of death: the short "¿Qué es tu vida, alma mía?" and the longer "Vendrá de noche." Both of these insights into death merit a close analysis which will demonstrate the level of lyric creation to which Unamuno brought two variations of the death theme in literature: the coming of death and the meaning of life when confronted by death. A formalistic and stylistic study of "Vendrá de noche" follows.

This poem was written in Paris on May 31, 1925. The repetition of the title and motif—Vendrá de noche—of this poem is reminiscent of the litanies of church ritual. However, in a litany the repetition is in the response to the invocation, while in this poem the repetition is in the series of descriptive evocations. The lyric *yo,* speaking as a third-person observer, is in a descriptive position, sometimes predicting, sometimes doubting, always commenting on "it" that will come by night.

On the level of sound the litany-like atmosphere is produced by the repetition of *ch* thirty-five times and *rá* as the second accented syllable twenty-five times. There are also several instances of words repeated within the same line and several excellent examples of internal rhyme, such as: "vendrá a su *hora,* cuando el aire *llora* / *llora* y medita." These repeated sounds accentuate the full rhyme of the stanzas and produce a very regular sound sequence, such as: "noche desnu*da* / que pasa y que*da* y que se que*da* al lado / y nunca mu*da* / vendrá de noche, cuando el tiempo aguar*da,* / cuando la tarde en las tinieblas tar*da*." Another factor that will be noted is that *do, ra,* and *da* are used for the rhyme of one-half of the verses. If one can say that sounds themselves can be used to create moods, the pattern of sounds in this poem certainly evokes a serious and somber mood of foreboding.

The use of the future tense throughout the poem creates the sensation of waiting, of expectation. This sensation together with the insistent sound pattern of regular repetition builds up in a crescendo, much in the same way Ravel creates a crescendo by repetition in his *Bolero.* In the reading of the poem, the rhythmic high point is reached in line 55, where the motif is repeated very emphatically, ending the expectation: "Vendrá de noche, sí, vendrá de noche." The intensity is somewhat less in the next line, but the rhyme of *noche* with *broche* keeps it strong. Then slowly in lines 58 and 59 the intensity is dissipated until line 60: "vendrá la calma." The movement almost ends, then as a last gasp of sound there is again the motif: "vendrá la noche."

Leaving behind the formal aspects, the study of the strange world of the lyric poem itself can be undertaken.

> 1 Vendrá de noche cuando todo duerma,
>   vendrá de noche cuando el alma enferma
>   se emboce en vida,
>   vendrá de noche con su paso quedo,
>   vendrá de noche y posará su dedo
>   sobre la herida.

This is the beginning of the creation of the ambient of "it." Quietness is the first attribute. "It" will come by night when everything sleeps, when nothing is aware of "it." "It" will come when the dying soul wraps itself in its last illusion of life. This is the first outward condition that must exist, for "it" will creep up and insistently point a finger at the veil of illusion with which the soul covers the wound.

> 7 Vendrá de noche y su fugaz vislumbre
>   volverá lumbre la fatal quejumbre;
>   vendrá de noche
>   con su rosario, soltará las perlas
>   del negro sol que da ceguera verlas,
>   ¡todo un derroche!

The powers of "it" are clearly in evidence here, for with a fleeting glimpse "it" tears the veil of illusion. The fatal moan turns to

fire. Again one can see the expression of "it." Now it is portrayed
as the black sun that will, at the proper time, cut the string of life
and let loose the beads of human experience so painfully and
slowly gathered together to form the rosary that is human existence.
It is blinding to see them spill; they are the accumulation of
thoughts, suffering, and experiences that is life now suddenly
dispersed—a total loss.

> 13 Vendrá de noche, noche nuestra madre,
>   cuando a lo lejos el recuerdo ladre
>   perdido agüero;
>   vendrá de noche; apagará su paso
>   mortal ladrido y dejará al ocaso
>   largo agujero...

"It" will come at night. "It" must come under the protection of
night when in the distance the awesome barking of the memory can
be heard; an omen is lost in the night. Man's individuality rests
in memory; the barking in the night is an omen of impending
destruction, but it is lost under the cover of night. "It" will silence
its step, for "it" must not be heard. What is heard again is the
mortal bark of memory. "It" will leave a large hole in the sunset,
for "it" must come in the protection of the darkness of night; thus,
by removing the sun from the sunset, "it" can come.

> 31 Vendrá de noche, en una noche clara,
>   noche de luna que al dolor ampara,
>   noche desnuda,
>   vendrá... venir es porvenir... pasado
>   que pasa y queda y que se queda al lado
>   y nunca muda...

This must be a clear night, a moonlit night that can give refuge
to sorrow under its maternal protection. The sorrow that the air
weeps for is the sorrow of the memory barking. This must be a
naked night. "It" will come, yet one must see that although this
coming is still to come (that is, still in the future), "it" is also in
the past for it has always been coming. Again, one must not lose
sight of the true essence of time as man's dimension, for "it" is
outside of time. "It" never moves, is always there at man's moment.
What is man's moment?

> 55 Vendrá de noche, sí, vendrá de noche,
>   su negro sello servirá de broche
>   que cierra el alma;
>   vendrá de noche sin hacer ruido,
>   se apagará a lo lejos el ladrido,
>   vendrá la calma...
>   vendrá la noche... [*RD*, 15-17].

"It" will come at night. Yes. "It" will come at night. "It" will come with its black seal being the seal that encloses the soul. "It" will come without a sound. In the distance the bark of memory will die out, for individuality will have ended. The sound of the wind that weeps will die out—the calm will come... the night will come...

Such is the world of this poem. The theme throughout is the anticipation of death, and yet death is never named directly, for if it were named, the expectation would have ended and death would have been evoked by the narrator. In the poem the narrator never meets death face to face, even at the climax in line 55; instead, there is a projection of the senses beyond death to what will follow death —calm, night, nothing... This is the creation of the atmosphere of the coming of death. Man awaits death because it must come, but he does not know when; all he has is the situation for its coming built up with lyric intensity. The coming by night, the silence, the omen of the distant barking are all mood-setting images. The sick soul wrapping itself up in a disguise of life and the exhausted heart delivering itself are the exterior conditions for the coming of death. Death will point its finger at the wound, it will turn the fatal moan to fire, it will cut the string of the rosary dispersing the beads, it will leave a long hole in the sunset, and death will seal life with its black seal enclosing the soul.

This is a poem of the anguish of man when he anticipates his death. It is Unamuno's re-creation through poetry of that inner moment of crisis that gives the *yo* the awareness of death which will transform his life either negatively or positively depending on his choice: surrender or struggle.

On August 11, 1926, Unamuno wrote the following short poem in what must have been a moment of poetic insight, for he never reworked it. The final form was written that day:

> ¿Qué es tu vida, alma mía?
> ¿Qué es tu vida, alma mía? ¿cuál tu pago?
> ¡Lluvia en el lago!
> ¿Qué es tu vida, alma mía, tu costumbre?
> ¡Viento en la cumbre!
> ¿Cómo tu vida, mi alma, se renueva?
> ¡Sombra en la cueva!
> ¡Lluvia en el lago!
> ¡Viento en la cumbre!
> ¡Sombra en la cueva!
> Lágrimas es la lluvia desde el cielo,
> y es el viento sollozo sin partida,
> pesar la sombra sin ningún consuelo,
> y lluvia y viento y sombra hacen la vida [*RD*, 81].

An indication of the spectrum of Unamuno's creative genius can be seen in this poem. In the first line the lyric *yo* asks two questions—what is life and what is the soul's reward. Only the second question is answered with the metaphor of "¡lluvia en el lago!" Man's reward is to be lost in the flux of existence as water onto water is lost. With this answer the soul anticipates the loss of individuality. Again the lyric *yo* asks two questions: What is life? Is it your way of life? And again only the second part is answered with "¡viento en la cumbre!" Man's way of life is also a passing wind, but it has force and is felt as he, the individual, encounters the world. Finally, for the third time, the *yo* interrogates the soul: How is life renewed? And the third metaphor responds: "¡sombra en la cueva!" Man is re-created as the shadows on the wall of the cave reflect the real man to others; such shadows of man are the writings of that man. The initial question of what is life remains unanswered. The *yo* has received three exclamatory metaphors but no answer. The smooth-flowing last quatrain serenely gives the *yo* his answer. First, the three metaphors are humanized; they are made into the world of the *yo* as tears, sobs, and sorrow. Once the three different points of view have been remade into the internal perspective of the *yo,* the answer is clear. The three—rain, wind, and shadow—make life. The rain (annihilation), the wind (*yo*-will), and the shadow (re-creation in others) all function together to make the life for the soul. Thus, the life of the soul is seen from three facets of death, and these are known to the *yo* only through the emotive reception of suffering as tears, sobs, and sorrow.

Cancionero (1928–36)

This posthumous publication has the most diverse thematic contents of any Unamunian collection of poems. The explanation is clear. This was a personal poetic diary which don Miguel wrote during his last nine years as the result of his day to day experiences. García Blanco has best captured the essence of this corpus:

. . . la actualidad está ahí, es la que le da el autor de estos versos. Que por eso, entiendo, fueron precisamente así y no de otra manera. O dicho con sus propias palabras:

> Dios mío, este yo, ¡ay de mí!,
> se me está yendo en cantares;
> pero en mi mundo es así:
> los seres se hacen estares.[41]

The following poems, like most of those in this poetic diary,

[41] *Don Miguel de Unamuno y sus poesías,* pp. 363–364.

appear simply numbered without a title. These poems are exemplary of hundreds that appear of equal value and that express this same attitude of death to the personal *yo*.

> Tú me has hecho encontrarme, Cristo mío;
> por la gracia bendita de tu Padre
> soy lo que soy: un dios, un yo, un hombre!
> Más dentro aún que mis entrañas arde
> el fuego eterno que encendió los soles
> e hizo la luz, un fuego de diamante.
> Hombre me has hecho, Cristo, nada menos
> que todo un hombre, todo un dios, un padre [C, 27].

The identification of Unamuno with the lyric *yo* is evident in this poem. The existentialist values are implicit in such verses as: "Tú me has hecho encontrarme, Cristo mío." The *yo* is authentic, having elevated himself above the endless progression of existence to realize that he is one, unique, and irreplaceable *yo*. Christ has become the living symbol of immortality, which, when put into discourse or practice, comes from Unamuno as the tragic sense of life.

The fecund source of inspiration that St. Paul was throughout Unamuno's life is put into this poem:

> Pablo, me muero cada día,
> y cada día resucito;
> mas ay de la pobre alma mía,
> que va a perderse en lo infinito.
>
> .   .   .
>
> En ti el Cristo y en mí tú vives;
> viviremos en El después? [C, 456–457].

Once again, the shadow of death gives only a sense of nothingness to the poet. He realizes how empty it is to say that the *yo* will live in history, for it will not be the *yo* of *carne y hueso,* but only the *yo* that others think he is. Paul lives in Unamuno and Christ in Paul. Could it be that they all will live in God? The next chapter will explore this train of feeling and thought.

Poemas inéditos

The latest anthology of 1954, presenting unpublished or lost poems of Unamuno, has given further evidence of his lifelong fascination with poetry and the rôle that it played as his means of literary expression. Since these poems now fill the gaps between the published poetic works, a trajectory of lyric development can be studied by the scholar.

Although the majority of these poems are part of the other attitudes of Unamuno, there is one striking example to mention here.
This is the poetic dialogue entitled "La despedida final." The dramatic intensity in this poetic anticipation of death is of the greatest
force. There are three characters in this small play within a poem
—Juan who is dying, Isabel his beloved, and the narrating *yo*. The
dialogued verse creates all of the dramatic anticipation of death.
A metaphorical image of the setting sun as the man dies gives the
yo's narration the lyrical expression of the death scene.

In the narrative prose studied in this chapter, the death theme
fulfills two functions: the development of plot and the creation of
complexity in the characters. As a part of plot, death provides
background atmosphere in such instances as the battles of *Paz en la
guerra* or the deaths of Rosa and Apolodoro in *Amor y pedagogía*.
Death realizes one of its primary functions in the creation of fictional characters. Those characters who have an awareness of death
—like Apolodoro, Pachico, Augusto Pérez, Joaquín Monegro, or
Manuel Bueno—are fully developed and complex individuals. But
those characters who are oblivious of their impending death—like
Pedro Antonio (*Paz en la guerra*), Avito Carrascal, or Abel Sánchez
—are all single-faceted.

Death in Unamuno's dramatic prose also serves two functions.
It creates the principal dramatic situation, as can be seen in the
last scene of each *La esfinge*, *La venda*, and *Fedra*. Also, death
causes the inner struggle in Unamuno's *agonistas*, like Angel (*La
esfinge*), or in the speakers of the *monodiálogos*, like those of *¡Vae
Victoribus!*

The lyric expression of death has several basic moods that are
adopted by the *yo*. Death is at times treated with sorrowful resignation, as in the fatigued *yo*'s evocation of the sleep that brings
eternal rest in "Duerme, alma mía" (*Poesías*). In other poems, like
"Vendrá de noche," the anticipation of the moment when death
will come to the *yo* is seen. There are other poems like those in the
collection of *El Cristo de Velázquez* where the *yo* struggles to cling
to a thread of hope for immortality. But there are also those
expressions that ring out with the furor of the desperate struggle
against nothingness, as, for example, in "Irresignación" (*Rosario de
sonetos líricos*).

All of the literature studied directly or indirectly in this chapter
is an esthetic creation of the *yo*'s confrontation with his impending

end in death. The personal *yo,* if authentic, responds in many ways, but these are all agonizing, for even the surrender to sleep is the desperate resolution of an agonizing *yo.* The unauthentic expressions within this literature are also a part of the awareness of death, for they represent the negative, empty *yo* that contrasts with the authentic *yo.*

The literature of this second attitude represents Unamuno's progressive concentration on the philosophical position of the individual and the radical re-orientation of the world into an existential relationship to the *yo.* Reality as "being-in-struggle" is known by the *yo* when he is threatened and made aware of his being. This is essentially the truth Unamuno felt and had to express. Consequently the changes wrought on the literary structure were all necessities for the creation of this attitude from which *Del sentimiento trágico* was formulated.

CHAPTER FOUR

THE LITERARY EXPRESSION OF DEATH FOR THE *YO* THAT IS RE-CREATED IN OTHERS

The idea that man can achieve a measure of immortality through his fame is one of the oldest in Western civilization.[1] In the literature of Spain it reaches classical expression in Jorge Manrique's *Coplas a la muerte de su padre*. There is also another approach, perhaps older than fame, to immortality in the less intellectual belief that man leaves a part of himself in his children.[2] Both of these beliefs, one intellectual, the other sentimental, are taken up by Unamuno as being expressive of man's attempt to defy death by remaining in the world in some active way. The literary creation of this attempted survival takes the form of two related themes: *los hijos espirituales* and *los hijos de carne y hueso*. Both are presented in narratives, in dramas, and, to a more limited extent, in poetry. They are, essentially, the attempt to save the personal *yo* through the *yo* that exists in others. Intellectually the effort is crude, but emotionally it has great intensity. This *yo* that exists in others, taken as a substitute for the personal *yo*, first appears in *Amor y pedagogia* (1902), where it leads to Apolodoro's frustration.

This third literary attitude receives another development in the form of doubt. An agonizing doubt is voiced as to the validity of the premise of the *yo*'s survival in others. This doubt, which results

[1] For a fundamental study of immortality through fame, see M. R. Lida de Malkiel, *La idea de la fama en la Edad Media castellana* (México: Fondo de cultura económica, 1952).

[2] For the mother symbol in Unamuno, see Blanco Aguinaga, *El Unamuno contemplativo*, pp. 123–163; also Richard Predmore, "Flesh and Spirit in the Works of Unamuno," *PMLA*, LXX, 4 (1955), 587–605.

in the Unamunian theme of "el otro," destroys the value of the *yo*-in-others as a substitute for personal immortality.

The last development of the attitude comes in the novel-essay *Cómo se hace una novela* as the spiritual re-creation of the *yo* in others through the written word. This last phase does not give any solace or sense of escape from death through re-creation, but rather imparts the meaning of an active participation in a spiritual brotherhood. Within this current, the images of men, fictional characters, and myths all share an equal status as the active agents in moving their re-creators to feel thoughts and to think feelings. Thus, once again, the literary attitude creates the atmosphere for a philosophical perspective. This is the struggle of the *yo*'s words to continue the re-creation and not to fall into oblivion. The philosophy goes on to consider man's work and expression as a unique part of the current.

NARRATIVE PROSE

The various developments of the third attitude all find expression in the narratives beginning with *Amor y pedagogía* and ending with *La novela de Don Sandalio, jugador de ajedrez*. In this chapter, as with most of Unamuno's literature, there is no suppression or supplanting of one literary mood by another. Instead, Unamuno keeps adding to the initial theme development until he has created a complex and profound work of art. This is the case with *Cómo se hace una novela*, where the emotive drive of works like *Dos madres* or *La tía Tula* is united with the dramatic situation of *Tulio Montalbán y Julio Macedo* and then made into the expression of multiple levels of reality. Thus, this attitude leads to a positive participation of the re-created *yo* in the re-creators.

The Theme Development of "los hijos":
Amor y pedagogía, "Los hijos espirituales," *Dos madres*,
El marqués de Lumbría, *La tía Tula*

In the prologue to the second edition (1934) of *Amor y pedagogía*, Unamuno indicated that much of his literature was already expressed in an embryonic form in this novel of 1902. And from Unamuno's correspondence it can also be ascertained that he began to write *La tía Tula* at the same time. However, this latter novel was not given its final form until 1921. Thus, while *Amor y pedagogía* is the genesis for this development of the yearning for the re-creation of the *yo*, *La tía Tula* is the culmination.

Apolodoro, the aborted genius of *Amor y pedagogía,* had two goals set before him: to re-create his *yo* through literature and to leave a part of himself in children. Both of these accomplishments would be assurances of Apolodoro's immortality, not only in name as could be expected, but in this tragic satire they become rationalizations of scientism; they are means of achieving a continued existence for the personal *yo.* The frustration is complete when Apolodoro's short story is ignored as being mediocre and he loses the love of Clarita. The failure to attain these goals makes Apolodoro choose the surrender to suicide, but before dying he answers the call "haz hijos." Although there is a child born, the attempt at a re-creation of the *yo* is completely frustrated as the use of logic and reason to cope with the emotive dread of death is satirized.

Years later, in 1916, Unamuno wrote "Los hijos espirituales," a *relato,* which he intended to rework into a drama. Here, the desire for children is set against the writer's creation of literature. The desire for maternity in the wife, Eulalia, reaches the breaking point of frustration when she begins to buy dolls which she treats like children. The husband, Federico, is concerned with the attainment of immortality through his poems and short stories, which he calls his "hijos espirituales." After the death of Federico's mother, Eulalia, who senses the impending end, tells her husband: "Ahora escribe una elegía a la muerte de tu madre . . . ya que no puedes escribir una oda triunfante al natalicio de tu primer hijo" (*OC*, 2a, IX, 257).

From this moment Eulalia becomes increasingly demented, as she throws out his books and places dolls in their place, she says: "son mis hijos... espirituales." Finally the timid little man explodes in a burst of emotion and begins to destroy the dolls. Together they throw their respective *hijos* out the windows—she what remains of his books and he the collection of dolls. The result is complete frustration for both husband and wife as he roams through the world hating literature and she locks herself up where she can never see a child.

Contained in the publication of *Tres novelas ejemplares* (1920) are the two short novels *Dos madres* and *El marqués de Lumbría,* which present the theme of motherhood once more. In *Dos madres,* Raquel, who was tormented because she had never had children, found a way to overcome the frustration by acting as the *celestina* between her own lover, Juan, and her candidate for motherhood, Berta. She controlled every step of the procreation of the child, and, once born, had Juan name the infant girl Raquel. The helpless Juan was torn between the two mothers—the spiritual one and the physical bearer—and had no other way out but to die. After his death Raquel easily bought the right of adoption from Berta and her parents. Thus, the frustrated mother not only caused the birth of the child but gave her her own name and therefore achieved a measure of re-creation of herself.

Carolina, the eldest daughter of *El marqués de Lumbría,* is another Unamunian woman with the furor of maternity. She completely dominates her lover, who later marries her younger sister. She is more than the bearer of the child; she is the will that begets the child and later claims and wins his birthright as the future Marqués. Carolina tells Tristán:

—¡Fuí yo quien te seduje! ¡Yo! . . . Yo quise ser la madre del marqués. . . . Tú despertaste mi carne y con ella mi orgullo de mayorazga. . . . Y cuando entraste aquí te hice sentir que la mujer era yo, yo, y no mi hermana... ¿Quieres que te recuerde la caída? [*OC,* 2a, IX, 469–470].

The *yo*-will of the mother has been passed on to her son, who not only is her flesh and blood but also the heir of the family name as the *Marqués.*

The novel *La tía Tula,* which was started in 1902 but was not completed until 1921, is the Unamunian narration of the longest gestation. The plot itself was already established in 1902, as can be seen from Unamuno's letter of that year to the Catalan poet Juan Maragall:

Ahora ando metido en una nueva novela, *La tía,* historia de una joven que rechazando novios se queda soltera para cuidar a unos sobrinos, hijos de una hermana que se le muere. Vive con el cuñado, a quien rechaza para marido, pues no quiere *manchar* con el débito conyugal el recinto en que respiran aire de castidad sus *hijos.* Satisfecho el instinto de maternidad, ¿para qué ha de perder su virginidad? Es virgen madre.[3]

What Unamuno adds to this initial outline is the intimate convent atmosphere which the spiritual mother, Tula, instills in the household after the death of the physical mother, Rosa. Unamuno wrote in the prologue that he was not aware of this mother superior rôle which was adopted by Tula until he reread it after its completion in 1921. It is clear that the influence of Santa Teresa enters into the novel slowly and is not marked until the later chapters. In the review of the world of this novel, its own development will

[3] See *Epistolario entre Miguel de Unamuno y Juan Maragall* (Barcelona: Edimar, 1951), pp. 13–14.

be followed so that the multiple factors of the re-creation of the *yo* can be seen in the novel's own trajectory.

The basic drive behind Tula, manifested from the opening lines, is an overwhelming desire for maternity. For Tula the only end in life is to have children and thus to create and re-create the personal *yo*. This iron-willed woman, like Raquel of *Dos madres*, precipitates the marriage of Rosa to Ramiro, who is the first suitor to approach her. She remains aloof from the married couple until their first child is about to be born; at this time Tula moves in to direct and safeguard the birth of the child, who is more important to her than her sister. After assisting the doctor in delivering the child, she declares: "Y en cuanto a éste—y al decirlo apretábalo contra su seno palpitante—, corre ya de mi cuenta, y o poco he de poder o haré de él un hombre" (*OC*, 2a, IX, 543). Unamuno does not let the image of maternity slip from the forceful Tula as he adds: "La casa le daba vueltas en derredor a Ramiro. Y del fondo de su alma salíale una voz diciendo: '¿Cuál es la madre?'" (p. 543). And when she takes the child into the room of the exhausted mother, Tula whispers in her ear: "Este se llamará Ramiro, como su padre . . . y la otra, porque la siguiente será niña, Gertrudis, como yo" (p. 544).[4]

Tula takes over the complete care of the child and insists that her sister devote herself to her husband and to the procreation of the next child. As Tula gives her entire energy to the care of the child, she is careful to keep him well separated from the spirit of the physical love of the parents:

Era como una preocupación en la tía la de ir sustrayendo al niño, ya desde su más tierna edad de inconciencia, de conocer, ni en las más leves y remotas señales, el amor de que había brotado. Colgóle al cuello, desde luego, una medalla de la Santísima Virgen, de la Virgen Madre, con su Niño en brazos [*OC*, 2a, IX, 545].

Thus, from the beginning of her life in the house, Tula establishes in her own mind her status of the virgin mother. Her designs pay dividends as Rosa has a second child and then a third. By this time, the division of labor that she had established from the start makes her conscious of her rôle as the worker bee whose mission is the care and upbringing of the brood of the queen bee. It must be mentioned that the various symbols that characterize Tula's chang-

---

[4] Although Tula proclaims that the next child would be named after her, Unamuno shows the effects of a long period of composition in that the second child is sometimes called Gertrudis and at other times Rosa or Rosita; see pp. 559, 573, 626.

ing rôle in the household are not a mere narrative descriptive technique; they are conscious states of mind that Tula accepts.

Rosa dies after the birth of the third child, and once more in Unamuno's literature the Leopardi verses of the proximity of love and death are recalled. Now Ramiro, the widower, turns to his sister-in-law, seeking to make her his wife as well as the spiritual mother of his children, but she refuses him: "No insistas; ya te tengo dicho que no debo casarme ni contigo ni con otro menos" (p. 565).

Slowly Tula takes on the new status of the mother superior of the convent-like house: "En la ciudad estaba su convento, su hogar, y en él su celda. Allí adormecería mejor a su cuñado. . . . Gertrudis leía mucho a Santa Teresa" (p. 577). It is during this period that the moon symbol of the Matriarch goddess is applied to Tula, for she is not only the unquestioned ruler of the house but is now becoming a household divinity.[5]

When she discovers that Ramiro has found sexual satisfaction with the young maid, she forces him into marriage for the second time. Two more children are added to the three of Rosa, and all five are equally the children of Tula, the virgin mother. Ramiro dies shortly before the last child is born. In his last words he speaks to Tula: "La madre de mis hijos eres tú, tú, tú." Then he asks her if she thinks he will be reunited with Rosa beyond death, but Tula can only reassure him with this inner confession of her maternal drive: "Piensa en vivir, en tus hijos" (p. 594). Shortly after Ramiro's death, the maid, the last concubine for the virgin mother, dies in childbirth. Tula is now alone with her convent of children. Her prayer to the Blessed Virgin that she might also become a mother without having to know man is now granted.

Unamuno describes the passage of time in these words: "Corrieron unos años apacibles y serenos. La orfandad daba a aquel hogar, en el que de nada de bienestar se carecía, una íntima luz espiritual de serena calma."

Finally, when the oldest son, Ramiro, reaches manhood, Tula moves him into marriage with Caridad, another fecund partner for the creation of men and the re-creation of Tula. The young bride immediately becomes part of the family group and is soon pregnant.

[5] For the implications of the moon in antiquity see Robert Graves, *The Greek Myths* (Baltimore: Penguin Books, 1957), I, 9–23; also Erich Neumann, *The Great Mother: An Analysis of Archetype*, trans., Ralph Manheim (New York: Pantheon Books, 1955). For the moon as a symbol in Unamuno, see Carlos Clavería, "Don Miguel y la luna," *Temas de Unamuno*, pp. 137–156.

But before this last child can be born, the Matriarch Tula dies. Unamuno then writes:

¿Murió la tía Tula? No, sino que empezó a vivir en la familia, e irradiando de ella, con una nueva vida más entrañada y más vivífica, con la vida eterna de la familiaridad inmortal. Ahora era ya para sus hijos, sus sobrinos, la Tía, no más que la Tía, ni *madre* ya ni *mamá*, ni aún tía Tula, sino sólo la Tía. Fué este nombre de invocación, de verdadera invocación religiosa, como el canonizamiento doméstico de una santidad de hogar [*OC*, 2a, IX, 625].

The re-creation of the *yo* in others, which in this section has been examined from the point of view of heredity, both physical and spiritual, has been developed by Unamuno from the ridiculous logical abstractions of *Amor y pedagogía* to the sublime emotional drive of *La tía Tula*. However, the need for the re-creation has dominated in this exposition, for although frustrations have been felt by the characters, there has been no agonizing doubt as to the effectiveness of the re-creation for the continued existence of the personal *yo*. This type of destructive doubt is an agony of the inner thoughts of the *yo* which has been seen in the second attitude. But here, the dramatic situation which confronts the *yo*, who has been re-created, is the basis for the Unamunian theme of "el otro."

The Theme Development of "el otro": "El que se enterró," *Tulio Montalbán*

The first narrative where this theme predominates is "El que se enterró" of 1908. This narrative, like a few others, was intended for theatrical adaptation.[6] In this story the narrator presents his conversation with the protagonist, Emilio:

Hace cosa de año y medio, meses antes del misterio, caí enfermo de terror. . . . Sentía a todas horas la presencia invisible de la muerte, pero de la verdadera muerte, es decir, del anonadamiento [*OC*, 2a, IX, 195].

He suffered in this state of terror before death until one day, as he sat alone locked in his room, someone opened the door and walked in:

El que estaba ahí, de pie, delante mío, era yo mismo, por lo menos en imagen. Figúrate que estando delante de un espejo, la imagen que de ti se refleja en el cristal se desprende de éste, toma cuerpo y se te viene encima... [*OC*, 2a, IX, 197].

The other one sat in front of Emilio and looked into his eyes. When Emilio heard him whisper his name, he felt death, and died. But

---

6 See *Teatro completo*, pp. 187–188.

he was re-created in the other one, for he regained consciousness in the body of the other one. And where he had been sitting before was the corpse of his former self. The terror was gone; he had known death and had returned to life. Emilio buried the corpse of his former *yo* and began to live life as an authentic *yo*. The question that remained unanswered was: which is the true *yo*, the Emilio who died and was buried or the Emilio who was re-created in the other one.

In *Tulio Montalbán y Julio Macedo* (1920) there is a perfect example of the Unamunian narrative that was intended for the theatre, for in 1926 he reworked it as a drama by the same title and in 1930 again as *Sombras de sueño*. Here, the personal *yo* is confronted by the *yo* that lives in others. The battle between the historical figure of Tulio Montalbán and the man of flesh and blood, Julio Macedo, is a direct outcome of the re-creation of the *yo*. Since the definitive creation is the drama which Unamuno completed in 1930, the more detailed study of this work will be postponed for the next section of this chapter.

It is quite evident that the theme of the re-created *yo* confronting the personal *yo* is basically a dramatic situation. And thus, it is in these works that Unamuno achieves his finest writings for the theatre. He is no longer hampered with the presentation of only the personal *yo*'s crisis before death, as was the case in the second literary attitude, but here there is the dramatic exchange of the *yo* one thinks he is and the *yo* others think one to be.

Cómo se hace una novela (1924–27)

This novel-essay is Unamuno's masterpiece of the third literary attitude, but, quite ironically, it was almost completely ignored until 1960, when Armando Zubizarreta contributed to Unamunian studies with his *Unamuno en su "nivola."* The present examination of Unamuno's literary creation makes use of part of the discoveries and insights achieved by Zubizarreta. This scholar divides the work into three levels of examination: "La circunstancia política," "La situación espiritual," and "El fruto autobiográfico." [7] And it is the third level that has the novelistic creation; this is the re-creation of Miguel de Unamuno together with his character U. Jugo de la Raza, whose name Unamuno made up from his surnames of U[namuno], Jugo, and Larraza.

[7] Armando F. Zubizarreta, *Unamuno en su "nivola"* (Madrid: Taurus, 1960), pp. 21–90, 167–244.

The novel is, in fact, three novels in one. There is novel one, the story which U. Jugo de la Raza starts to read; novel two is the reading of the book 1 by Jugo; and finally, novel three is the above activity of Jugo, as well as the interspersed autobiographical data which Unamuno mixes into the writing. Thus, a concentric progression is established: the protagonist of the romantic book is re-created by Jugo as Jugo is being created by Unamuno for the readers, the others, to re-create the creator—Unamuno—together with his creation—Jugo. These multiple levels of reality are better appreciated if seen in the Unamunian language with personal awareness as the motive force moving the narration. The novel begins with these words: "Héteme aquí ante estas blancas páginas—blancas como el negro porvenir: ¡terrible blancura!—buscando retener el tiempo que pasa, fijar el huidero hoy, eternizarme o inmortalizarme" *(OC,* 2a, X, 857).

And the idea for an auto-novel begins a few pages later:

Me dió la ocurrencia . . . de ponerme en una novela que vendría a ser una autobiografía. Pero ¿no son acaso autobiografías todas las novelas que se eternizan y duran eternizando y haciendo durar a sus autores y a sus antagonistas? [*OC,* 2a, X, 860].

¡Mi novela!, ¡mi leyenda! El Unamuno de mi leyenda, de mi novela, el que hemos hecho juntos mi yo amigo y mi yo enemigo [i.e., the dialectic struggle] y los demás, mis amigos y mis enemigos [i.e., the re-creators], este Unamuno me da vida y muerte [i.e., re-creation by others, but a denial of the personal *yo*] me crea y me destruye, me sostiene y me ahoga [*OC,* 2a, X, 865].

At this point the novel of Jugo begins as he wanders through the bookstalls on the banks of the Seine, bored as he browses through the books. Suddenly he is struck with a novel that begins to pull him into its world:

Le saca de sí, le introduce en el personaje de la novela—la novela de una confesión autobiográfico-romántica—le identifica con aquel otro, le da una historia, en fin. . . . Y he aquí que da con un pasaje, pasaje eterno, en que lee estas palabras proféticas: "Cuando el lector llegue al fin de esta dolorosa historia se morirá conmigo" [*OC,* 2a, X, 866–867].

Thus, the participating levels of this novel within a novel that is another novel are now complete. Jugo flees from the bookstall vowing never to read again. But Jugo could not live without the book, for he had already re-created the fictional character of the novel. Here, Unamuno suspends the novel of Jugo to present his own life in exile. Upon resumption of the narration, Unamuno introduces it with the following opening: "Volvamos, pues, a la

novela de Jugo de la Raza, a la novela de su lectura de la novela"
(p. 870). Jugo could not resist any longer; he bought the book and
ran home, slowly ate his dinner, got into bed, prayed, and finally
opened the book and began to read. And, again he came across
the fatal lines: "Debo repetir a mi lector que se morirá conmigo."
The effect was even more pronounced than the first time, and in a
fit of terror he cast the book into the fireplace and burned it.
After another presentation of autobiography, Unamuno returns to
the narration:

Cuando se despertó a la mañana siguiente, en su lecho de agonía espiritual,
encontróse encalmado, se levantó y contempló un momento las cenizas del
libro fatídico de su vida. . . . Su tormento se renovó: ¿cómo acabaría la
historia? [*OC*, 2a, X, 876].

The question "¿Cómo acabará esa historia?" began to haunt Jugo
as he roamed through Paris, the mountains, and the sea; he had
to get another copy of the novel. At this point Unamuno moves to
his personal novel for several pages, and upon returning to the novel
of Jugo's reading, only the conditional tense of the verbs is used
as a situation of what-would-be-if-there-were-a-novel is established.
Thus, Unamuno draws himself, the creator, even closer to the
created Jugo, for he now narrates: "Pensaba hacerle emprender un
viaje . . . habría andado errante," and so forth. Finally, Jugo
would have found the book and returned to Paris with it:

El cual, así que yo le haría volver a París trayéndose el libro fatídico, se
propondría el terrible problema de o acabar de leer la novela que se había
convertido en su vida y morir en acabándola o renunciar a leerla y vivir,
vivir, y, por consiguiente, morirse también [*OC*, 2a, X, 887].

The thoughts of Jugo would appear in the following monologue:

Voy a continuar leyendo un poco hasta que al pobre diablo no le quede
más que un poco de vida, y entonces cuando haya previsto el fin viviré
pensando que le hago vivir [*OC*, 2a, X, 887–888].

As Unamuno, the creator, and his creation Jugo reach the position of the awareness of death as the only end of life, the problem
becomes clear: which shall come first, the end of the reading of the
novel by Jugo or Jugo's death. Unamuno rises to the challenge as
he transcends the limitations of a spatio-temporal existence to defy
death. He achieves the essence of the third attitude in the active
participation with the living company of man's thought. The
re-created Unamuno is no longer a threat to the personal living
Unamuno, for the re-created *yo* is not the substitute of the personal
yo but rather a working partner to make life which faces death have
meaning.

On the last pages of the book Unamuno moves his re-created *yo* into an active rôle of making the re-creator, the reader, sense that he, together with Unamuno and Jugo, have been the producers of the novel:

El hombre de dentro, el intra-hombre—y éste es más divino que el tras-hombre o sobre-hombre nietzscheniano—cuando se hace lector hácese por lo mismo autor, o sea actor; cuando lee una novela se hace novelista, cuando lee historia, historiador. Y todo lector que sea hombre de dentro, humano, es, lector, autor de lo que lee y está leyendo. Esto que ahora lees aquí, lector, te lo estás diciendo tú a ti mismo y es tan tuyo como mío (*OC*, 2a, X, 911].

Hence, it can now be seen that the radical structure of this narrative creation has given an expression of the attitude of the re-created *yo* that otherwise would have been impossible. By developing the concentric levels of literary creativity, Unamuno has brought the narrative from the most inner confines of the created work—the novel within the novel—to his created character Jugo. But Unamuno does not end at this creative level, for he also ties himself intimately to his literary creation of Jugo de la Raza. And he further instills the exterior reality of the creator Unamuno by interspersing his autobiography of exile. Thus, by making a fictional character into a living entity and himself into a fictional character, Unamuno can appeal to the readers for the re-creation of this *yo* in their consciousness. In the last entry of the narrative Unamuno states:

. . . para qué se hace una novela? Para hacerse el novelista. ¿Y para qué se hace el novelista? Para hacer al lector, para hacerse uno con el lector. Y sólo haciéndose uno el novelador y el lector de la novela se salvan ambos de su soledad radical. En cuanto se hacen uno se actualizan y actualizán-dose se eternizan [*OC*, 2a, X, 922].

La novela de Don Sandalio, jugador de ajedrez (1930)

This short novel was published in 1933, three years after it was written, together with *San Manuel Bueno, mártir* (1930), the short narrative *Un pobre hombre rico, o el sentimiento cómico de la vida* (1930), and an earlier short narrative *Una historia de amor* (1911). Thus, this publication marks Unamuno's last period of narrative creativity.

Don Sandalio is a *yo* who is presented as seen by the epistler narrator of the novel, as was the case in *San Manuel Bueno, mártir*, but this *yo* is not given any reality of his own, not even a depicted substance. It is through the narrator's comments in his letters to

a friend, Felipe, that the character of Don Sandalio is developed.
Since he only plays chess with the narrator and never speaks to him
or to anyone else, this *yo* becomes progressively an imaginative
creation by his observer until finally he has been completely re-
created in life and, to the narrator's astonishment, also in death.

The *yo*-development begins in the fourth letter as the narrator
writes to Felipe:

No he podido columbrar nada de su vida, ni en rigor me importa gran
cosa. Prefiero imaginármela. No viene al Casino más que a jugar al ajedrez,
y lo juega, sin pronunciar apenas palabra, con una avidez de enfermo.
Fuera del ajedrez parece no haber mundo para él [*OC*, la, II, 1238].

Through the imaginative capacity of the narrator, the *yo* of Don
Sandalio, as the narrator thinks he is, begins to take form. He continues writing:

"Y cuando no juega, ¿qué hace?"—me he preguntado—. ¿Cuál es la profe-
sión con que se gana la vida? ¿Tiene familia? ¿Quiere a alguien? ¿Guarda
dolores y desengaños? ¿Lleva alguna tragedia dentro? [*OC*, la, II, 1239].

As the letters continue, the *yo* begins to become fully developed in
the consciousness of the narrator so that the problem of his own
possible re-creation in this re-created *yo* appears: "¿Qué pensará
de mí? ¿Cómo seré yo para él?" (p. 1246). But the crucial question
is: "¿Quién seré yo para él?" (p. 1246). Here there is not only
the re-creation of a *yo* during life but also the complementary
problem of being re-created in the other.

When death comes to Don Sandalio, the existence of this re-
created *yo* does not end, for it had never depended on much more
than the imaginative capacity of the narrator to give a *yo* to this
figure before him.

In the eighteenth letter the narrator realizes what has happened:

¿Por qué de pronto me ha invadido una negra congoja y me he puesto a
llorar, así como lo oyes, Felipe, a llorar la muerte de mi Don Sandalio?
Sentía dentro de mí un vacío inmenso. . . . aquel hombre se me había
muerto a mí. Ya no le oiría callar mientras jugaba, ya no oiría su silencio
[*OC*, la, II, 1255–56].

The emptiness within the narrator is due to the loss of one who also
carried the narrator's *yo* within him just as he had done. But the
re-created *yo* of Don Sandalio was not dead, for he lived on in the
consciousness of the narrator. Letter twenty-two underscores this
state of the *yo*:

El problema más hondo de nuestra novela, de la tuya, Felipe, de la mía,
de la de Don Sandalio, es un problema de personalidad, de ser o no ser
[*OC*, la, II, 1263].

Consequently, during life the personal *yo* of a man is converted into a *yo* that others think he is, but upon death this can no longer be the case. Hence, the memory of the observer can recall and thus re-create the departed *yo* for some time, but as life goes on he, too, will be forgotten and lost in oblivion. Don Sandalio could not hope to have left more than a vestige of his *yo* since the remaking of his personality was completely divorced from the real *yo*. The narrator therefore sees the problem as being one of making the re-created *yo* an expression of the personal *yo*. This is the function of the novel of life, that is, living it in such a way that others may continue to re-create the *yo*. Unamuno expresses himself in these words in the epilogue:

Todo poeta, todo creador, todo novelador—novelar es crear—, al crear personajes se está creando a sí mismo, y si le nacen muertos es que él vive muerto [*OC,* 1a, II, 1267].

DRAMATIC PROSE

Within this third attitude of the re-creation of the *yo* are most of Unamuno's writings for the theatre, including the one-act farce *La princesa Doña Lambra* and the *sainete La difunta* of 1909, the drama *El pasado que vuelve* (1910), his dramatic achievements *Soledad* and *Raquel encadenada* of 1921, *El otro* (1926), *Sombras de sueño* (1926–30), and *El hermano Juan* (1929).

The basic difference between these plays and those of the other attitudes is that here the dramatic situations are exterior to the *yo* as well as interior. In the first attitude, it will be recalled, the *yo* was lost in the totality; thus, there was an almost complete absence of dramatic situation. And in the second attitude, the *yo* was a closed personalized world, making it difficult for the other characters to be active participants as dramatic exchange demands. This difference can be better appreciated by a comparison of *La esfinge* (1899) and *Soledad* (1921), where the same plot is developed. In the former, the dramatic conflict is the inner battle of Angel as he faced death, but in the latter the conflict is a mutual frustration felt by both Soledad and Agustín after the loss of their son. Here the dramatic situation is exterior as well as interior to the *yo*. This can be done because the two protagonists share a conflict: the frustrated desire for the creation and re-creation of the *yo* in children. Therefore, it can be realized that although most of Unamuno's literary creations have some elements of dramatic intensity, not all have the exterior situations to express the inner struggle of the *yo*.

The Anticipation of the Third Attitude:
Monodiálogos, La princesa Doña Lambra, La difunta

Among the *monodiálogos*, there are some direct anticipations of what later will be developed into the dramatic current of the third attitude.

In *Los lunes de El Imparcial* Unamuno published a series of five articles under the title "Diálogos del escritor y el político," the last of which was "La paradoja." In it Unamuno gives an insight into a writer's possibilities of being a re-created *yo*.

—Ni quiero jubilaciones ni patentes de inmortalidad, más o menos académicas, en vida; quiero acabar mi carrera con mi muerte, y si no con mi silencio voluntario, pero no que el público me jubile homenajeándome. No quiero que me entierren en vida. El homenaje que un escritor debe codiciar es ser leído [*OC*, 2a, IX, 706].

The man Unamuno is concerned with the created word that represents him and through which he will be re-created. He does not want to be honored and forgotten, but rather to be discussed and re-created. He wants his thought and feelings to have an active participation in the living thought of the *yos* who read his created word.

In a philosophical tone, Unamuno presents the meaning of literary glory and the interpretation of the creator in the *monodiálogo* entitled "Nuestro yo y el de los demás" of 1917.

La obra de un hombre público, es decir, de uno que viva en la historia, por la historia y para la historia debe ser depositar en las conciencias de aquellos sobre que ejerce su acción la semilla de un hombre nuevo. Lo eterno de cada uno de nosotros se hará en ellos. Pero esto no es, claro está, lo que de nosotros quieren y esperan los que nos rodean. Nuestro eterno yo futuro no es nuestro actual yo de los demás, aunque no sea nuestro yo propio, el que nosotros mismos nos hacemos [*OC*, 2a, IX, 900–901].

This momentary glimpse into Unamuno's thinking gives a clear indication of the direction taken toward the third attitude. This is the earliest statement which clearly separates the literary re-creation of the *yo* from the thirst for immortality by the personal *yo*.

Shortly after finishing the tragic satire of *Amor y pedagogía*, Unamuno began to consider the different forms of comedy as the best media for the type of theatre he wanted. In letters to his many friends, Unamuno refers to his comic vein: "Estoy en vena de cómico pero de un cómico sangriento y cínico" (Letter to Juan Arzadun, November, 1909).[8] "Y tanto me he enamorado de lo cómico, de un cómico algo triste, que ando buscando la tragedia bufa" (Letter to Juan Maragall, December, 1909).[9] Of the many comedies in process at that time, only two reached completion; others remained in manuscript notes,[10] in an initial short story form, or only remembered by title in correspondence.[11] The two that show early signs of the third attitude are *La princesa Doña Lambra,* written in 1909 but never presented on stage, and *La difunta* of 1909, staged in 1910.

Unamuno gives the setting and action of *La princesa Doña Lambra* in these words:

Un poeta arqueólogo, medio loco, enamorado de la estatua, va a hacerle el amor y se encuentra de noche y a oscuras con la hermana del conserje que espera la vuelta de un novio que se le fué hace veinte años al Paraguay. El cree que es la princesa resucitada, ella que es el novio, y el conserje, que les sorprende, les obliga a casarse [*OC,* 2a, XII, 75].

Sinforosa gives up the re-created *yo* of her long absent fiancé, and the poet, Don Eugenio, gives up the re-created *yo* of the princess. They will now have each other and also regain their own *yos,* which had been lost in the past of their re-creations. The brother, Fortunato, ends the farce with this note of Unamunian melancholy that comes out from behind the mask of the buffoon: "¡Lo que pude haber sido! También yo pude haber sido trágico y me he quedado en cómico" (*OC,* 2a, XII, 367).

In the light play *La difunta,* Unamuno humorously touches the same insights of human melancholy as shown in *La princesa Doña Lambra* by again using the ridiculous. He writes concerning this play: "Es realmente feroz, aunque muy cómico; los que lo han oído leer se ríen a mandíbula batiente, diciendo: '¡Qué barbaridad!' "[12]

The play presents a widower of four months who attempts to re-create his wife by having the maid dress up in her clothes and walk around the house for him. During the masquerade of the re-creation the widower begins to make love to the maid, as if she were his departed wife, but a friend and later the mother-in-law inter-

---

[8] See the complete letter in *OC,* 2a, XII, 76.

[9] *Epistolario Unamuno y Maragall,* p. 89.

[10] After García Blanco published *Teatro completo,* it was thought that all of Unamuno's dramas left in manuscript were published. However, traces of another have been found recently; see Ricardo Gullón, "Un drama inédito de Unamuno," *Insula,* 181 (December, 1961).

[11] For example, see "Obras dramáticas proyectadas," *OC,* 2a, XII, 168.

[12] This statement is in a letter to Arzadun; see *OC,* 2a, XII, 76.

rupt. When they are left alone, the girl takes full advantage of the situation; she throws off the guise of the re-created wife to become herself again and demands marriage in order to be his wife as herself and not as another.

El pasado que vuelve (1910–23)

This play does not have a *yo* with the driving emotional desire to leave part of himself in children, as will be seen in other Unamunian plays. However, there is an exchange of thoughts, opinions, and a way of looking at the world from Víctor I to Víctor II, his grandson. In the dialogue between the two in the third act they see their *yos* so closely united that they begin to talk as if they were the same person:

Víctor II.—No sé que me da oírte.

Víctor I.—Y yo me oigo cuando te oigo. Eres el que dejé hace cuarenta años en el camino de la vida. . . . Tú haras lo que yo no pude hacer; yo haré, yo haré de nuevo lo que entonces no hice, ¿verdad, Víctor, verdad?

Víctor II.—Sí, Víctor, sí; yo haré, yo haré lo que hace cuarenta años no pude [*OC,* 2a, XII, 562–563].

The grandfather explains that he inherited his mother's temperament (the Landeta characteristics)—but nothing of his father's personality (the Rodero line). However, his son is a Rodero. But now, with the fourth generation, the Landeta line is going to win out over the Roderos.

In the next scene, Víctor II and his fiancée are encouraged to go out and seek their own life by both Víctor I and his wife. As they do, they sense the parallel to their own courtship and their escape from the Rodero house. The conflict that has been growing between Víctor II and his father, Federico, is now coming to a climax since Víctor II has been threatened with imprisonment because of a pamphlet he wrote denouncing the government. At this point (scene XII) there is a suspension of the conflict of the generations when Víctor I's old friend, Alberto, returns to Spain from Chile after fifty years of absence. But after only two days he wants to return to America for he is alone: "Yo no me encontré. ¡Aquel Alberto ha muerto! Ni deje aquí semilla ni recuerdo" (p. 580).

The drama reaches its peak of intensity when Víctor II decides to leave his father's house *quijotescamente* to make the world a better place. Federico accuses Víctor I of having turned the boy's mind. The old man answers with pride: "¡Locos, sí, locos los dos!

Resucité, hijo, resucité." Federico reminds his father that he is old and will soon die, there, in the house that is his, only because of his filial charity. Víctor I replies:

¡Pues no, no moriré, no, no moriré! ¡Soy yo quien dejé morir solo a mi padre . . . y soy yo, yo, sí, yo quien te deja morir solo . . . [*OC*, 2a, XII, 586].

Víctor I will not die because his *yo* has been re-created in his grandson, but his son Federico will die just as the first Rodero, alone.

Soledad (1921)

In this drama, frustrated parenthood is made the vehicle for transforming the protagonist's life into a continuous struggle to re-create his *yo* in others. However, in contrast to other dramas where the *yo* is in anguish, here there is an exterior dramatic struggle of re-creation to mirror the inner struggle.[13]

This is the drama of Agustín's personal agony with death and his quest for re-creation. At the beginning he is a successful dramatist who has devoted himself almost completely to his work in order to forget the loss of his son. The wife, Soledad, has nothing to turn to and is dominated by abject pessimism. His mother, Sofía, who is living with the couple since the child's death, through wise counsel tries to keep the two from torturing each other. Gloria, who has been the principal interpreter of Agustín's tragic women, comes to see him about a rôle in one of his current plays. At this time Soledad and his friend Pablo are trying to convince Agustín to leave the theatre and dedicate himself to politics. But Gloria and Sofía advise him to continue as a dramatist. Enrique, a critic, also tells him that he is within reach of immortality if he remains in the theatre. But Agustín, moved by Soledad more than by Gloria, decides to enter the political arena.

As the second act begins it becomes obvious that he has been a failure in politics, for the police are seeking to arrest him, charging him with conspiracy against the state. Sofía is now almost completely insane and will soon die. Soledad realizes how mistaken she was in wanting Agustín to enter the political world. Before the act ends, in a scene that is reminiscent of the ending of *La esfinge*,

13 The drama *Soledad* and the farce *La difunta* have been produced in 1962 in Madrid's Teatro María Guerrero. For a critical review, see Rafael Vázquez Zamora, "García Lorca y Unamuno en dos teatros madrileños," *Insula*, 192 (November, 1962).

Gloria, Pablo, and Enrique have all tried to convince Agustín to flee. Finally, as the police arrive, Soledad tries to protect him. At this moment Sofía dies and Agustín goes out to meet his persecutors.

The third act finds Agustín alone with Soledad and suffering from disillusion and ill-health, both caused by his period of imprisonment. Again his friends come to visit him, attempting to pull him out of his depression. But Agustín slowly sinks into semi-consciousness and at the final curtain he is sinking into the eternal sleep that will unite him with his son.

The names of the three women are symbolic of the forces that battle within Agustín. Sofía, who has the wisdom of experience in the first act, is demented in the second act before she dies. During the first act Unamuno uses her to underscore or comment on the action with reason and common sense. Like a Greek chorus, she does not add to the tragedy, but rather dramatizes the dialogue of the other characters. However, in the second act, as the insane paralytic, her monologue acts as a piercing series of symbols of anguish and frustration that create the secondary meaning of the dialogue. Gloria, symbolically, is Agustín's achievement of immortality in name. She is to play the part of Hagar in his next play; this is the biblical slave girl who was brought to Abraham as a substitute by the sterile Sarah, but was then driven into the desert because of Sarah's jealousy. Since Gloria plays the tragic *yos* that Agustín creates, she is their spiritual mother. Although she comes to comfort Agustín, she is turned away. Soledad, who can no longer have children, is the embodiment of frustration and despair.

The tragedy is the struggle that Agustín suffers as he is torn between Gloria and Soledad, since both promise him the re-creation of his *yo* by others. He achieves a measure of re-creation in the characters to whom he gives life through Gloria, but when Soledad attempts to have him put his *yo* into the nation and the people to such an extent that they all will have re-created him, he fails. He is left alone with Soledad; no longer does he seek to create his *yo* in others as he sinks into the sleep of death.

From the outset, with Agustín's first lines, the dramatic situation is established as an atmosphere of death prevails: "No se me arranca. ¡Vaya! Que no se me arranca." Soledad answers: "¿Puedo ayudarte en algo?" Then she turns to Sofía, who is sitting near, and tells her: "Aunque mejor sería que se dejase de todo ello . . . se pone a escribir como un loco; ni me ve, ni me oye, ni siente otra cosa..." (*OC,* 2a, XII, 589). Sofía tells Soledad that she should make an effort to overcome her depressed state and not keep the dead child's photograph and cardboard horse in the center of the room:

Soledad.—Su obra no me devuelve...
Sofía.—Su obra te da a él más entero, y como creador...
Soledad.—¡Creador de ficciones! . . .
Agustín.—¿Cómo será otro, otro que yo...? Uno que me lleve como yo ahora le llevo... [*OC,* 2a, XII, 590].

Agustín feels that his characters must be apart from him, but yet infused with the life that reflects his *yo.* When these creations live, then his *yo* will be re-created through them. But Soledad coldly reminds him of its unimportance since he will also die. Agustín, intent on his dramatic creation, answers: "¡No importa! ¡Todo lo que nace, nace para morir!" What does matter is that the creation has the truth of his *yo* through which he can share with others his dramatic experience:

Es menester que sientan mis torturas, que mis criaturas palpiten de vida..., de vida y de goce y de dolor...; que pesen sobre las tablas... ¡No! ¡Sobre las almas!, que hinchan de pasión el escenario... Y éste es mi drama, el drama del dramaturgo, el drama del parto... [*OC,* 2a, XII, 592].

When Soledad and Pablo convince Agustín that his place is in politics, he has not changed his intimate yearning. He has merely changed the theatrical for the political stage. But neither Soledad nor Pablo have understood that Agustín's basic motivation is a search for immortality, which comes out in disconnected utterings like these:

Porque necesito crear almas..., necesito crear..., crearnos..., crearme..., y nada de tribuna ni de cátedra... [*OC,* 2a, XII, 611].

Therefore, when Agustín, in the second act, is defeated but not yet broken in spirit, he can accuse Soledad of having destroyed the only thing of value he had: his work. Agustín tells her that the cardboard horse—which is always on stage—is immortal for it is a symbol of the dead son, as Clavileño became an immortal symbol of Don Quixote. He feels the emptiness of his life without the created world of his spiritual sons:

Agustín.—Sí, me sacasteis de mi tablado..., del tablado que poblé con mis criaturas, con mis hijos... [*OC,* 2a, XII, 622].

The third act brings death's rest to the pathetic figure of the demented man. The creator of characters who were to carry his *yo* for others to re-create now dies demented and frustrated in the arms of Soledad.

Raquel encadenada (1921)

This play is the most severe presentation of maternal frustration in Unamuno's theatre. It has been compared to García Lorca's *Yerma* of thirteen years later because of the intensity of the emotional drive.[14] Unamuno's play does not create the blind passion of *Yerma*, but rather it builds up the dread of *la sima* as an apparently unconscious psychological state, until it materializes as the frustration of the empty womb.

The action is uncomplicated, revolving around the three characters who are presented in this manner: "Raquel, una violinista que da conciertos. Simón, su marido y administrador, usurero; no tienen hijos. Aurelio, primo y antiguo novio de Raquel, soltero, enriquecido últimamente, y con un hijo que tuvo con una muchacha que murió al darlo a luz" (*OC,* 2a, XII, 662). Raquel's biblical name is further underscored in the quotation that was to be read before the curtain opened: " '¡Dame hijos, o si no me muero!' (Génesis, cap. XXX, v. 1)" (p. 662).

The first act opens with a demonstration of marital devotion between Raquel and Simón, but as the action progresses it becomes clear that there is a wide gulf separating them:

Raquel.—Me siento desfallecer, Simón, me faltan las fuerzas... Paréceme ver siempre al lado una sima, una sima sin fondo, oscura y helada, llena de vacío, y que si caigo en ella he de estarme cayendo siempre, siempre, siempre, sin fin, sin fin, sin fin, en el vacío oscuro y helado... ¡Es peor que el infierno...! [*OC,* 2a, XII, 687].

The conflict materializes in the second act when Raquel agrees to go to Aurelio's house to care for his child Susín, who is dying. In the quarrel that this precipitates, Raquel cries out:

A Raquel, Simón, le ha llegado la hora de rebelarse. No quisiste traer a tu sobrino y así salvarnos; voy a ver si salvo al mío; si me salvo... ¡Estoy harta de tiranía! [*OC,* 2a, XII, 707].

And as the act ends, she cries:

¡Qué soledad, Dios mío! ¡Con sus besos [del niño], con sus risas, hasta con sus lloros llenaría mi alma..., taparía la sima...! ¡La sima, la sima...! ¡Qué soledad, Dios mío! [*OC,* 2a, XII, 710].

The child recovers, but Raquel has tasted the joys of being a mother and she cannot return to Simón. She confronts him and declares she is leaving: "¡Sí; Raquel viene de guerra! Raquel ha

---

[14] See *OC,* 2a, XII, 125–126; for a brief study of *Raquel encadenada,* see Frank Sedwick, "Unamuno and Womanhood: His Theatre," *Hispania,* XLII (1960), 311–313.

decidido irse a vivir con su hijo." As the three characters confront
each other, the drama reaches its climax. Raquel accuses her
husband:

> Raquel.— ¡El mulo, sí! ¡El violinisto! ¡El usurero! ¡El avaro!
> Simón.— ¡Y éste... el zángano!
> Aurelio.— ¡Simón! ¿Volvemos a las andadas?
> Raquel.— ¡Déjale! ¡Sí, tú, el zángano..., el zángano! Sin zánganos no
> habría abejas, ni colmenas, ni miel...
> Simón.—Ni reina.
> Raquel.—Ni reina. ¡Y yo... la reina! ¡Yo, la reina! ¡La reina de casa!
> ¡La madre! [*OC*, 2a, XII, 726].

She now understands *la sima* to be her frustrated maternal drive:

> . . . no quiso llenar este horrible vacío que ahora sé cuál era. . . .
> Aurelio.—Y acaso logres ahora lo que con éste...
> Simón.—¿Qué? (Pausa.) ¿Qué? (Pausa.) ¡Ah, sí! ¡El zángano es el macho
> de la colmena..., el padre! [*OC*, 2a, XII, 727].

Raquel leaves as Aurelio defends her against Simón's threats,
and she accepts willingly the public disgrace that will follow, as
well as the loss of all her property to Simón. She will now become
the queen bee to create men and re-create herself. Tula of *La tía
Tula* was the worker bee who became the virgin mother, but Raquel
will be both the spiritual and physical mother, for she has her
drone, Aurelio.

Sombras de sueño (1926–30)

As has been indicated above, this drama had its origin in a
relato of 1920, which was transformed by Unamuno into theatre in
1926, and was then reworked for the last time as *Sombras de sueño*
in 1930.

The play is set in an island, similar to Gran Canaria,[15] where
the Solórzano name has been the most prominent from the island's
earliest history. Don Juan Manuel de Solórzano, who lives with his
daughter, is the dedicated historian of the place. His life is
entirely devoted to history. His only truth is the recorded word
of the historical past. The daughter, Elvira, is also addicted to
the historical reality. However, she has re-created the figure of
Tulio Montalbán, the liberator of a small Latin American republic.
In the same manner in which the poet of *La princesa Doña Lambra*
had re-created and had fallen in love with the re-created *yo*, Elvira is

---

[15] García Blanco is of the opinion that this play was inspired by the story of
an incident in Gran Canaria; see *OC*, 2a, XII, 127.

emotionally dedicated to the re-creation of her hero. As the play begins, Solórzano's growing anxiety is that Elvira does not have any interest in marriage, for this endangers the continuation of the Solórzano family line.

Julio Macedo, a stranger who bears a striking resemblance to Tulio Montalbán, comes to the island, but he presents himself to Elvira Solórzano as the killer of Montalbán. In the biography that has turned Elvira's mind, the hero is said to have mysteriously disappeared crossing a river and is assumed to be dead. Macedo is, in reality, Montalbán. He exiled himself after his great victory so that he would not be swept into a dictatorship and, thus, deny everything he had fought for. He has come to this distant island hoping to find a new life, and thinking that the legend of Tulio Montalbán would not be known here. When he meets Elvira, who reminds him of his deceased wife, also named Elvira, he finds that he must compete with his other *yo* for her affections. The conflict is cast as the historic *yo*, in struggle against the personal *yo*, seeks to conquer the woman, the mother, whom the man needs:

Macedo.—Sí, me gustaría volver al seno materno, a su oscuridad y su silencio y su quietud...
Elvira.—¡Diga, pues, que a la muerte!
Macedo.—No, a la muerte, no; eso no es la muerte. Me gustaría "des-nacer," no morir... [*OC*, 2a, XII, 755].

The desire for prenatal sleep in the womb corresponds to that aspect of the second literary attitude where the *yo* seeks reassurance against annihilation. Also, the first attitude is present in the symbol of the sea, which is used extensively in this play; it is in the background for every scene, for it is the symbolic expression of the ever present flux of eternity. Thus, it incessantly diverts the characters' attention and drowns out their references to life and death. The new dimension in this play is in the struggle between the man and the myth in the quest for the meaning of death. The personal *yo* seeks the woman-mother in order to *des-nacer,* which is one way of defeating death. But the other *yo*, the one re-created by Elvira, tends to establish immortality not only in name but also in personality. Julio, the man, is frustrated in his desire to win Elvira from Tulio, the myth, when Elvira refuses to see the man again. The climax to this conflict comes in the fourth act, when Julio returns to the Solórzano home to inform father and daughter that he is leaving the island. After he confesses the truth of his past, Elvira pleads with him to stay; she offers to give him the solace he is seeking. But Julio rejects her: "¡No, tú no! ¡Tú no! Tú eres la del libro, ¡quítate de ahí!" As Julio speaks he notices the biography of his youth, his other *yo*, on a table. He hands it to Elvira and cries out: "¡Toma mi cadáver!" Elvira is stricken with terror since she anticipates his intentions. Julio Macedo, the man, has been defeated by Tulio Montalbán, the myth, in his search to find meaning for his existence: consequently, he chooses death: "Sí, es penoso decidirse... ¡Cuánto cuesta morir! ¡Y la mar tan tranquila! Como si no pasase nada... Adiós, Elvira, adiós" (p. 796). Julio shoots himself on the shores of the indifferent sea, and a tearful Elvira ends the play: "¡Mírala, padre, mírala! ¡Es como si no hubiese pasado nada!"

Julio's frustration and defeat by his other *yo* have negated his will to live. He had sought escape from death through the woman, but since this had been denied to him he turned to the sea. All that was left to Julio was to lose himself in the eternal flux, but Tulio, his own myth, would live on to be re-created in another.

El hermano Juan (1929)

This play is subtitled most significantly *El mundo es teatro, vieja comedia nueva*. The source materials for this play are the traditional Don Juan Tenorio theme and the love-death motif. However, the theme is drastically changed with the seduction of Don Juan by death. Death is personified in this play as a woman who pursues the traditional lover. This is an inversion of Espronceda's *El estudiante de Salamanca*, where Don Félix pursues a female personification of death to the gates of hell. However, the love-death motif has come to Unamuno from Leopardi's poetry, especially *Amore e Morte*. In the prologue to the 1934 publication of this play, Unamuno explained these sources:

El goce de reproducirse—carnal o espiritualmente, en hijos o en obras—es un éxtasis, un rapto, un enajenamiento y un goce de muerte. De muerte y de resurrección. Es anonadarse como individuo separado y distinto. Y Don Juan, aun sin saberlo, se buscaba en sus víctimas. No quería morirse sin más.

En aquel estupendo canto de Leopardi al amor y la muerte—*Amore e Morte*—nos dice cómo donde llega al corazón el amor se desprecia la vida y se siente uno pronto a peligrar por él y nace el coraje, y la prole humana se hace sabia en obras, y no en pensamientos vanos [*OC*, 2a, XII, 875–876].

In the three short acts of *El hermano Juan* Unamuno presents Don Juan symbolically as the separation of love from the procreation of children. He never is a true *yo,* but only the representation of a *yo;* he cries out to Inés: "Nací condenado a no poder hacer mujer a mujer alguna, ni a mí hombre" (p. 886). In the second act Elvira's fiancé charges that Don Juan is not a man: "¿Hombre?— que vive buscándose a sí mismo, rebuscando al hombre en sí y sin encontrarlo" (p. 943). Finally, in the third act, Don Juan, now converted to "el hermano Juan," acts as the go-between with Inés and Elvira and their respective lovers. He sees himself in his true dimension as sterile love and not as the virile rôle he plays over and over again in the theatre, which is his world. He has only one rendezvous and only one lover: "ella," who is death. When Don Juan dies, one of the characters turns to the audience and declares: "¡Se consumó la boda!" Thus, Don Juan has not died but rather love has married death.

The play has ended; love has found its fulfillment in union with death, but Don Juan will return many times in many forms since he must play his rôle in the theatre of life. The Don Juan of this play is therefore a re-creation that is immortal. Don Juan knows that he is only the myth of a man and that he is a re-created *yo.* He lives owing to the imaginative re-creation by others who see in him all the virile traits that man needs to attract and conquer women. However, each re-creation ends with death and must be conjured up again in the theatre at another time. In conclusion, just as Don Quixote saw reality as the idealist (the *yo* one wants to be) and Segismundo as the dreamer (the *yo* one thinks he is), Don Juan approaches life as the actor who is re-created to play the rôle of love that ends in death (the *yo* others think one to be).

El otro (1926–32)

This drama was first written in 1926 together with *Tulio Montalbán y Julio Macedo,* but *El otro* was reworked with considerable changes for its 1932 presentation. Therefore, only the 1932 definitive version is considered here. The play deals with the mystery behind the levels of personality in the *yo.* There is an intense dramatic situation throughout the play which is increasingly made more profound as new dimensions are added.

The first act opens with Laura's brother, Ernesto, and Don Juan, the doctor, discussing the demented state of Laura's husband. The theatrical technique of this opening creates a sense of mystery for the rapidly moving scenes of the entire first act. Ernesto confronts

Laura and makes her admit that her husband is insane, that he will have nothing to do with her, and that he calls himself "el otro." Laura informs Ernesto that she suddenly found him in this state of delusion. "El otro" comes in and Ernesto begins to question him; he rapidly agrees to confess himself to Ernesto, but he insists that Laura must leave the room. Scene IV, which ends the act, is the reworking of the *relato* of 1908, "El que se enterró." In both versions the inquisitor is asked to sit down in front of the speaker as he relates his experience: one day, while the speaker was at home working, someone entered the room. He was the mirror image of the speaker. After this meeting the speaker passed out, and when he regained consciousness he was in the place where the other had been and the other, that is, the mirror image of himself, was dead where he had been. The speaker, after regaining his composure, reassures the inquisitor that he is safe with him, but insists on taking him to see the body. In "El que se enterró" the corpse is buried, but in this play it is in the cellar. At this point the parallel ends, for the agonizing *yo* of "El que se enterró" becomes an authentic *yo* with a living awareness of death. Here, the *yo* is torn apart with the doubts of his personality: is he himself, or is he now "el otro." He not only lost consciousness, but also had the sensation of losing his *yo* as he plunged back into his past, toward his birth, until he felt himself *des-nacer*.

Therefore, in the first act, Unamuno has reworked older material to create a dramatic situation of the deepest tension. The second act brings into the play two other Unamunian subjects: the Cain and Abel fratricide of *Abel Sánchez* and the duel between the women for their man of *Dos madres*. Again, here, there are significant changes as the material is transformed to the situations of the stage. Cosme and Damián were identical twin brothers whose mutual hatred had come to the surface in their furious struggle to win the love of Laura. She loved them both and could not distinguish; thus, she left the choice up to them. They reached their decision alone, one stayed, the other left, for they had feared that if they did not separate they would kill each other. Now that one is dead the mystery should clear up, simply as a matter of Cain killing Abel; however, this is not the case, for "el otro" is neither Cosme nor Damián, but both. The situation that precipitates the accusation of "el otro" is the arrival of Damiana, the pregnant wife of Damián, who comes to find her husband.

All of the previously mentioned materials are given a new dimension in the third act, where the shadow of death begins to bear down on "el otro." His *yo* is lost in the *des-nacer* of his experience and is therefore an example of the living dead. The agony now becomes "yo no sé quién soy," which is unbearable and results in his suicide.

The epilogue extends the mystery of the duel of personalities from "el otro" to Unamuno and to the audience:

Ama.—¡El misterio! Yo no sé quién soy, vosotros no sabéis quiénes sois, el historiador no sabe quién es (Donde dice: "El historiador no sabe quién es," puede decirse: "Unamuno no sabe quién es."), no sabe quién es ninguno de los que nos oyen [*OC*, 2a, XII, 862].

The ultimate question remains: what is death to the personal *yo* and his relation to the other *yo*. Each *yo* that dies carries with him all the other *yos* that are within him. Thus, every man who dies kills the *yo* of all whom he knew or re-created from reading. This aspect is further developed by the narrator of *Don Sandalio, jugador de ajedrez.*

LYRIC VERSE

This last section of Unamuno's literature in the third attitude follows the general development which has been discussed in this chapter. Here, the re-creation of the *yo* in others has its culmination as poetic expression in *Teresa* (1924), but it is already in gestation in *Poesías* (1907). Throughout these years the attitude uses various lyric forms; in general, the following are seen: the evocation of the possibility of the re-creation of the *yo* in others, the apostrophe of lyric address by the re-creator to the re-created, and the enunciation of the lyric expresser who seeks to participate in the living tradition of the written word.

Poems from 1906 to 1911

In 1906 the last poems, which comprise the section titled *Introducción,* were written for *Poesías;* here the first poetic expressions of the re-created *yo* are found. The first is "Id con Dios!" In the classical tradition this poem would be the invocation to the muses for inspiration, but here it is the appeal from the creator to the *cantos* for his re-creation. This striking *romance* of hendecasyllables introduces the poet Unamuno to the literary world:

Por cada uno de estos pobres cantos,
hijos del alma, que con ella os dejo,
¡cuántos en el primer vagido endeble
faltos de aire de ritmo se murieron!
Estos que os doy logré sacar á vida,
y á luchar por la eterna aquí os los dejo;
quieren vivir, cantar en vuestras mentes,
y les confío el logro de su intento.
Les pongo en el camino de la gloria
ó del olvido, hice ya por ellos
lo que debía hacer, que por mí hagan
ellos lo que me deban, justicieros.

.   .   .   .

y que al morir, en mi postrer jornada
me forméis, cual calzada, mi sendero [*P*, 7–9].

The poet's verses are the living survivors of the many thoughts and emotions that have been felt but lost into oblivion. Those experiences that have survived through the writing of poetry carry in them the seeds of their creator. These seeds are the means of re-creation for the poet in the mind of his reader or listener. Consequently, the poet's *cantares* will live long after their creator is dead; they will live and he will live through them and in them.

This thought is still rather elementary in its scope, but it is the beginning for what will develop into the third attitude and into a theory of esthetics.

In another poem from this *Introducción,* the moving "Para después de mi muerte," Unamuno gives a more direct expression of the re-creation through poetry. This is a lyric apostrophe aimed at the reader:

12 Oye tú que lees esto
después de estar yo en tierra,
cuando yo que lo he escrito
no puedo ya al espejo contemplarme;
¡oye y medita!

.   .   .   .

Sí, lector solitario, que así atiendes
la voz de un muerto,
tuyas serán estas palabras mías
que sonarán acaso
desde otra boca,
sobre mi polvo
sin que las oiga yo que soy su fuente.
¡Cuando yo ya no sea,
serás tú, canto mío! [*P*, 18–19].

The forceful directness of the twelfth verse startles the reader into the frame of mind the poet wants: "Oye y medita." Unamuno is giving the attitude of re-creation. He must be certain that the reader will not take these poems for granted without stopping to consider the creative force from whence they came. For this shadow of the *yo* will *be* only if the reader listens to the verses and meditates. The series of personality traits and characteristics must be sought or this *yo* will not exist in others. Here there is the mere enumeration of the parts of the *yo*. This poem is, thus, introductory in nature since in itself it does not give any part of the Unamunian *yo*, but serves to make the reader look for Unamuno in the poems that follow.

The poem "Pobre Miguel, tus hijos de silencio," written in 1908 and later published in *Rimas de dentro* (1923), contains another indication of the creator's poetic expression as his *hijos*. Here there is a distinction made between the poems written that were inspired by the poetic tradition and those of the intimate personal expression of the poet himself. The former are part of the sea of human endeavor and have almost become separated from their creators as traditional thoughts, but the latter are the unique facets that can re-create Unamuno.

Rosario de sonetos líricos (1910–11)

This book has been examined in the previous chapters regarding the lyric manifestations of the first two attitudes. Here only the first steps of the third attitude can be seen; however, these poems dealing with the re-creation of the *yo* follow directly from those of the earlier writings of *Poesías* and *Rimas de dentro* in anticipation of the poematic masterpiece of *Teresa*.

In "La palabra" the philosophical implications of the gospel according to St. John are brought to bear on the lyric verse:

> Con la palabra, como Dios, el hombre
> su realidad de ideas forja y labra:
> nunca la profanéis á huero ripio [*RSL*, 99].

In a more solemn tone, the poematic word is also seen as the basis for the *yo*'s making. Man is capable of making his image and likeness as God has done. But it is in the sonnet "¡Siémbrate!" that Unamuno gives the full impact of this third attitude. The basic thought here is that all that remains after death is man's work; thus, he must leave part of his *yo* in his accomplishments:

Ve sembrándote al paso y con tu propio arado
sin volver la vista que es volverla á la muerte,
y no á lo por andar sea peso lo andado.

En los surcos lo vivo, en tí deja lo inerte,
pues la vida no pasa al paso de un nublado;
de tus obras podrás un día recojerte [*RSL*, 140–141].

Teresa (1924)

This book was Unamuno's last publication in Spain before his exile in February, 1924. It is a poetic creation of prose and verse. The prose consists of a *presentación* at the outset, *notas*, and a *despedida* at the end, framing the verse body of the book. The verse consists of a series of ninety-eight *rimas* and a concluding *epístola*. In the *presentación* Unamuno introduces the verses as the work of a young unknown poet, Rafael, who has left the manuscript in his care. Consequently, the *notas* are a commentary on the contents and verse form of the manuscript, as well as the poematic reactions that the commentator had from this work of editing Rafael's *rimas*.

Before examining ·the lyric work itself, it is important to note Unamuno's thinking regarding his book; he wrote to Alfonso Reyes the following account of his progress in 1923:

Un solo refugio hacia el ideal he hallado en este año. He escrito unas rimas románticas de un supuesto poeta—algo como Stechetti—y las he enmarcado en una historia. Se llamará *Teresa*. Son cerca de...—no se asuste usted—2,500 versos.[16]

The poetic affinities acknowledged by Unamuno, in his rôle as editor and critic of the manuscript, are indicative of the tone and contents of the work. The most important source of inspiration is Bécquer's *Rimas*, but along with these Romantic poems are Leopardi's *Amore e Morte*, Jorge Manrique's *Coplas a la muerte de su padre*, Ausias March's *Cantos*, and Gabriela Mistral's *Los sonetos de la muerte*.[17]

Unamuno begins the prose frame with the story of the love and death of Rafael and Teresa:

Hará cosa de año y medio recibí de una pequeña villa, cuyo nombre, fiel a una promesa, que estimo sagrada, no he de revelar, una carta de un muchacho herido de mal de amor y de muerte, de amor de muerte y de muerte de amor [*T*,15].

---

[16] *Don Miguel y sus poesías*, p. 266. For the most penetrating study of *Teresa*, see Ricardo Gullón, "Autobiografías de Unamuno: 'Teresa,' novela de amor," *Cuadernos*, 65 (October, 1962), 38–51.

[17] *Don Miguel y sus poesías*, pp. 257–263.

It is the story of a tragic love that ended in death, first for "la Teresa de Rafael," and later, for the poet, "el Rafael de Teresa." The story is told through the narrator, Unamuno, but it is brought to life, that is, re-created through the poems that Rafael left behind. Unamuno gives a subtle indication that Rafael is the other *yo* that he might have been:

Era como si a más de la mitad del camino de la vida, traspuesto ya el puerto serrano que separa la solana de la umbría y bajando la cuesta del ocaso hacia los campos de gamonas, hubiese topado con uno de mis yos ex-futuros, con uno de los míos que dejé al borde del sendero al pasar de los veinticinco [*T*, 15–16].

The story itself, Unamuno asserts, is a most simple and commonplace idyl, with its roots set in Romanticism. A boy and a girl are in love from their earliest childhood; they reach the age when their long vigil can finally be consummated in marriage, but she dies from consumption before they can marry. He dies soon after from the same disease, which he probably contracted from her. But something happens that is not commonplace: the boy, Rafael, becomes a poet, a creator of the word, that is, "amante de la verdadera sabiduría, de la de saber vivir muriendo—o morir viviendo—, o sea filósofo" (*T*, 16). By thinking his emotions and feeling his thoughts, Rafael could transcend death and re-create his Teresa: "Ya que no había podido tener hijos de carne y sangre y hueso en su Teresa, quería tenerlos en espíritu, quería inmortalizarse o más bien inmortalizar a su huidera novia" (*T*, 17). This is the simple plot that serves as the subject for the collection of *Rimas*.

Unamuno intends to keep the level of reality of Rafael and Teresa from becoming a subreality to the reader. Consequently, he writes:

Te aseguro, lector, que este Rafael de Teresa cuyas rimas te ofrezco, ha existido real y verdaderamente, así como la Teresa de Rafael [*T*, 20].

Unamuno is not inventing a fictional character who speaks Unamuno's ideas, but rather he is forging his *yo*, his other *yo*, for the reader to re-create: "Te he hablado ya, lector, de un presunto ex-futuro Unamuno" (*T*, 20). And just as Unamuno has created Rafael in order that he, the creator, may be re-created, Rafael has also created the symbol of the eternal woman in his Teresa so that she may re-create him: "Es que Rafael no quería morir, anhelaba vivir en su obra, no en su nombre" (*T*, 22).

As Unamuno moves closer to the poetic core of his book, he begins to insert poems which he had written to his Rafael. Also, the long tradition of the love-death poetry is slowly brought to the fore.

Teresa is not the mere remembrance of a young girl, for she is transformed into a poetic inspiration; she becomes a symbol of the eternal woman, the giver of life and beauty. But most important she also becomes the hope for immortality through the re-creation of the poet. Thus, Teresa is more than Dante's Beatriz, Petrarca's Laura, or Tasso's Leonor; she is also the virgin mother.[18]

Unamuno's poems in this book are all expressions of the attitude of study in this chapter: death for the re-created *yo*. It can also be said that they are the most traditional Unamuno wrote, since the models have been Bécquer and Ausias March. With the understanding that nothing short of a detailed analysis of every poem can give the complete picture, the following representative examples can give an indication of the various tone patterns that exist within the poematic whole:

> Tú sabes que moriste, vida mía
> pero tienes sentido
> de que vives en mí, y viva aguardas
> que a ti torne yo vivo.
> Por el amor supimos de la muerte,
> por el amor supimos
> que se muere; sabemos que se vive
> cuando llega el morirnos [*T*, 69].

The motif of love-death becomes the basis for Teresa's re-creation by Rafael and, at the same time, Rafael's poetic creation of his Teresa also gives him another level of reality: death has meaning because love has given values and meaning to life.[19]

The following *rima* contains an expression of the idea of *desnacer*. The *yo* wants to return to the peace of innocence; thus, he implores the Virgin mother, who gave birth to God, to cast the blanket of the moon's eternal rest upon him. The moon, as has been commented upon (Chapter Four, p. 132, n. 5), is also a symbol for the powers of the goddess mother of antiquity:

> Tú, Señora, que a Dios hiciste niño
> hazme niño al morirme
> y cúbreme con el manto de armiño
> de tu luna al oírme
> con tu sonrisa [*T*, 150].

---

[18] For the tradition of the formalized love, see J. Huizinga, *The Waning of the Middle Ages* (New York: Doubleday and Co., 1924), pp. 107–138.

[19] The metaphorical union of Eros and Thanatos is a traditional theme in Spanish literature; Ausias March's *Cantos*, Garcilasso's *Sonetos*, and Lope de Vega's *El caballero de Olmedo* are only a few outstanding expressions of the theme. However, it must be noted that Unamuno has made this theme—beginning with the invocation to Leopardi—a vehicle for the re-creation of his other *yo*, that is, the one that exists in his readers.

In the next *rima,* a lyric dialogue is presented as Rafael searches for the significance of death and Teresa answers him with the promise of the eternal participation. Teresa is fully re-created here by Rafael, yet more important is the fact that she brings only the hope of a nameless union with God. Rafael wants also to leave his name and hers linked for eternity.

> Ten valor y paciencia, Rafael mío,
>   y aprende a esperar;
> Dios vive en las aguas; todo río
>   se pierde en la mar...! [*T,* 182–183].

But by the end of his worldly existence, Rafael has come to believe in the promise of God's eternal cradle; he expresses these last thoughts to Unamuno in the *Epistola:*

> Y ya que Dios nos niega la fortuna
> de ser mía Teresa y yo su hombre,
> su tumba séanos bendita cuna
> de la inmortalidad, ¿qué importa el nombre? [*T,* 191].

The full dimensions of the book are brought out by Unamuno, the commentator, in the *Despedida:* "Enmarcando este cuadro lo he vivido. Y he vivido" (*T,* 224). Unamuno is re-created through his literary creation of Rafael in two dimensions: the Unamuno of 1923, embattled opponent of the political powers of that moment, and also the Unamuno who might have been in his youth. The two dimensions end together with these lines:

> Y ahora tengo que dejar estas queridas cuartillas. Y ¡adiós, lector!
> ¡Adiós, Rafael! ¡Adiós, Teresa! ¡Adiós, mocedad!
> No lloro, ¡no! ¡Miradme a los ojos! [*T,* 227].

Poems from 1924 to 1928

The two outstanding books of this period of exile were *De Fuerteventura a París* (1925) and *Romancero del destierro* (1928), both of which have been studied at length in the previous chapters. They are subsequent to the third attitude's most extensive creation, *Teresa.* Therefore, what appears here is only further proof that the maturity achieved in *Teresa* was continued.

In sonnet LXXVI of the first collection, Unamuno gives the following lyric enunciation:

> sólo espero de Ti—¡Señor, perdona!—
> des a mi vida, des a mi obra en pago
> una muerte inmortal como corona [*FP,* 121–122].

The *Romancero del destierro,* which contains so many excellent examples of the other attitudes, also has the poem "Filosofemas."

This poem, which was written in Paris in 1925, carries over the verse form of *Teresa* (consonantal rhyme); it also expresses the third attitude that will soon find its philosophical statement in *La agonía del Cristianismo* (1925). In "Filosofemas" there are seven stanzas of rhymed hendecasyllables in an ABAB sequence (*serventesios*). In a tone of sad melancholy, Unamuno is considering the personal *yo*'s work: "Nace la raya sobre un punto fijo / y sobre él muere, como tú, alma mía." But this life history is seen here in conjunction with the totality of existence, where it becomes an insignificant repetition: "La vida es toda un redivivo luego; / tan sólo lo que pasa sólo dura." However, the sixth stanza makes the fundamental clarification that both oblivion and renown are nothing to the personal *yo,* if he be dead. Finally, the last stanza places the third attitude into a meaningful unity with the first and second:

> Decir de nuevo lo que ya se dijo,
> crear de nuevo la palabra muerta,
> darle otra vuelta más al acertijo
> y hacer con sombra y luz la muerte incierta [*RD,* 22].

Both the re-creation of the *yo* of others as well as the creation of the word that enables Unamuno's *yo* to be re-created take on the positive meaning of making life. This re-created *yo* which is left behind is only the shadow of the personal *yo,* but together the shadow and the light, that is, the personal *yo,* can make life have meaning in the face of death.

Cancionero (1928–36)

This poetic diary of the last eight years of don Miguel's life offers many excellent examples of the third attitude in poetry. Two small poems are brought into this chapter as exemplary of the others. The first, of 1929, starts with Unamuno's re-creation of other *yos* and ends with his interrogation as to his own re-creation by others.

> Leer, leer, leer; vivir la vida
>   que otros soñaron;
> leer, leer, leer; el alma olvida
>   los que pasaron;
> se queda en las que quedan, las ficciones,
>   las flores de la pluma,
> las solas, las humanas creaciones,
>   el poso de la espuma.
> Leer, leer, leer; ¿seré lectura
>   mañana también yo?
> Seré mi creador, mi criatura?
>   Seré lo que pasó? [*C,* 330].

Unamuno made three significant changes in this poem, as his manuscript seems to indicate. Lines 4, 5, and 7 were given the form they
have above after first having appeared in the following form
[emphasis added]:

> 4 *las cosas* que pasaron;
> 5 Se *quedan*...las que quedan, las ficciones
> 7 *las olas,* las humanas creaciones [20]

It will be noted that all three changes move the poem further into
the third attitude, since *yos* are replacing things, and the loneliness
replaces the waves of the sea metaphor. But of greatest importance
is the change in line 5, for in the first version the things of human
creation remained, but in the second version the third person reflexive refers back to "el alma" in line 3; thus, the soul of the *yo*
remains in the fictional creations.

In contrast, the second poem, of 1934, begins with the re-creation
and ends with the consideration of the re-created others.

> Aquí quedáis, mis momentos;
> con el ritmo aquí os fijé;
> ¿o es que en vuestros fundamentos
> también yo me quedaré?
> Dios mío, este yo ¡ay de mí!
> se me está yendo en cantares;
> pero en mi mundo es así;
> los seres se hacen estares [*C,* 457–458].

The last quartet is the distant echo of the "Id con Dios!" of 1906.

At the beginning of this chapter, it was remarked that the literary
attitude of the *yo*'s re-creation has its roots in the concept of fame
which was given classical expression by Jorge Manrique. Unamuno
compounds this basis with the emotional and psychological desire
for maternity and paternity which is a fundamental drive in man.
Such narratives as *Amor y pedagogía,* "Los hijos espirituales," *Dos
madres, El marqués de Lumbría,* and *La tía Tula,* as well as such
dramas as *El pasado que vuelve, Soledad,* and *Raquel encadenada,*
all partake of the emotive drive for reproduction of a part of the
yo. The focus in these works is on the *yo* who does not want to
die utterly; consequently, he wants to be re-created by others. The
cantares of *Poesías* are poetic sons that are called upon to re-create
the poet after his death.

[20] For the variation of this poem, compare Luis F. Vivanco's earlier version of
Antología poética, p. 414, with that of Federico de Onís' *Cancionero.*

Allied to the above literature is the focus on the others, who are doing the actual re-creating; the husband in *La difunta*, the poet in *La princesa Doña Lambra*, the narrator in *Don Sandalio, jugador de ajedrez*, and Rafael in *Teresa*. The concentration on the fictional character, who is the go-between for the re-creation of the writer, is seen only in *El hermano Juan*.

The next development in the attitude comes when the re-created *yo* is examined in the light of the various levels of personality. Obviously, when the *yo* is re-created by others, the *yo* that is given viability is the *yo* they think Unamuno is; thus, there will be at least two Unamunos confronting each other. The personal *yo*, who is made up of the *yo* Unamuno thinks he is and the *yo* he would want to be, comes face to face with the other *yo*, the one others think Unamuno is. The literary creations of this aspect are the narratives: "El que se enterró," "Tulio Montalbán," and the dramas: *Sombras de sueño* and *El otro*. The poem "Pobre Miguel, tus hijos de silencio" of *Rimas de dentro* provides the lyrical counterpart of this aspect.

Finally, this third attitude reaches its most complex statement as the participation of man's thoughts and emotions in the living current of tradition through his achievements. The outstanding works of this culmination are *Cómo se hace una novela* and *Teresa*, written in 1924, shortly before the third philosophical perspective was to take form in *La agonía del Cristianismo*.

Lyric verse is used for the most part to express the emotions corresponding to the desired re-creation, and drama is used to develop the situation of oppositions that results from the re-creation, but only prose gives the actual re-creation in the literary work itself. This latter can be seen both in the prose frame of *Teresa* and in the novel within *Cómo se hace una novela*.

Consequently, the third attitude is the literary quest for immortality of more than the *yo*'s name or image. The reflective culmination of this literature brings us to the third sphere of Unamuno's reality which we have called a philosophical perspective. It is clear that this is a transcendence of death and is only operative within the second perspective of the *yo*'s world. Unamuno's frequent comments about the reality of fictional characters are not to be dismissed lightly as mere whim, for fictional characters are an "in-struggle" reality.

CHAPTER FIVE

CONCLUSION

It has been remarked in the course of this study that Unamuno's literature contains the essence of his philosophical truth. This statement was made with the realization of the many implications and problems inherent in it. Fundamentally, Unamuno's literature is the creation of the world which he meditates on and explains in philosophical discourse. However, this imaginative creation is not synonymous with the psychotemporal world in which Unamuno lived, for that died in 1936. The literary world is of another dimension, one of esthetic experience, born in the emotive and intellectual complex that was the man, Unamuno, and expressed through language. Hence, in order to understand the essence of this esthetic experience, the language of its expression has been studied. The linguistic elements examined are the highly specialized means available in Spanish that do not so much express as create. In other words, Unamuno's literary creation does not state that *this* is true or *that* is false, but rather it builds viable situations. Some consist only of mountains, sea, and trees in the endless flux of existence; others are peopled with *yos* like Pachico, Apolodoro, San Manuel, or Raquel, Soledad, Tula; and still others have *yos* together with re-created *yos*, like Rafael and Teresa, or U. Jugo de la Raza. These situations are all representations of the inner truth, for Unamuno thought with his emotions.

THE CORRELATION OF UNAMUNO'S PHILOSOPHY TO HIS LITERATURE

The chronological correlation of the literary attitude to the philosophical perspective has a pattern of development: the literature came first and built up a direction of tone, form, and meaning which passed into the philosophical statement.

It would be grossly erroneous for us to leave the slightest impression that the perspectives of thought reconstructed in Chapter One are different frameworks of intellectual effort. They are neither separate nor equal. What we have presented is the anatomy of a philosophy as it developed, each step opening new dimensions to the original basis. This is a philosophy concerned with reality. Unamuno always strove to encounter the real and not an abstraction of reason. In this philosophy the real is the continuous "in-struggle" of being and non-being. We could thus say that to Unamuno reality is the unceasing conquest of its own being. In other words, that which is continues to be through its struggle with non-being. This—the broadest ontological truth of Unamuno's philosophy—is never supplanted by the following perspectives: it is only applied to new dimensions. The second perspective is different insofar as it concentrates on the one aspect of reality directly encountered by man —his being. The ontological position of the *yo* now replaces the consideration of being itself. The *yo* is "in-struggle" reality as the continuous conquest of death. The *yo*'s existence precedes his world's essence since all in the *yo*'s world exists in the *yo*. The anthropology that follows is one of awareness and authenticity leading to the existential commitment to fellowman and world. The last perspective is the being of the *yo*'s thoughts as formulated outside himself by his words. Thus, in a very precise manner the third perspective deals with the being of the word. The "in-struggle" capacity of the word is in the re-creation of the *yo* and the constant reconquering of its being from oblivion.

In summation, reality is the "in-struggle" affirmation of being which is manifest in three spheres of consideration: being itself, the *yo* as being in his world, and the re-created *yo* as being in other *yos*. Death is only meaningful to the *yo* for only the *yo* "exists" and can become aware of his projection unto death. Thus death is the guarantee of the *yo*'s existence.

The table on the next page demonstrates the chronology of Unamuno's writings—philosophical and literary—and substantiates the initial hypothesis that the corpus of literature could be better understood in relation to the directions of thought.

EVALUATION OF DEATH IN UNAMUNO'S
LITERATURE

Unamuno did not write in categories or classifications; these are merely critical tools employed for analytic purposes. Consequently, the perspectives and the attitudes are reunited and treated as the whole which they are in Unamuno in order to arrive at the values and meaning of the death theme in his work.

The Ethereal Negation

When Unamuno loses himself in the contemplation of nature, death loses all significance. The overwhelming spectacle of life seems to be saying that nothing dies, it merely changes. This frame of mind is not resignation before death; it is the very negation of death. This spirit is not far removed from that of the religious mystics, who do not yearn to participate in the divinity as much as to lose themselves, to lose their *yo* in the beatific vision. In other words, it is not a question of the *yo*'s salvation, but rather an appreciation of the unlimited power and glory of God.

Man is reduced to a mere insignificant speck which can be likened to a drop of water in a bottomless sea. Since the individual focus is not present in this part of Unamuno's emotive thinking, it can only contrast with the spatio-temporal existence of the reader. The only exception is the novel *Paz en la guerra,* which was written from 1887 to 1897, and presents both the *todo* and the individual, side by side. The evocation itself concentrates on the *todo* and is not concerned with man. This ethereal mood is evoked in Unamuno when he is contemplating specific scenes; it moves him to go beyond death and the *yo.* When Unamuno observed a man digging a trench by the side of a river, amidst the shadows of the mountains, he did not see a man but rather human-sediment-to-be which would change, not die, and contribute to the eternal current of *intrahistoria.*

This view of death as an insignificant change is presented in many forms, but the most enduring is the symbol of the sea. In *Sombras de sueño,* after the protagonist has taken his life and the monotonous sound of the ocean is heard, Elvira turns to the ocean and sees only indifference, just as if nothing had happened, for in the view of totality death has lost all meaning; it is negated. Other variations of this symbol were seen in the familiar poetic response "lluvia en el lago," in "Qué es tu vida, alma mía" of *Romancero del destierro,* and in *San Manuel Bueno, mártir,* where the rain on the lake presents the totality of existence. When death is approached from an ethereal evocation of the all, its basic meaning—the termination of life—gradually vanishes. What is lost with death is personal consciousness, and that is not being considered.

SYMBOLIC CHARACTERISTICS OF THE LITERARY ATTITUDES	FIRST APPEARANCE OF THE LITERARY ATTITUDE	FORMULATION OF THE PHILOSOPHICAL PERSPECTIVE	FULLEST EXPRESSION OF THE LITERARY ATTITUDE
First attitude			
Sea (lake) and rain, or snow	*Paz en la guerra* (1887–97)		The sea is used as the symbol of the totality in *Sombras de sueño* (1926–30) / *San Manuel . . .* (1930)
Nature cycles: dust to clay, to rock, etc.	"Humiles," *Paisajes* (1891)	*En torno al casticismo* (1895)	*Andanzas y visiones españolas* (1922)
Landscape evocations	"Pompeya," *Paisajes del alma* (1892)		*Paisajes del alma* (1918)
Second attitude			
Non-awareness of death	"La beca," "Juan Manso," *El espejo de la muerte* (1891–1900)		*Amor y pedagogía* (1902)
Awareness of death / death desired / death dreaded	*Paz en la guerra* (1897) Pedro Antonio Pachico	*Del sentimiento trágico de la vida* (1912)	*Cristo de Velázquez* (1913–20) / *Niebla* (1914) / Also poems from *Romancero del destierro* (1925–27) / *San Manuel . . .* (1930)
Authentic awareness of death	*El que se enterró* (1908)		
Third attitude			
Maternity and parenthood	*Amor y pedagogía* (1902)		*La tía Tula* (1921) / *Raquel encadenada* (1921)
The *yo* of *el otro*	*El que se enterró* (1908)	*La agonía del Cristianismo* (1925–27)	*Sombras de sueño* (1926–30) / *El otro* (1926–32)
Man's work as survival in others: re-creation	"Id con Dios," "Para después de mi muerte" *Poesías* (1906)		*Teresa* (1924) / *Cómo se hace una novela* (1924–27)

The development in time of the literary forms that express these ideas and sentiments has been seen in the following: narrative prose tends to pass from an ethereal evocation to an emotive intuition as the style becomes more direct and personal; the dramatic prose of the *Monodiálogos* also progressively loses the *mono* and becomes more of an open exchange; and the lyric verse goes from the Unamunian *silva*, sonnet, and *romance* to the openness of free verse. All of these factors point out a progressive elimination of the limitations of discursive language in favor of what Unamuno considered the viable force of the spoken language.

The Intense Anticipation

When Unamuno, the *agonista*, becomes aware of death as a personal threat, he reacts violently, like Augusto Pérez. He wants to live; he wills to live, but he knows he must die. In this state of mind the *yo* is very much in evidence. The man is aware of his *yo* because it pains him to have to lose it. The result is a struggle that cannot be avoided or dismissed: the will demands immortality, but the rational faculties reply that this is an absurd desire. From the depths of this abyss, Unamuno returned with the existential authenticity of the tragic sense of life, but along the way one can find many authentic and unauthentic Unamunian creations like Pachico, Pedro Antonio, Apolodoro, Avito Carrascal, Alejandro Gómez, Joaquín Monegro, Angel (*La esfinge*), and San Manuel.

Consequently, death not only marks the end of life, as when it is observed in another, but it is, in this case, the corrosive force that cuts the blinders from man and makes life meaningful, that is, authentic. In the strict sense of the word, this is not death but the anticipation of death. This sentiment of death has two faces when man imagines its coming: there is the angel of death who brings solace to the dying Pedro Antonio with the promise of another better life; and, also, there is the demon of death who comes to Teresa's Rafael "con sus alas, cual gigante murciélago, para hundirme en la tierra, cerrado piélago."

Unamuno presses for an answer to the question: is death the end of the personal *yo*. "Aldebarán" answers *todo es nada*. The paradox is only one on the surface, for it is clear that the star has evoked the realization in Unamuno that to the personal *yo* of "carne y hueso" there is no difference between the Spinozian God and the Leopardian nothingness: both mean annihilation. Una-

muno's answer to the dilemma is demonstrated by San Manuel:
Let us live in such a way that if there be nothing beyond death
our death will have been a gross injustice. This is the path to
existential authenticity; Unamuno feels himself—as does San
Manuel—to be committed to his world with all the unique irreplaceable *yos* that inhabit it. Thus, each authentic *yo* has personalized his world in his commitment and is deemed to live by
this self-realization. In this way the personal *yo* is unique and completely irreplaceable. Only the *yo* who is unauthentic, like Avito
Carrascal, is not aware of death; he sees it as an event in another's
historical presence.

The anticipation of death takes on many forms and expressions,
but there is none more intense nor more penetrating than "Vendrá
de noche." This poem creates the atmosphere of anticipation with
an insistent crescendo of images and omens.

The literary form used in these creations of the sense of death
has been the narrative prose which after *Paz en la guerra* bifurcates
into the *paisaje* and the "nivola"; it is the "nivola," with its naked
passions and inner reality, that expresses death; and the lyric verse
of death which develops from an enunciation, in the earlier poems,
to a litany-like, repetitious pattern. As a whole, all of these developments lead to a greater, more direct creation of intensity in the
anticipation of death.

The Esthetic Survival

Although the sentiment of leaving a remembrance of himself had
been with Unamuno since early writings, like *Poesías* and *Amor y
pedagogía,* the full meaning of death in this relation was not felt
until the years shortly before and during his exile. In this focus
death is the destructive force of oblivion, for if man wants his
thoughts and sentiments to survive, he must write them in such a
way that they will not be forgotten. This is the task that every
man accomplishes when he leaves a part of himself in his work. But
there is no survival as meaningful as the survival of the re-created
word. In everything that Unamuno writes, he is sowing the seeds
for his re-creation by others. Death is the threat that moves Unamuno to write, but also it is a continuing threat to his created
works. The most emotional expression of this need to survive in
others comes with the theme of motherhood, both spiritual and
physical. Such women as Tula, Raquel, and Soledad feel the need

of surviving from the *sima* of frustrated re-creation through children. The more intellectual level of the survival of one's ideas leads to the doubt as to who is re-created, the personal *yo* or the other *yo*. The survival from death reaches its full development in the interior duplication which was touched upon in *Niebla,* but is at the core of *Teresa* and *Cómo se hace una novela*. For example, in *Teresa* Unamuno creates Rafael so that Unamuno may be re-created by Rafael's story, and, in turn, Rafael creates his Teresa in the poems so that she may re-create him when they are read. In this manner both Unamuno and Rafael will be re-created by the reader. But it is Unamuno who has survived the threat of the second death— oblivion. Unamuno, thus, in his lifetime saw himself become another *yo* who lived in his readers and who lives today.

Finally, it has been seen that death has had three different realities in the literature studied: death of the totality of existence which is negated; death of the personal *yo* and his world, which is making a better man of the *yo;* and death of the works and the other *yo* they carry within, which is survived only through the living expression.

The esthetic doctrine that has been in development throughout Unamuno's works can be summed up in these terms: the ethereal transcendence of the earlier writings slowly becomes an emotive evocation of the glories of existence; the personal response to death becomes a very intense anticipation; and the survival so longingly sought for reaches the complexity of interior duplication, with the other two factors implicitly contained. By the last decade of his life, Unamuno had all three manifestations of death fully operative in the creation of his world.

INDEX